HOBO JUNGLE

HOBO JUNGLE

A Homeless Community in Paradise

Michele Wakin

LYNNE
RIENNER
PUBLISHERS

BOULDER
LONDON

Published in the United States of America in 2020 by
Lynne Rienner Publishers, Inc.
1800 30th Street, Boulder, Colorado 80301
www.rienner.com

and in the United Kingdom by
Lynne Rienner Publishers, Inc.
Gray's Inn House, 127 Clerkenwell Road, London EC1 5DB

Library of Congress Cataloging-in-Publication Data
A Cataloging-in-Publication record for this book
is available from the Library of Congress.

ISBN 978-1-62637-871-1 (hc.)
ISBN 978-1-62637-872-8 (pbk.)

British Cataloguing in Publication Data
A Cataloguing in Publication record for this book
is available from the British Library.

Printed and bound in the United States of America

The paper used in this publication meets the requirements
of the American National Standard for Permanence of
Paper for Printed Library Materials Z39.48-1992.

5 4 3 2 1

Contents

Acknowledgments

I will keep this short and sweet because these sections can be pretentious. What is this, the Oscars? Of course, acknowledgments are a chance to say thank you, which is good and genuine, but higher education can also be exclusive and entitled, making acknowledgments a who's who of academic superstars. Of course, I'm jealous. I have never had a famous mentor for any duration, and I have never had a woman as a mentor. If I had, maybe things would've been different.

Like it or not, "you academics you" are still my tribe and I'm grateful, so I want to spell it out. The Center for Advancement of Research and Scholarship at Bridgewater State University (BSU) awarded generous grants to make my research for this book possible. BSU colleagues Walter Carroll and Pamela Witcher, and author David Wagner, read early versions of the work and offered wonderful contributions. Michael Redmon, director of research at the Santa Barbara Historical Museum, put up with my ongoing inquiries with patience and aplomb. Santa Barbara hippy activist Chuck Blitz, writer Peter Marin, and the original Mesa Lane Gang not only put up with me but empowered me. Thank you all. This research was never boring.

The people who shaped this book the most are people who dedicate their lives to working on positive solutions for people in poverty. They are people who strive to assist others, even when they themselves are struggling. They are the people on the street who fear or believe that they are not worth saving.

By publishing this book, I acknowledge all people experiencing homelessness in California, a huge and growing number, and especially those in Santa Barbara, my home away from home. I may not like all of you, but I am grateful for you and I admire you. You made me feel at home when I was lonely. You offered me food when I was hungry. You made me laugh and didn't judge me. You played music for me and with me. You shared your ideas and I shared mine. You listened to me and I listened to you. What you had, you gave openly. It wasn't all positive. Some of you scared me. Some of you threatened me. Some of you hurt me. But for the most part, you accepted me and protected me. You allowed me into your world and trusted me to tell your story. I am profoundly grateful to you and I want you to know that you have changed me. I acknowledge you and I promise you this: I will always work to make life better for people who are struggling, whether I like them or not. Thank you for making the need for this clear to me. It is a lesson I will never forget.

1

My Welcome to the Jungle

Arriving in Santa Barbara from the East Coast was unsettling. After living in Boston, an admittedly small, walkable city, I had gotten used to large multistory buildings and the bustle of city life. Santa Barbara, by contrast, is a random collection of one- and two-story stucco buildings laid out grid style downtown and nestled in the foothills in completely unplanned curves and angles. It feels lonely and untamed, with only the ocean and the mountains framing its grandeur. I was studying sociology at the University of California, Santa Barbara, focusing on homelessness, but did not yet have formal research questions, only the beginnings of a study and a growing interest in the themes of criminalization and shelter. Santa Barbara's hobo jungle immediately drew my attention as a mysterious camping area along the railroad tracks by the ocean, where it has existed in some form from the early 1900s to the present. In this book, the jungle offers a window through which to understand and track changes in the meaning and experience of living unsheltered for yesterday's hoboes and today's homeless people.[1]

Studying the jungle and understanding the resources and risks associated with different types of makeshift housing solutions led me on a journey that spans several years and encompasses multiple time periods, methodologies, and settings. The result is that this book is not only about the jungle but also about our changing understanding of unsheltered homelessness and how this understanding shapes policy, public opinion, and overall life chances for homeless people. The intent here is to explore the experience of being homeless and unsheltered, rather than seeing it as a quality, a condition, or a characteristic of a person. This approach incorporates elements of both symbolic interactionism and historical comparative research to shape and interpret the common categories of experience used to understand jungle living. Data sources in the chapters that follow include historical archives, ethnographic fieldwork, and applied advocacy research. I use these sources to trace the persistence of the jungle for over seven decades in one of the most opulent cities on California's South Coast.

The early chapters of this book include historical archives kept by men living in the jungle in the 1940s and 1950s. Access to the writings and opinions of the men, in poems, letters, and short stories, informs the focus on mobility that characterizes the hobo lifestyle during this era. I supplement these data with research on the historical preservation and commercial development of the waterfront area, where the jungle is located. Using maps, photographs, and city planning documents to track the evolution of the waterfront shows the confluence of environmental preservation and luxury tourism that are its signature features, making the jungle's endurance that much more surprising. In a city hoping to attract tourist revenue and using the railroad and eventually the freeway to do so, Santa Barbara was also attracting hoboes, and one of the city's most prominent property owners invited them to stay. This ignited debate in the community, portrayed in local newspapers, showing how the jungle was understood and managed.

Exploring the jungle's next rise to prominence in the 1980s relies on a combination of published scholarly sources, thirty interviews with people active in the protest movement, and over 300 newspaper articles to illustrate the rise of the shelter industry and its impact on the local homeless population. Tracking the evolution of the jungle community is easier in the 1980s, relative to earlier decades, because of the proliferation of media accounts, scholarly research, and policy and advocacy work, as well as the prevalence of activism throughout the nation and the local community. This decade is also pivotal in defining and dividing people experiencing homelessness and linking policy with rewards and punishments for categories of people seen as deserving or undeserving, a divide that will widen by the early 2000s.

It is during these later years, from 2000 to 2005, that I spend over 450 hours in the field, conduct thirty-five formal interviews with people living in the jungle, and carry a digital audiotape recorder for approximately nine months, recording hundreds of conversations. I also take countless photographs and extensive field notes throughout, in addition to transcribing the recordings. To elucidate the experience of jungle living and focus a diverse and fluid data set, I examine the representative experience of three relationships between people living in the jungle. These relationships help situate the jungle within a larger context of public space and criminalization, survival, and resistance. To further explore these themes, I work with the Committee for Social Justice as an advocate and volunteer expert witness in fifteen court cases in which homeless people are cited for sleeping and camping offenses. I also conduct fieldwork at the day-labor line and employ people seeking work there to assist me in translation and data gathering as I explore the changing shape of migratory labor and how immigration status, language, and culture shape criminalization.[2]

To focus on local policies and responses to homelessness, I start working extensively with the Santa Barbara City Council, Santa Barbara County Board of Supervisors, Police Advisory Board, Coalition to End Hunger and Homelessness, and other regional and local service boards in charge of setting policy and offering punishment and provision to homeless people. My involvement with these groups is advocacy based and includes monthly if not weekly meetings with each, directly related to setting policy and arguing for increased rights and privileges. To enhance this work, in 2005 and 2006, I organize a series of classes called The People's Institute, for people living in the jungle, and evaluate their efficacy and impact on overall quality of life. I return to Santa Barbara in 2008 and 2016 to revisit its shelters, jungles, and beaches, to interview activists, advocates, and people experiencing homelessness and to attend meetings related to policy and protest movements. I also conduct comparative research in Santa Cruz and Sonoma Counties for three-week stints in 2006 and 2008 to see how prevalent unsheltered homelessness is in comparison with Santa Barbara, and to gauge the differences in the local response to criminalization and resistance activities within these communities.

Although this additional research is important in establishing a more current context for examining jungle living and tracking its evolution, it is also limited because of my inability to gain the trust of such a hidden population, particularly as I was always new in town. As a result, this research enhances the present analysis of the jungle, but the bulk of the fieldwork presented here was conducted earlier and in Santa Barbara, which are related limitations. My lack of unfettered access to the jungle, discussed in more detail in Chapter 4 and the appendix, and the timing and diversity of data sources are an added weakness. I address but perhaps don't completely solve these problems by using historical data to view the societal trends that influence our ideas of the jungle and policies used to manage populations seen as marginal or dangerous. What results, however flawed, is a focus on the power dynamics involved in living unsheltered and understanding and managing its exigencies.

In the field, I go from being a "buddy researcher" to a legal advocate and service provider to a lifelong friend, confidante, and champion of homeless rights. While conducting participant observation, I become immersed in the lives of the people included in these chapters. I take them to appointments, listen to their daily struggles and triumphs, and share my own. I become part of their relationships and routines and care deeply about what happens to them. When they get separated from one another, I remain in contact with both sides and carry information back and forth. In some cases, I am in touch with their families. Although I conduct formal interviews, I learn far more by listening and becoming a part of people's daily lives, leaving them in control of what and how much they want to tell me. I also elicit their stories and opinions, formally and informally. I bring newspaper clippings about homelessness, of which I have hundreds, for people to comment on. I learn to play pinochle and to speak passable Spanish. I hire people, when I can, to assist me with data collection, and I incorporate their insights, expertise, and direction throughout this research. All of these things help as I try to become a part of an environment so different from my own, as I strive to understand its various dimensions.

My approach to fieldwork allows the interests and pursuits of the individuals and small groups I study to inform my goals and methodology. Rather than viewing homeless people as subjects, this research collaborates with them as experts, setting a course for both research and action, key features of a participatory action approach (Foote Whyte et al. 1991; Gomez and Ryan 2016). Although I contextualize the Santa Barbara jungle within statewide and national trends and explore its history, the heart of this work relies on naturally occurring interaction and the voices of homeless people to inform more general claims about jungle living. The methodology in this book is exploratory, allowing initial inquiry to become gradually focused through field observations and through using a diverse set of methodological tools (Blumer 1969). It is also directly linked to wider questions of social inequality and social justice (Humphries, Mertens, and Truman 2000, 13).

For me, the lure of the jungle is in the idea of an unfiltered sense of loyalty homeless people seem to have for one another and the idea of questioning societal rules and structures and developing alternatives. The questions that drive this inquiry are: How do people living in the jungle develop a sense of community and identity? How do they understand and explain themselves in relationship to other homeless people and to housed society, and how are these explanations received? And finally, how does the experience of geographic and social mobility change over time to allow different forms of survival and resistance? This study of the Santa Barbara jungle explores answers to these questions and examines the changing nature of work, mobility, and urban spaces. It focuses on outlining a framework through which to understand how the structural and individual causes of homelessness converge on everyday life experience, shaping both the problem and the solution.

Experiencing Unsheltered Homelessness

Having a private, backstage area in which to relax and let down your guard is central to the idea of home. People also view living spaces as reflections of self-worth and social value (Goffman 1959; Reitzes et al. 2015). Just as those living in luxury homes in gated communities are seen as social and economic elites, those living in jungles and ghetto neighborhoods are seen as social and economic failures (Anderson 2012). Equating failed spaces with marginal people means that they become synonymous referents for one another, melding personal, social, and political stigmatization (Jones and Jackson 2012). Stigma is a status we ascribe to various groups based on presumed differences and deficiencies rather than inherent qualities, and it changes over time, depending on social and cultural preferences, although some forms of stigma seem immutable. Understanding the stigma of homelessness through experiential categories is a way of highlighting its constructed meaning by tracking changes in society's treatment of it over time.

Homelessness is often seen as a combination of personal and structural issues that make accessing housing out of reach. Emphasizing personal over structural causes means viewing homeless people as culpable, as causing or deserving their present state. This is part of the stigma theory that justifies the cruel and unusual punishment of homeless people (National Law Center on Homelessness and Poverty 2013). After all, one of the worst characteristics of stigma is that we see the bearer as tainted, discounted, less than human, and deserving what they get (Goffman 1963, 3). It is in this context that the jungle is a place to hide, to be accepted, and to develop a sense of identity and community. These features of jungle living remain constant, yet the way it intersects with other city areas, with transportation routes, and in the context of mainstream shelter and housing and employment markets, fluctuates over time. Living in makeshift settings like the jungle means negotiating a complex nexus of space, time, and mobility mapped onto the development of identity, community, and resistance, and it is never a one-sided game. People experiencing homelessness must negotiate the power dynamics that dictate the legality of public space and codes of conduct, which threaten their existence.

The experiential categories outlined in Table 1.1 represent the most constant and enduring features that set hoboes and unsheltered homeless people apart from the mainstream while still being applicable to the mainstream. Space, time, and any of the other categories do not belong to or define homeless people but characterize their experience, instead of focusing on problematic identities, characteristics, or maladies. In so doing, they explain the effects of macro-level policies on the lived experience of the jungle. These categories also correspond with the methodological approach employed here, in the attempt to balance the need for representativeness with the singularity of the Santa Barbara jungle and the disparate time periods this book covers. Using experiential categories over other modes of analysis allows for fluidity and flexibility, rather than reifying the binaries so prevalent in research, service, and policy approaches to homelessness: deserving/undeserving, good/bad, worthy/unworthy. Treating homelessness as an experience one goes through rather than as an identity characteristic removes the blame, moral judgment, repentance, and even valorization that go with examining street liv-

Table 1.1 Experiential Categories: Living Unsheltered

Space	1940s–1950s	Skid row housing, jungles, migrant labor camps, jails
	1980s	Makeshifts, streets, shelters, jails, prisons
	2000s	Shelters, jails, prisons, service organizations, makeshifts, encampments, tent cities
Time	1940s–1950s	Periods of work and rest, harvest cycles, train schedules
	1980s	Survival and protest, submission to institutional routines
	2000s	Time-stretch, lack of control, submission to institutional routines
Mobility	1940s–1950s	Regular, nationwide travel, automobile over railroad
	1980s	Circumscribed, urban spaces and service areas, cyclical
	2000s	Circumscribed, urban and rural spaces, service areas, cyclical, confined
Identity	1940s–1950s	Stigmatized, older, "disaffiliated"
	1980s	Stigmatized, diverse, split: deserving/undeserving
	2000s	Stigmatized, criminalized, polarized, marginalized
Survival and resistance	1940s–1950s	Skid row, service driven
	1980s	Advocacy driven, organized protest, shelterization, criminalization
	2000s	Advocacy driven, muted protest, shelterization, criminalization

ing. It is a way of capturing the lived experience of the jungle, then and now, as a place of sanctuary and marginalization with punitive and protective aspects, similar to other marginal spaces and defined in relationship to the mainstream (Waquant 2012).

In this chapter, I track changes in how homeless people occupy public, city spaces and how makeshift living areas like the jungle proliferate. I examine changing housing options, from skid row to prisons and shelters, as the nation's understanding of public space becomes more overtly based on fear, control, and resource protection (Davis 1990; Blakely and Snyder 1997) rather than public interaction and discourse. Over time, mobility in the jungle becomes limited and cyclical, rather than geographic or social, and it is shaped by various means of repression and punishment that exclude homeless people from city spaces or repeatedly punish their visibility and behavior there (Wright 1997; Ellickson 2001; Mitchell 2001; National Coalition for the Homeless 2004; National Law Center on Homelessness and Poverty 2009). This creates and exacerbates the stress and trauma that make transcending homelessness difficult, as it is associated with a problematic identity and survival eclipses resistance. To understand how the experience of jungle living changes over time, I examine the Santa Barbara jungle in the context of the social, political, and economic changes that take place over the decades of interest and compare it with other forms of unsheltered homelessness to situate the Santa Barbara location within a hierarchy of makeshift settings.

Jungle Meaning, Jungle Beginning

The word *jungle* conjures up images of a primitive and unruly place, where outsiders face hidden dangers and even those who live there face the unknown (Conrad 1899; Kipling 1984; Sinclair 1906). The jungle is primordial but replicates itself expertly into modern urban consciousness. The jungle is the home of the indigenous other and the darkness inside us all. It lives within the ghetto, skid row, and the encampments, tent cities, and shadow cities that proliferate today and in the feeling of marginality that pervades them. It exists in the interstices of urban, suburban, and rural spaces and in the hearts and minds, the words and deeds of people who live there. The jungle is beaten back, but it grows just the same, flourishing in its wild expression of beauty. It uses the grid but remains separate from it, threatening its values and structure. This threat, albeit imagined, is used to justify various forms of exclusion that lock people up, silence them, and strip away their opportunities, even their hopes, until there is nothing left but to give in to societal expectations and let the jungle take over. How do people who live in the jungle survive? Is survival enough or is something closer to revolution needed to change their perilous situation? These larger questions are addressed through an exploration of the jungle as an outdoor camp for people without shelter.

Hobo jungles begin as a home for itinerant laborers in the late 1800s, in part as an outgrowth of Civil War bivouacs, which taught men to live off the land (DePastino 2003). The jungle is a public but hidden setting, a temporary camp close to the railroad and the main stem, with the city lights twinkling in the distance. It is a place to learn about life riding the rails, to access temporary seasonal employment, to spend time in the company of one's fellows and share a mulligan stew. The jungle overlaps with more permanent urban areas such as skid row, but men who live in the jungle are typically passing through. It serves, in a sense, as a poor man's Motel 6, where the bed is always available, the light is always on, and you can count on at least this small measure of comfort from the dangers of life on the road. But, as its name implies, the jungle is off the beaten track and designed to remain hidden. Men who live there adhere to the unspoken rules of anonymity and reciprocity, often leaving standard cooking and camping supplies behind for incoming men to find respite (Anderson 1923, 1930). Temporary and permanent camps differ, although the former are more common, and men who live in the jungles are "domesticated without the aid of women" (Anderson 1923, 18). As hoboing becomes more widespread from the turn of the century into the early 1900s, these features of jungle life ensure basic standards of domesticity and help facilitate a life on the move.

The jungle is an island of stability in an otherwise transient existence, yet hobo life holds hidden dangers for the unaware. Jackrollers and jungle buzzards are two kinds of transients, waiting to part young hoboes from their money or their virtue (Shaw 1930). And trains themselves pose imminent danger for those who fail to prop open boxcars or who ride in cars with shifting cargoes. Even railroad workers are at risk, with 2,550 deaths recorded in 1900 alone (Caplow 1940). In addition to fatalities, many hoboes lose limbs because they are not fast enough or do not jump high enough to reach the moving train. Still others ride the rods underneath the train or cross paths with "bulls" (transportation workers), police, or townspeople, and risk various forms of danger or sanction. If jungles can be considered a home base, the rest of the world requires a performance: to convince employers to hire you, housewives to feed you, and police and citizens to leave you alone. When unsuccessful in winning over any of these constituents, hoboes face violence, fines, or jail time, or merely go hungry. Jungles are a place to learn about these dangers and to learn from the experts how to negotiate a life on the road.

The hobo himself, his employment patterns, culture, and place in society is the focus of early Chicago School sociologist Nels Anderson. His work was funded, in part, by Ben Reitman, noted for developing a Chicago branch of the Hobo Colleges that were an outgrowth of the International Brotherhood Welfare Association (Burgess and Bogue 1964, 6), one of the last times anyone would seriously consider offering educational opportunities for homeless adults.[3] Anderson's books include *The Hobo: The Sociology of the*

Homeless Man (1923), *The Milk and Honey Route: A Handbook for Hobos* (as Dean Stiff) (1930)*, and *Men on the Move* (1940). His work explains the hobo as a social category enjoying heightened mobility because of employment circumstances but also enduring a marginalized, degraded status. Anderson focuses on the services and accommodations that skid row provides for working, wandering men. He describes the jungle as a flat, shady sleeping area, close to a railroad division point, a water source, wood for a fire, and a town to supply basic needs.

Unlike skid row areas, where women also live, early jungles are almost exclusively a man's domain.[4] Although jungles are more racially diverse than skid row areas, Anderson's pronouncement that they are "the melting pot of trampdom" is perhaps an overstatement (Flynt 1972). Although jungles are more inclusive than skid rows, a hobo's life is defined by motion between the two, facilitated by railroad travel and seasonal labor, periods of work and rest. One of the essential differences between skid row and the jungle is that the latter is seen as a place where the informal relations governing city life hold less sway. In the context of being a feared, marginalized group of workers, the jungle provides a place to shed these constraints. As a result, "the hobo enters this life as he does no other. Here he turns his back on the world and faces his fellows and is at ease" (Anderson 1923, 44). This sense of freedom, community, and danger, coupled with a simple and anonymous "no strings attached" form of domesticity, is and remains central to the jungle's appeal.

Tracking the use of the jungle over time is difficult, as both its form and meaning undergo change, and it is more difficult to access and study than traditional shelter or skid row settings. The use of jungles is widespread throughout the mid- to late 1800s, surging during the Great Depression and waning precipitously until the 1970s, only to proliferate again in the 1980s and endure into the twenty-first century, in many forms and under many different names, including encampments and tent cities. What kind of place is the jungle, as a makeshift camp, in comparison to other kinds of housing and shelter options? Does it offer a site for community and resistance or for vice and suffering? How can we understand the jungle and the people who live there in the context of changes in the national economy, employment, and housing markets? And how can we understand, through the experience of jungle living, what kind of home unsheltered homeless people are striving for?

Space, Time, and Mobility

In this section, I briefly explore the advent of hoboing and early attempts to reintegrate wandering men in the early 1900s, focusing on the degree of control hoboes have over space, time, and mobility, relative to later decades. Because they have more time than their wage-earning, head-of-household counterparts and more choices about where to work and rest, hoboes have a greater sense of freedom. Despite this, they are still at the mercy of train schedules, the waxing and waning of seasonal labor, and the threat of physical harm, jail, or other forms of danger or sanction. Whereas skid rows are crowded urban thoroughfares that mirror the routines of city life, hobo jungles take on a rugged and romantic quality, where these routines hold less sway. Over time, the larger, nationwide circles hoboes travel, between harvest work and rest, become smaller, localized, and controlled and defined by agencies of assistance or correction, or both. Freedom eventually turns to submission by luck, punishment, or choice, and living in alternative makeshift settings like the jungle reinforces a cycle of marginality. Part of this is informed by the hobo's changing experience of space, time, and mobility.

The idea of space-time compression is central to mobility theory (Harvey 1989). Tim Cresswell describes this as "the effective shrinking of the globe by ever-increasing mobility at speed enabled by innovations in transportation and communications technology" (2006, 4). Perhaps this is why there is initially some romance in the idea of the hobo—someone who can be in Chicago tonight and California tomorrow. Railroads are the first emergent, transformative technology to open the American West, and hard as it is to imagine in an age when plane travel is commonplace, the excitement of a railroad connecting the nation so that cross-country travel becomes a matter of days instead of months was unprecedented. Beginning in the late 1800s, the railroad as a mobility system facilitated the hobo as a social category (Anderson 1930; Urry 2007), containing the now famous distinction between tramps, bums, and seasonal laborers (Anderson 1923; Cresswell 2001).[5] With hundreds of people riding boxcars in search of work, what would eventually be termed the "migrancy problem" is just "an extended job hunt in the casual labor market" (Anderson 1940, 273), in which the conditions, duration, and even availability of work are unpredictable.

In this context, mobility is essential. It informs the very culture and identity of the hobo, as it is a "thoroughly social facet of life imbued with meaning and power" (Cresswell 2006, 4). It involves the blending of geographic and social movement and gives rise to and reinforces social inequality (Urry 2007), marking hoboes as different and suspect (Monkkonen 1984). The power of the hobo, albeit limited, is in the degree of mobility, flexibility, and choice that accompanies his lifestyle and employment patterns (Anderson 1930). But this power is not without limits. While he is working, the hobo is tolerated, but when work is over, he is unwelcome and sent packing. Hoboes as mobile subjects are made meaningful through interaction with the established order, telling the hobo to move on or inviting him to the table. Although often maligned as dirty, dangerous, dishonest, or merely a drain on resources (Uys 1999), hoboes in the early 1900s have options that place them in control, in motion, and with choices. When they cease to be mobile, or when they enter towns and cities without employment, they are beaten, jailed, and barred from entry or forced to leave (Pacific Rural Press 1880; Cresswell 2001). This rejection and regulation increases in the decades leading up to the 1940s and 1950s, where this book begins, reflecting the changing value of the hobo in society (Chambliss 1964).

Our appreciation of the hobo as a social category starts to fade as early as the 1920s, by which time he has become "a man out of time, a relic from a world that had once rewarded freewheeling masculinity" (DePastino 2003, 128). Mobility begins to take on an ironic meaning still associated with adventure but threatening the establishment of a traditional home base and subject to sanction or rehabilitation, or both (Davenport 1915). Part of this has to do with cultural standards of masculinity. Todd DePastino (2003) describes the shifting definition of masculinity with the closing of the Gilded Age and the triumph of corporate capitalism in the late 1800s and early 1900s. The idea of the "self-made man," defined by "success in the market, individual achievement, mobility, wealth" (Kimmel 2012, 18) wanes with increasing industrialization and the fear and self-doubt that accompany the loss of autonomy and submission to wage labor. The identity of the hobo—a man without a traditional home to retreat to—becomes fused with wandering and transience, threat, and questioning of the wage system, unfair labor practices, and capitalism, more broadly speaking. It is also associated with protest.

Early attempts at social protest through uniting with the Industrial Workers of the World (IWW) helped turn hoboes into slightly more respectable transient workers, formulating what Robert Park calls a

masculinist "group consciousness" for men wandering "without destination" (Park 1967, 159). The IWW focused on direct economic
action through strike and sabotage, justifying and valorizing the physical prowess needed to sustain both work and protest. Ironically, the
very traits that marginalized hoboes in the eyes of housed citizens
made them powerful men among their fellows and friends of the
IWW. Pairing hoboes with the IWW also brought a culture of protest
to the fore in the form of songs and spoken word, fomenting revolution (DePastino 2003; Garon and Tomko 2006; Industrial Workers of
the World 1905). Yet the tactics and schisms within the IWW, along
with government opposition, made its reign in the jungle short-lived.

Depression and Reintegration

The federal government intervened during the Great Depression to
provide for transients and workers, connecting the idea of assistance
with identities or populations deemed acceptable, in this case "transients" (Higbie 2003). The Federal Transient Program, established in
1933, when an estimated one-third of the workforce was unemployed, attempted to reintegrate transients by granting state aid for
communities willing to shelter them. It was also an early attempt at a
comprehensive census of homeless people, as by 1934, all states
except Vermont were participating in the program (Anderson 1940,
302). Program administrators identified several kinds of transients,
including boys, girls and young women, men, families, persons and
families seeking employment and healthier climates, the aged and
handicapped, the mentally ill, and persons who had been institutionalized (Reed and Potter 1934). They also separated people for federal
aid based on a definition of "transience" as having been in a state for
less than twelve months. Those not meeting this requirement had to
rely on state aid and on missions and almshouses or depend on
friends and family, as in the case of black or "negro" transients who
faced overt racism, limiting or directing their overall mobility.[6]

In an attempt to stem the growing tide of transients during the
Depression, the federal government provided funding for states to
offer shelters, camps, and rented rooms, as well as an impressive
array of services, including those providing basic needs such as food
and clothing to those addressing the root causes of long-term poverty,
including unequal access to education and employment. The idea was

that tailoring services and programs to meet people's needs would help them reintegrate more quickly and become part of their host communities or return to their city of origin. Federal transient camps were particularly effective in serving working young men and clustered in the warmer states, such as California, where outdoor living is tolerable on an almost year-round basis. There is some evidence to suggest that the Federal Transient Program reduced the number of young men living in jungles, a solution they turned to because jungle life was preferred "rather than submit to the humiliation of forced contact with the degrading atmosphere of the indiscriminate shelter and soup kitchen" (Reed and Potter 1934, 46).

Here we see a distinction between the deserving and undeserving beginning to take shape through federal policy. One group is employable, flexible, and amenable to physical labor, and the other is limited by a combination of factors including age and infirmity. Although geared to serve those considered the most vulnerable, most acceptable, and/or the easiest to reintegrate, there is general recognition that the increase in migrancy in the 1930s is need driven by a "socially valuable and enterprising people willing and anxious to work" (Reed and Potter 1934, 31). There is also a keen understanding that services need to be attractive to the service population. Making services need driven and attractive are sentiments that will bear repeating in the 1980s and beyond. And finally, there is the recognition that wandering can be reduced or eliminated entirely by a combination of reintegrative strategies that reinforce community membership and long-term buy in, something the Federal Transient Program was not always successful in doing (Caplow 1940). Despite its gains and the promise of its ideology, the administration of this federal program turned out to be poorly coordinated and short-lived.

The end of the Federal Transient Program and failure to plan for its future means a resurgence in jungle areas (Kusmer 2002), which overlap with the Hoovervilles commonly seen on the outskirts of cities, full of people seeking work. As a result of these developments, states become even more hostile to hoboes, whom they now see as crossing their borders to draw on resources, with Florida and California leading the pack. Along with receiving support from the Federal Transient Program, which lasted from 1933 to 1942, younger men on relief also enlist in the Civilian Conservation Corps (CCC), a program that grew out of legislation that was part of the Works Progress Administration (WPA), designed to provide environmentally based employment programs for young men. Focusing on education and vocational training as keys to family stability, the CCC builds 46,000 bridges, plants more than 2 billion trees, slows soil erosion on 40 million acres of farmland, and develops 800 state parks (Maher 2008, 43). Not only does the CCC transform the landscape, it also transforms boys into men rather than leaving them stuck in a state of dependence, or a life without achievable, mainstream goals (Suzik 1999). Instead of joining the hobo ranks, young men receive training, employment, and wages to send home to their families, and the focus on youth and physical fitness serves as a counter to "the lure of the open road." Although the CCC is administered like a military program and is overseen, in part, by the Department of War, its explicit disconnect with the armed forces is eventually called into question in a prewar era that makes it seem superfluous (Suzik 1999).

The nation's understanding of poverty during the Depression and the solutions that arose to handle it are indicative of the struggle to define and manage a problematic social category. Whether labeled "transients, wanderers, hoboes, homeless," there is a subtle and growing distinction between those who fit in and those who, in part because of their poverty and mobility, do not. In fact, for some time, mobility itself is associated with "nomadism," "feeble mindedness," or "wanderlust" as quasi-psychological conditions (Solenberger 1911; Davenport 1915). Even before the Depression, sociologists wonder: "What, if anything, is the matter with the hobo's mind?" (Park 1925, 158). Why, instead of setting down roots, does the hobo seem to wander for wandering's sake without contributing more to society than struggle-inspired poetry and hard physical labor? And, more important, how can hoboes be reintegrated into society? The Depression-era response to these questions is to ground the hobo and limit his mobility and to direct and focus his labor through social policy, traditional family building, and community reintegration. This also happens through technological progress, as the mechanization of agricultural work and the ever-increasing use of automobiles over railroads conspire to keep wandering men close to home.

During the 1930s, migration to California differed from the prior decade, when people moved because of a mix of push-pull factors ranging from the strain of poverty and unemployment to the promise of a better life, a healthy climate, and greater economic prospects.

By the 1930s, push factors prevail and people are migrating in search of work over adventure and with a sense of urgency, if not panic. Individuals and families flock to California from Dust Bowl and Cotton Belt states, with 400,000 from the Southwest alone and the majority moving to Los Angeles and the more rural San Joaquin Valley (Gregory 1989, 12). Many migrants on the move do not find work, and squatter encampments known as Hoovervilles become an embarrassing national symbol of a dream gone wrong (Gravelle 2015). Throughout California, the agricultural labor that hoboes once sought is gradually replaced with service and semi-skilled jobs, with Mexican and Asian families preferred for the most arduous farm work (Wyman 2010). With the onset of World War II, everything changes again, and the fear that accompanied being a receiving state for migrants from other areas is replaced with a renewed interest in attracting workers, this time for wartime industry.

1940s–1950s: War and Decline

As the country pulls itself out of Depression-era poverty to face World War II, able-bodied young men become soldiers and support workers. Those who cannot work or cannot fight are left to fend for themselves without a fully developed safety net. Although Social Security benefits for the aged and unemployed are signed into law in 1935, they only become payable by 1942, and many low-wage earners, including agricultural workers, are not eligible for benefits (Piven and Cloward 1979, 114). Making states the arbiters of federal work relief through the Works Progress Administration is informed by the same ideology informing the English Poor Laws: relief is a local responsibility, allowances should be lower than wages, and settlement should be a prerequisite for aid (Piven and Cloward 1979, 130; Morris 1994; Wagner 2005). Localities manage the terms of work relief, requiring place-based loyalty and loyalty to industry as keys to long-term stability. Geographic mobility is sublimated for a presumed increase in social mobility, a goal Stephan Thernstrom (1964) points out can mean property ownership or the move to white-collar professions and is often elusive.

With the onset of war, eligible men are called to military service and women are employed in greater numbers than ever before, with the participation of women in the workforce jumping from

13.8 to 19.1 million from 1940 to 1944 (Gregory 1974). The country also tightens its belt, rationing food, clothing, gas, and other commodities, and ideologically tightens its belt to focus on an external threat.[7] When servicemen return from war, several federal programs assist in reintegrating them into mainstream society as breadwinners, and a combination of government policy and popular culture sells the idea of suburbia and the private automobile to the populace. The GI Bill facilitates reintegration by offering over 2 million men college and university training, 3.5 million school training, and 3.4 million on-the-job training (Servicemen's Readjustment Act 1944). It also targets home ownership, business loans, and employment as keys to a good and stable family life. This thwarts a feared repopulation of skid row by former servicemen, but not everyone participates equally in these programs. A combination of factors, including a legacy of racial oppression and overt discrimination, limits the preparedness of and opportunities available to black servicemen (Onkst 1998). These inequalities set the stage for growing racial disparities, segregated urban housing, and an overrepresentation of people of color within the homeless community for years to come.[8] With the push toward domestic prosperity, homeownership, and employment, those who do not enjoy these rewards are themselves thought to be somehow deficient.

The postwar era sees both skid row and jungle areas begin the slide into obscurity, and the embrace of the domestic ideals hoboes once shunned is never stronger. Skid row populations plummet accordingly during this decade (Hoch and Slayton 1989), and the adventure that characterized the hobo lifestyle, embodied in images of hobohemia and soapbox orators, fades into memory (Brundage 1997).[9] Skid row becomes isolated, segregated, and detached, while the country embraces the nuclear family, living in a home with a white picket fence, with women as homemakers and men as breadwinners. Disaffiliation theories of the time describe homeless people as having "low social attachment" and being generally prone to retreatism (Bahr 1973). Although this is not an entirely fair reading of why people are homeless or of the social ties they maintain (Grigsby et al. 1990), they are still seen as a category apart from the mainstream and fixed in urban spaces. Homelessness is increasingly viewed as an individual problem of a group of old men drinking and going nowhere, costing cities needed revenue (Bogue 1963; Spradley 1970; Bahr and Caplow 1973).

Skid Row: The Hobo's Urban Home

Skid row provides an urban counterpart to the more rustic jungle areas, making it easier to study as representative of hobo life. The organization and evolution of skid row and its residents is the subject of many studies and figures centrally into the urban sociological paradigm developed through the Chicago School in the early to mid 1900s. Some of the ideas initially posed about urban change and development boil down to a simple question: Is it a good thing or a bad thing? Does it make us more diversified in thinking and acting or more fragmented, disconnected, and unhappy?

Unlike the jungle, which exists in the interstices of urban development, skid row is seen as a negative part of urban change, a "zone of penury" for the highly mobile, disaffiliated subject (Burgess 1925). Skid row residents are pathologized and divided into various social categories. Their most common traits include "the nature of a man's employment and his propensity to travel about" (Bahr 1973, 112; Anderson 1923). As long as mobility and employment are used to characterize hoboes, they are respected slightly more than mere wanderers. Once this link is broken, those who cannot work are stagnant, tied to localities for shelter, service, and correction, and with dwindling opportunities.

Skid row helps fix the hobo in space and time and connects him to various organizations designed to cater to his needs. These same organizations also further his alienation, as the bar for service is gradually raised, vices are catered to, and money-making schemes part hoboes from the spoils of their labor. Particularly as shelter and service organizations grow within skid row, hoboes and eventually homeless people find themselves becoming passive clients, rather than active workers or consumers (Berger, Berger, and Kellner 1973). In Bahr's (1973, 120) view, one of primary challenges homeless people face is the effect of "occupying several stigmatized statuses at once," causing the embrace of skid row values in an act of self-preservation, a precursor for identity work (Snow and Anderson 1993). Bahr (1973) draws on Robert Merton's theory of anomie to explain disaffiliation among hoboes as a way of coping with their own inability to forge and sustain productive social ties. He also examines the lack of power among hoboes as a reason for disaffiliation:

> Power is control over environment—both the physical and the social environment . . . affiliations can be conceived as reflections

of power . . . power is manifest through organizations. A homeless man lacks the power to influence others or to mold his own future. It is an unenviable, and at the same time, a threatening condition. Skid row is reputed to be full of men in this state. (Bahr 1973, 31)

Skid row caters to the needs of the homeless traveler, but as consumers, hoboes have little power and engaging with service organizations reaffirms their marginality. At the same time, authorities develop new ways of rounding up, sheltering, and policing a seemingly permanent troublesome population and redeveloping city areas to make them more lucrative, exchangeable spaces. Laws against loitering, trespassing, and other nuisance offenses proliferate, restricting the movement and behavior of skid row residents and replacing the anti-tramp laws that regulated mobility in the late 1800s and early 1900s (Cresswell 2006). Instead of mobility being the primary problem with hoboes, occupying public space and performing private activities in public become the most poignant issues, as hoboes negotiate their position in a changing urban environment (Amster 2008).

What happens to the jungles during the postwar period is difficult to track, as few detailed records exist of them, even in their heyday. The Santa Barbara jungle is a semipermanent community that provides a unique view of what life was like from the perspective of its residents. Existing on private land in the downtown waterfront area, this jungle offers a setting through which to explore ideas of masculinity, domesticity, and how a marginalized group, of both men and eventually women, fits into a town that doesn't want them. Neatly situated between the beach, the dump, and the railroad station, the early jungle is a collection of twenty to sixty shacks, surviving until the late 1950s, when it fades out of existence only to resurface in the 1980s and endure to 2020, the present year. It provides an understanding of the hobo population; why the jungle is preferable to skid row, shelters, or a life on the move; and how marginal men develop social ties among one another and with the local community.

The 1980s: Survival and Resistance

By the 1980s, the jungle has risen to prominence, along with homelessness in general, as a nationwide problem of crisis proportions. Primary causes include deinstitutionalization, the 1981–1982 recession, polarized housing and employment markets, inadequate public assistance, domestic violence, mental illness, and changes in family structure (Baxter and Hopper 1981; Burt 1991, 1992; Wolch and Dear 1993; Baumohl 1996). The 1980s also inherit the loss of shared prosperity that occurs with widening income inequality beginning in the 1970s, when income gains at the top economic sector begin to flourish and continue to grow exponentially faster than in other sectors (Stone et al. 2018). But it is more than just increasing economic polarization that causes the immediate crisis; it is the four-pronged attack of inadequate housing, inaccessible employment, criminalization, and individual risk factors that set the scene for disaster. Employment trends show increasing levels of training and education needed to access the growing professional and service sectors (Wyatt and Hecker 2006; Fisk 2003). The housing market shows a lack of affordable units, stagnant growth, the elimination of subsidies, and the lack of a shelter safety net. And to make matters worse, jails and prisons, inevitable way stations for the marginal, explode during this decade and into the 1990s, with changing policies that promise a war on drugs and a get-tough-on-crime approach (Western 2001). The result is that the seasonal manual labor that hoboes relied on is either gone or provides just enough to survive on, but not enough to procure housing, which is not available anyway, and they are at risk on the street.

Understanding unsheltered homelessness in the 1980s is a challenge, particularly in terms of quantifying and regulating a large, diverse, and less mobile population. Instead of reducing mobility by restricting travel, regulation in this decade focuses on stagnation or mere visibility in public spaces; people experiencing homelessness are seen as a problem that won't go away. With the homeless ranks growing to Depression-era proportions, the nation's response comes from a sense of helplessness, and because of the volume and diversity of the population, structural factors are considered the most likely cause. But the focus on individual causes and vulnerabilities never disappears entirely. Some categories of homeless people are seen as undeserving, sympathetic victims, incapable of providing for themselves, and are offered a handout. Others are seen as people who are too lazy, addicted, or otherwise weak or flawed to merit assistance or are considered a threat to public safety. Service in the 1980s means minimally providing for sympathetic victims and leaving the rest to fight criminalization and struggle to survive on the streets. This inherent split between good and bad informs the creation of shelters and services for specific segments of the population, making entry requirements exclusive and confusing. Focusing on specific categories of homeless people rather than the overall population supports the status quo view of poverty as a permanent part of society (DiFazio 2006).

The first and only major federal response to homelessness, the McKinney-Vento Homeless Assistance Act of 1987 (Pub. L. 100-77, July 22, 1987, 101 Stat. 482, 42 U.S.C. § 11301 et seq.) is designed to offer immediate assistance as well as a continuum of care, implemented in 1994, to move people up a stepwise ladder beginning with behavioral compliance and emergency shelter and advancing to transitional and perhaps eventually permanent housing. People who are unsheltered are initially treated in a nuanced way as living in "a temporary makeshift accommodation in the residence of another individual, or a public/private place not . . . ordinarily used as . . . a regular sleeping accommodation for human beings" (S. Res. 813, Sess. of 1987), but wording is simplified in the final version to lacking a "fixed nighttime residence." Understanding exactly who people living unsheltered are, what they need, and what society is prepared to give them is up for grabs in the 1980s and beyond. But whatever its flaws and inadequacies, McKinney-Vento offers some ameliorative solutions to the immediate and growing crisis directing the most aid to those seen as undeserving victims of structural inequalities. It also begins the complicated process of defining unsheltered homelessness ideologically as needing service participation but increasingly unable to access welfare benefits, reintegrative strategies, or mainstream housing and employment. As a result of limited shelter space and directing resources to vulnerable populations, single men are last in line to receive federal assistance (Passaro 1996) and the face of unsheltered homelessness remains predominantly male.

In the midst of this crisis, many new enforcement measures are developed to protect citizens from the damage that seeing homeless people can cause. These measures reinforce the social, spatial, and behavioral norms that make public spaces the domain of housed citizens (Feldman 2004; Arnold 2004) and further marginalize people experiencing homelessness. This legal response assists municipalities in protecting themselves from the discomfort caused by homeless people in public, as well as any dangers and risks they may pose, including a loss of revenue. These laws are enacted locally but have federal implications, as they directly challenge the fundamental rights of citizenship embodied in several Constitutional Amendments (Feldman 2004; National Law Center on Homelessness and Poverty and the National Coalition for the Homeless 2009, 2013). They are also flexible, as they can be tailored to the needs and concerns of specific municipalities to address local issues related to the appearance and behavior of homeless people in public. Despite its effectiveness in removing homeless people from public places, anti-homeless criminalization ensures a lack of all but cyclical mobility, as homeless people are easy to find and cite repeatedly, reinforcing the cycle known as "churning" (Hudson 2015). This makes it more difficult to escape homelessness, prolongs time on the street, and creates enduring barriers to housing and employment.

For many people experiencing homelessness in this era, makeshift solutions are the only option, as even by conservative estimates, the need for housing greatly outpaces the resources, to the tune of at least a quarter of a million people without shelter (Hopper, Susser, and Conover 1985; Burt 1992). Along with emergency shelter provisions come questions about the moral worth of people experiencing homelessness, their culpability, and the basic questions: Are they honest or not? Will assistance be rehabilitative or will it reinforce laziness and dependence, possible reasons for homelessness in the first place? Many policies developed in the 1980s are geared toward ensuring that homeless people do not get too comfortable in an easy, taxpayer-supported lifestyle. And new, ugly stereotypes proliferate to corroborate this fear, including President Ronald Reagan's infamous "welfare queen," supporting the idea that black women, in particular, are milking the system. This skepticism, always racialized, about the overall moral character of benefit recipients sets the stage for favoring shorter subsidies with higher deliverables, for example, replacing Aid to Families with Dependent Children with Temporary Assistance for Needy Families (Ozawa and Yoon 2005; Danielson and Klerman 2008), and for service interactions fraught with mistrust and a legacy of personal and structural oppression.

The one thing people experiencing homelessness have going for them in the 1980s is that they gain national attention on an unprecedented scale. As the nation's cause célèbre, homelessness inspires scholarly research, federal policy changes, films, protest activities, and other forms of cultural, political, and social expression.[10] Protest focuses on the structural conditions leading to homelessness, arguing for shelter, services, and a moratorium on regulation strategies targeting individual behavior and the occupation of public space. Basic rights are also a focus, as many of the offenses homeless people are targeted for are life-sustaining activities or those considered central to citizenship and survival, such as sleeping and voting (Mitchell 2001). To address these issues, several national organizations are founded during this decade, including the United States Interagency Council on Homelessness, the National Alliance to End Homelessness, the National Coalition for the Homeless, and the National Law Center on Homelessness and Poverty, emphasizing the overwhelming consensus that homelessness is an emergency that needs to be remedied and demonstrating the strength of grassroots advocacy in establishing a national platform. Advocacy groups such as the Community for Creative Non-Violence (CCNV), headed by activist Mitch Snyder, and the National Coalition for the Homeless, founded by lawyer Robert Hayes, are the primary advocates for change and provisions on the federal level during this era.

In part because advocates have greater resources, higher political profiles, and the ability to negotiate eloquently on behalf of homeless people, homeless leaders never fully emerge. The logic behind silencing homeless people or speaking for them is part of a set of authoritative strategies designed to manage and exclude the unruly (Wright 1997, 182–183), even when used by advocates. For the CCNV and the National Coalition for the Homeless, the politics of compassion that characterizes homeless people as having a host of structural and individual vulnerabilities leading to homelessness is replaced by the politics of entitlement that argues for increased rights as a social justice issue that should be available to all regardless of status or identity (Hoch and Slayton 1989). Both approaches contest the idea that homelessness is an individual failing, but compassion leads to a loss of agency for homeless people who are pitied as victims of forces beyond their control, and entitlement is a threatening idea, as many Americans feel that they too struggle to make ends meet without assistance or handouts and homeless people should be able to do the same. As a result, and with Snyder at the helm of the CCNV, anti-homeless protest is both powerful and threatening, directed to offering immediate emergency services and shelter, and protesting unfair conditions.

Because of the compliance involved in seeking service, as well as the squalid conditions and a lack of shelter beds, unsheltered homelessness and makeshift living are seen as viable, preferable alternatives, and also as a form of resistance (Wagner 1993). Ethnographic work in the 1980s and 1990s examines the distinction between sheltered and unsheltered homelessness, emphasizing the need to retain a sense of control, acceptance, and community as key reasons for going unsheltered (Dordick 1997; Underwood 1993). Resistance activities by homeless people include makeshift sleeping as part of a larger set of urban survival strategies used to manage any combination of hunger, shelter, poverty, disability, trauma, and abuse, not to mention the more controversial problems of addiction and mental illness. "Economies of makeshift" describes a series of strategies designed to adapt under duress (Hopper, Susser, and Conover 1985). They exemplify homeless people's resilience and ability to create their own solutions to various problems and can be characterized by their ad hoc character, mobility, resort to public relief, parochial charity or begging, and participation in the underground economy (Hopper, Susser, and Conover 1985, 214). They are, by nature, adaptive to the immediate environment, whether that means having a good line to ask for spare change in cities nationwide or knowing which dumpsters have clean food in one's home city. They also take into account one's marginal status and the work needed to avoid regulation and get basic needs met, whether that means hiding or acting deferent or otherwise supplicatory to authorities.

The types of makeshift sleeping arrangements people use, as opposed to public and private shelters, vary widely depending on resources and availability and can include vehicles, buildings, sidewalk spaces like doorways, benches, aqueducts, tunnels, or other semipublic areas, tent cities, and jungles (Dehavenon 1996; Dordick 1997; Wakin 2014). Establishing these settings as an alternative to emergency shelter is a form of identity work that allows occupants to build self-esteem through minimizing contact with individuals and groups that reinforce stigma and marginality (Wright 1997). The jungle allows people experiencing homelessness to avoid the pain that goes with "mixed contacts," between stigmatized and normal, and the negative public attention that reinforces a degraded status and invites police attention. The idea of "mixed contacts," detailed in Chapter 4, draws attention to the discomfort involved in most service situations, where homeless people must account for their stigma and agree to fix it as a condition of seeking service (Goffman 1963). The shame and emotional work that often characterizes service interactions is a barrier to shelter and makes alternative living situations preferable.

The primary new space developed for people experiencing homelessness during this decade, and which they and advocates argue for vehemently, is the emergency shelter. Without a direct path to housing, emergency shelters are often empty warehouse spaces with cots or mats on the floor and a soup kitchen or other ad hoc services, when available. Instead of acting to immediately reduce the stress that homeless people are under or protect them from the dangerous conditions on the streets, shelters re-create the sense of emergency while ironically being seen as a precious resource. Homeless people entering emergency shelter in the 1980s begin a long path of service and compliance to prove their worth, which everyone doubts, and expend emotional and physical energy, which they don't have, and the promise of housing is often elusive.

The proliferation of service institutions for homeless people in the 1980s has the effect of making shelter itself synonymous with the general category "homeless." Skid row serves a similar function in earlier decades and is a much more homogenous and fixed part of the urban landscape, but beginning in the 1980s, the very definition of homelessness rests largely on service participation, or more specifically, shelter bed use. No longer able to count on skid row areas because of gentrification and other factors, homeless people are beholden to the organizations designed to serve them and are increasingly submissive to daily rules and schedules. At the same time, the increase in anti-homeless criminalization makes city spaces unsafe and makes unsheltered homeless people spend their days avoiding law enforcement. Instead of choosing periods of work and rest, people experiencing homelessness in the 1980s become accustomed to institutional routines at the expense of long-term planning or developing community, as they do more readily in makeshift settings. They also endure the duress of living a life on the run (Goffman 2014) and often avoid staying in one place for any length of time, or they opt out of service institutions entirely, and live life "off the grid."

The jungle is an "off the grid" place in the sense that people who live there often avoid services that require any intake procedure, identification, or record keeping beyond a head count. Most do not have credit cards, cell phones, or other means of ready identification indicating their position in the marketplace, as consumers. They are, in Mitchell Duneier's (2000) terminology, "men without accounts." The scavenging that they do to find food and the trappings of shelter is often time consuming, as it involves dodging police and avoiding trouble. One citation can topple the fragile apple cart of makeshift strategies many homeless people use to meet their needs for food, shelter, and basic resources. Because their possessions may be discarded during an arrest, homeless people often find themselves without even the meager possessions they have accumulated, and the time and effort it takes to reestablish credit or obtain identification causes many to give up. This is one way that people experiencing homelessness can become trapped in a revolving door of temporal and spatial control that punishes problematic identities and prevents social mobility.

But the 1980s is also a time for social protest and for pro-homeless advocacy at the local and national levels. Santa Barbara's jungle is at the center of the controversy for its anti-sleeping laws and hostile attitude toward "street people." Although the 1980s jungle there exists on public land, instead of the private property the early jungle enjoyed, the active social protest movement emboldens homeless people to take over other city areas, to protest unfair conditions, and to work with local and national advocates to do so. In this sense, it shares a legacy with the early jungle of community building with housed advocates who wield substantial power within the movement. But the loss of a private space and the different demographics of the 1980s Santa Barbara jungle community both solidify the idea of danger and threat associated with a troublesome population.

Millennial Jungle

It used to be the case that hoboes could travel the country surreptitiously on the same rail routes as paying customers. They had skid row as well as jungle areas and could afford cheap lodging, arranging their lives with periods of work and rest. In the 1980s, homelessness becomes a national crisis, and policy is directed toward filling emergency needs and protecting housed citizens. By contrast, homeless people today, in the second decade of the twenty-first century, are living in the shadows of global cities and do not hop trains (Von Mahs 2013). They watch trains go by and hide in the bushes, drinking and beating each other to death.[11] They are the failures of late capitalism, unable or unwilling to embrace consumerism, spatially and socially marginalized, and shuttling back and forth between prison and public shelters or the slightly more benevolent jail and county hospital. We valorize them only as the broken alter egos of corporate men gone wrong. In today's world, like Tyler Derden's character in the 1999 film *Fight Club*, those who do not buy into corporate capitalism completely are seen as psychotic. An ultraviolent, uber-masculine man free of the bonds of wage labor is, in the twenty-first century, just a mirage that exists in a buried part of the corporate imagination. The desire to revolt is kept down, in most cases, by the fear of becoming a social outcast, a failure, or at best a moral traffic light designed to keep us all in line.[12]

In this context, the jungle is a stigmatized zone where homeless in-groups not only survive but create a community of acceptance and resistance in the face of radical marginalization. Their only other options are correctional, institutional, and shelter spaces, whose proliferation is staggering. There is no valorizing or romanticizing the jungles of today, aside from the idea of freedom from responsibility, which is simply a misunderstanding. Unfettered travel and adventure are not associated with unsheltered homelessness as we now know it. Drifting and transience are only admired when done on private jets, by choice, or in the context of a youthful adventure (Krakauer 1996), but not when they involve filthy, dangerous conditions, trauma, addiction, and mental illness. Then, it's a trap (Kerr 2016). Comparing the jungles of yesterday and today tracks the change from mobility to stagnation and the resulting confines of cyclical motion and examines how alternative notions of identity and community are constructed in the context of living unsheltered.

Jungle spaces in the early 2000s are privatized and polarized, and people refer to them with a sense of ownership, "my jungle," rather than the more collective expression of "the jungle." They are also organized according to drug use and preference and overlap intimately with the organizational structure and culture of prison. People living in today's jungles are typically tethered to institutional and organizational spaces that provide resources they cannot procure on their own, including showers, meals, medical and support services, mail, and clothing and laundry facilities. Because jungle living is not legal in most areas, residents are also subject to police sweeps and receive citations for trespassing and other nuisance crimes (National Coalition for the Homeless 2004; National Law Center on Homelessness and Poverty and the National Coalition for the Homeless 2009, 2013; Mitchell 2001). Mobility, therefore, becomes more difficult over time, as city spaces become more and more regulated, policed, and gentrified, and homeless people's time is circumscribed according to institutional routines (Mitchell 2003). The physical danger of riding the rails is replaced with the drudgery of constant walking and movement without the excitement of possibility or new destinations and with accompanying illnesses, disabilities, and other forms of risk that make it that much more difficult (Dear and Wolch 1987; Wolch 1995). Even when homeless people buy automobiles to live in, they are chased around city areas, and new ordinances crop up that force them to remain in constant motion to avoid citation but without the means to escape entirely (Wakin 2014).

In the 2000s, how homeless people spend their time is of less interest than the length of time they remain homeless. Like the emergency, transitional, and permanent supportive housing nomenclature that differentiates types of shelter, time on the street is also quantified into "transitional, episodic, or chronic" (Murphy and Tobin 2011). People in the "chronic" category are defined as having a disabling condition and having been continuously homeless for one year or more, or having had four episodes of homelessness in the last three years (United States Department of Housing and Urban Development 2007). As complicated as this definition is, "disabling" is further broken down to include one or more of the following issues: substance abuse, serious mental illness, developmental disability, or chronic physical illness or disability, and an "episode" is a "separate, distinct, sustained stay" on the streets or in an emergency shelter (United States Department of Housing and Urban Development 2008). Research corroborates the idea that people who are chronically homeless are more likely to experience mental health issues and that these are exacerbated by life experiences and coping strategies prior to and while experiencing homelessness (Lippert and Lee 2015), so it is difficult to discern which comes first. Determining mental illness is also difficult, unless you have clinical expertise, so estimates often rely on guesses by "experts" and homeless service providers, and no official diagnosis.

The first point-in-time (PIT) count was implemented in January 2005, but these definitions make it difficult to understand and put a count into practice. The first 123-page guide to counting unsheltered homeless people, released in 2004, outlines possible counting methodologies, definitions, and the background and purpose of the count. Quantifying unsheltered homelessness remains a daunting task, as counting is often done in the dark, when seeing is a challenge, not to mention conducting interviews or diagnosing mental health or substance abuse issues or determining the length of homeless "episodes." Weather also significantly affects the count, as warm-weather areas have greater numbers of people who are unsheltered, and cold-weather areas have greater numbers of people indoors in January, when the count is conducted. As a result, unsheltered counts are the least accurate, consistent, and generalizable, and that population remains the most difficult to quantify or serve.

The length of time people experience homelessness is of interest primarily in light of the expense it causes, as chronically homeless people consume a disproportionate amount of service and tax dollars and can be more affordably housed in apartments than left on the street (Culhane, Park, and Metraux 2011). This explicit linkage recalls the classic phrase "time is money," except that homeless people's time is seen as other people's money. Ending or shortening the length of time people are homeless becomes a primary means of saving tax dollars. Reducing time on the street also saves lives, evidenced by the now well-utilized vulnerability index that measures mortality risk and prioritizes people for housing on this basis (O'Connell et al. 2010). Along with the housing-first initiative (Padgett, Henwood, and Tsemberis 2016), this approach foregrounds the voices, needs, and concerns of the most vulnerable segment of the homeless population, rather than eclipsing them in favor of economic savings. But whether reducing the amount of time people experience homelessness saves money or saves lives, both approaches agree that it is beneficial to shorten the length of time on the street.

As they did in the 1980s, people living in jungles in the 2000s remain unsheltered in part because of the degradation involved in seeking public assistance and in part because of the confusing and inadequate array of housing and service choices and eligibility requirements, and for many other reasons too numerous to describe (Donley and Wright 2012). People also resist shelter because increased time on the streets can result in an embrace of street culture and the homeless label (Snow and Anderson 1993; Wagner 1993). Embracing the values and survival strategies employed on the street, and even the modes of dress and communication, makes it more difficult for people to reintegrate into housed society. Both existence and resistance, in the form of occupying public spaces and communicating or behaving in ways that are not sanctioned by authority (Wright 1997), are risky as they result in jail and prison stays and other forms of institutional cycling (DeVerteuil 2003). The physical, emotional, and psychological toll that criminalization takes, not to mention legal complications, is a significant barrier to exiting homelessness (Kerr 2016).

In cities nationwide, there is still an acknowledged lack of shelter or affordable housing, leaving thousands of homeless people to find makeshift locations to sleep in on a nightly basis.[13] Whether they do so as an act of resistance or as a necessity, those who are unsheltered must know where to hide, as the most frequent citations are for performing bodily functions in public, including sitting, eating, sleeping, and going to the bathroom (National Law Center on Homelessness and Poverty and the National Coalition for the Homeless 2009). For people experiencing homelessness, the inevitable cycle of one's daily routine is done under constant scrutiny and the fear of persecution, what Tate (2015) calls "policing comfort." Targeting offers a two-pronged attack against the intellectual and emotional offenses homeless people may cause, collectively referred to as "quality of life" offenses (Kelling and Coles 1996; Vitale 2005). Criminalization strategies, now far more numerous and targeted than in the 1980s, reinforce the idea that people experiencing homelessness don't merit the rights or comforts the rest of us take for granted, not even the right to vote, sit down, sleep, or rest (Mitchell 2001; Ellickson 2001). And it may also be that there is still the lingering idea that perhaps homeless people don't even understand, appreciate, or deserve these basic rights (Feldman 2004). For these reasons, the National Law Center on Homelessness and Poverty (2013) calls the criminalization of homelessness "cruel, inhuman, and degrading."

Relegating people who are already stigmatized and often traumatized to marginal areas reinforces their marginality, rather than letting them blend in and disappear, as even chronically homeless people with acute mental illness can do with the housing-first principle today (Padgett, Henwood, and Tsemberis 2016). This innovative approach is now mainstreamed through the federal funding application process. But the brilliance of the "housing first" idea is that it treats homeless people with acute mental illness as consumers (Tsemberis, Gulcur, and Nakae 2004). This strategy works, on an interactional level, because people experiencing homelessness are given the one thing they need above all else, with relatively few conditions and high chances for success, when properly implemented. Housing first allows for control over time and space, for the most part, and its impact on identity is often transformative. The overall long-term goals are safe housing and individual and social betterment.

Without a steady income from employment or public assistance, all that homeless people usually have to pay is of themselves. They are expected to pay emotionally, in deference and submission to authority, by being detained in jail and/or serving prison time for transgressions of public space laws and behavioral norms. They may also pay physically in violence and sex work, which they are victims of or which they use to procure things, increasing exposure to various, insidious forms of risk, and making exit that much more difficult (Purser, Mowbray, and O'Shields 2017). These ways of paying fundamentally inform and structure the experience of unsheltered homelessness, leaving little time for long-term planning, employment, sobriety, or anything else that might lead to reintegration. Aside from the payment of public assistance and participation in weekly case management that housing first requires, it eliminates all other forms of behavioral compliance, which are not treated as a prerequisite for procuring or sustaining housing (Padgett, Henwood, and Tsemberis 2016). Eliminating this kind of high-barrier physical and emotional work and providing safety with minimal risk allows residents to focus on long-term goals and think of themselves as consumers with choices.

The farther people retreat from shelters, city streets, or housed society in general, the more they are insulated from all but targeted regulation. Despite their relative isolation, jungles overlap with tent cities (Udelsman 2011; Heben 2014) and encampments (Herring 2014; United States Interagency Council on Homelessness 2015). Whereas jungles are almost always hidden, tent cities are sometimes located in more prominent areas and may be designed to draw attention to homelessness as a problematic condition in need of remedy (Herring and Lutz 2015). Tent cities also have some overlap with more explicitly political movements, for example, Occupy Wall Street (OWS), and its national and global counterparts (Schein 2012). For these initiatives, occupying space makes overlapping claims: public space belongs to all, those in power do not represent the people, the system has failed the people, and change is possible (Gould-Wartofsky 2015, 31). The revolutionary potential of these more organized and explicitly political tent cities is reminiscent of early attempts to organize hoboes under the IWW. They are also reminiscent of the 1980s reliance on advocates to focus and deliver the movement's message and goals. Today's jungles, by contrast, do not want attention. They may share some of the sentiments expressed by Occupy, and many joined the movement, but as sleeping spaces go, they are designed to remain hidden.

A Jungle in Paradise

Unsheltered homelessness today is still the domain of single men. About 35 percent of the total nationwide homeless population is unsheltered and 71 percent are male (Annual Homeless Assessment Report 2017). Half of all unsheltered homeless people in the country live in California, and 66 percent of the statewide homeless population is unsheltered. California has also been named the "meanest" state with respect to anti-homeless criminalization and having the least-affordable housing market (National Coalition for the Homeless 2004). Unsheltered homeless people living in California today face competition for scarce resources and a host of regulation measures that limit their mobility and punish their visibility in public. Does this mean they are "disaffiliated," that they lack productive social ties, or that we ensure disaffiliation by breaking down their sense of agency through constrained mobility, high-barrier shelters, and repeat interaction with law enforcement and other agencies of correction?

First appearing in the early 1900s, the Santa Barbara jungle is a collection of shacks on the property of Lillian Child, a wealthy widow and owner of prime waterfront land. It differs from most jungles of the time because of its spatial and temporal permanence. Its population ranges from a high of approximately sixty men in the 1930s to only three in the 1960s, and its collection of shacks swells and dwindles accordingly. The jungle is protected because it exists on private property, and its sense of community and social structure are allowed to flourish. After Child's death in 1951, the estate, including the jungle, is deeded to the city for the construction of a public park, and when the land is eventually developed, all of the men relocate. The jungle reemerges in virtually the same area, on publicly owned but still undeveloped land in the 1980s, when it becomes a site for social protest and a symbol of the fear and danger associated with homeless street people. By the early 2000s, jungles are more fragmented camps, still scattered along the railroad tracks and in close proximity to the jungle of old. The fights, sweeps, and fires that occur in the jungle of the early 2000s show that it is a place where street justice holds sway.

In Chapter 2, I introduce the Santa Barbara jungle as a literal and figurative anchor point for men on the road. Using two first-hand accounts from men who live in the jungle, I explore how they survive and create a sense of community. The first account is from a resident known as the "Bookman," who lives in the jungle from 1940 to 1943, along with approximately forty to sixty others. He writes a series of letters on daily life, an overview of survival strategies, and descriptions of the personalities and routines of the men. The second account is from Edward Anderson, who serves as mayor of the jungle from 1951 to 1958. He acts as the jungle's spokesperson and arbiter of any conflicts that occur therein. He is also a prolific writer, and his letters appear in the local press even after his tenure as mayor comes to an end. These letters, along with two scrapbooks abundantly stocked with photos, clippings, poems, and short stories, are used in this chapter to explore the culture and community of the jungle, survival strategies, and interaction with the housed community.

Chapter 3 focuses on power and protest in the jungle in the 1980s. During this time, the jungle exists on public property and is a highly controversial site. This chapter draws on a seventy-five-page manuscript by author, activist, and Santa Barbara resident Peter Marin, which examines the structure and culture of the jungle. It also includes information from thirty interviews with homeless people and advocates active in the protest movement of the 1980s, and the summaries provided in Rob Rosenthal's (1994) *Homeless in Paradise: A Map of the Terrain,* and Jane Haggstrom's (1994) dissertation, "The Santa Barbara Sleeping Law Controversy: A Study of the Empowerment of the Homeless." These sources are used to explore the protest activities that take place in Santa Barbara in the 1980s with particular emphasis on the right to sleep and vote. By this time, the existence of the jungle and everyone in it is challenged, and mobility and transiency become central concerns for authorities seeking to regulate the local homeless community. This debate plays out in local newspapers, and this chapter draws on over 300 articles to illustrate the battle. Overall, this decade raises questions about citizenship, entitlement, identity, protest, and advocacy that will be key concerns for homeless people for years to come.

Chapter 4 incorporates fieldwork I conducted from 2000 to 2005 and includes twenty visits to jungle camps and extended interviews with thirty-five jungle residents, detailed in the body of the chapter. Similar to the early chapters, initial questions that structure these interviews include pathways into and out of homelessness, current survival strategies, and forms of identity work. These issues are also explored through fieldwork, as people often furnish better answers to questions when they go unasked (Van Maanen 1991). Exploring how people in the jungle see themselves in relation to society, to law enforcement, and to their former and future selves offers a comparison with earlier years. This chapter uses three sets of partners who live together in the jungle to examine these issues in greater depth. With the rise of shelterization and criminalization as strategies of containment, the focus here is on the limited, cyclical mobility that people experiencing homelessness find themselves trapped within and on possible ways out.

Chapter 5 offers an updated view of makeshift housing solutions and includes data collected in 2006, 2008, and 2016 to trace the lives of long-term jungle residents. Using interviews, surveys, and fieldwork, I examine the evolution of the legal battle over public space in Santa Barbara and the provision of shelter and services for people living unsheltered. A comparison of different forms of unsheltered homelessness from an ethnographic perspective provides a detailed view of the reasons people choose to live in makeshifts like jungles and vehicles over other alternatives. I address the issue of how different makeshifts foster resistance and examine local advocacy efforts to assist people living in the jungle in contesting criminalization, accessing education, and preserving stable housing. I also examine grassroots efforts to offer community and support to the jungle's long-term residents, focusing on quality of life and reintegration. Finally, I explore how the experience of living unsheltered affects identity, community, and chances for survival and resistance. Chapter 6 continues this exploration and suggests that understanding the experience of jungle living warrants refocusing policies and services to address rebuilding identity and community over survival and punishment.

2

A Protected Community: 1940s–1950s

In the 1940s, the Santa Barbara Waterfront is a premiere tourist destination, with the railroad running parallel to the ocean, along East Beach, on to State Street for shopping and dining, and out to West Beach to stay the night and travel on to all points north. The jungle is located on the Child Estate, a sixteen-acre plot of land bordered by the railroad and the Pacific Ocean and stretching from the luxurious Mar Monte Hotel to the Andrée Clark Bird Refuge. It is in one of three distinct, adjacent neighborhoods along the compact enclaves of East Beach.[1] In the early 1940s, as the United States enters World War II, control of the waterfront is turned over to the US government, and although some improvements are made, a plan for developing the area isn't seriously considered until the late 1950s. The reason for this is limited funding along with the local desire to keep the waterfront pristine, as a corrective to the more commercial atmosphere of the Santa Monica and Santa Cruz waterfront areas. It is in this context that locals pose the question: What will Santa Barbara do with a hobo jungle in the middle of its premier estate neighborhood?

Answering this question helps identify the image of the waterfront Santa Barbara is cultivating, which the men of the jungle must answer to. As early as the 1920s and 1930s, wealthy citizens begin to fear the influence of outside developers and aggressively purchase waterfront property for public use.[2] Development focuses on a

Figure 2.1 Santa Barbara Waterfront: 1940s–1950s

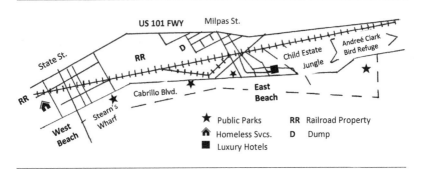

combination of luxury and preservation, "entrepreneurial" and "aesthetic" uses, causing one author to comment, "Santa Barbara has inspired an image of an ideal residential retreat from the grime, poverty, and inclemency associated with other human settlements" (Bookspan 1982, 2). But does this mean inclusion or an isolated, elite city neighborhood? Although there is still significant undeveloped land along the waterfront in the 1940s, and a good deal of it is owned by the railroad, the jungle's existence goes against the dual ideals of commercial development and environmental preservation. The following discussion examines how the city manages the odd, ironic presence of the jungle in the East Beach area in the 1940s and 1950s and how the men of the jungle survive and persevere.

Two firsthand accounts from men living in the jungle at this time illustrate how it flourishes, wanes, and eventually fades into memory. The first is a handwritten series of fourteen letters and a fifty-five-page diary written by a man calling himself the Bookman, a jungle resident from 1940 to 1943. Through the Bookman, we learn about daily survival, jungle culture, and the sense of identity and community fostered among the men. An ethnographer at heart, the Bookman writes in meticulous detail about how he came to live in and eventually leave the jungle to pursue employment. The second account includes a scrapbook and a collection of letters, stories, and poems penned by one of the last jungle mayors, Edward Anderson, who lived there from 1951 to 1958. In comparison with the Bookman, the jungle mayor is an important person in the jungle, with status and prestige to accompany his title. Anderson's writing is not in the form of a daily report but takes the form of a scrapbook of personal letters, photographs, and newspaper clippings that chronicle his life. He speaks for the men of the jungle but does not write about them as much as the Bookman does, preferring to use his role as jungle leader to negotiate for increased provisions for the men and explain their way of life to the local community. After the jungle fades, Anderson moves to an apartment in town and continues to be active in the civic life of the city. The stories of the Bookman and Anderson illustrate the time during which hoboing, skid row, and the jungle itself become obsolete.

The detailed writings these men leave behind characterize their jungle as they saw it. Historical documents are also used to explore the development of the waterfront and the jungle, and local newspapers help show how the men interact with the local community. But so many questions remain: Who were the Bookman and Edward Anderson before and after they came to live in the jungle? How did they survive there? And what kind of culture and community did they create? Although these questions may never be fully answered, through these research materials we can begin to form a unique, sustained portrait of a usually hidden and transient community.

Having space and a benefactor, along with rules and a hierarchy, informs the culture and community of the jungle and makes it tolerable for the rest of the city. The men of the jungle, for the most part, stay in their place. They are older men, pensioners and veterans, several of whom live there for decades. Their sense of identity derives from control and community but not from "success," which revolves around financial gain and supporting the nuclear family. These men are not breadwinners or potential soldiers. Most of them do not find or sustain gainful employment, beyond the odd or temporary jobs they hold in the casual labor market. Their spatial permanence and age mean that neither their masculinity nor their mobility is seen as threatening, and by the early 1960s, the last remaining jungle residents are in their seventies and eighties, making the town's tolerance seem that much more benevolent.

Examining the nexus of space, time, and mobility in the Santa Barbara jungle shows that what sets it apart from its transient counterparts and leads to its endurance is a combination of the unique features of living collectively, on private land, with access to various subsistence needs and items and time to pursue and accumulate them. This, in turn, affects the men's sense of themselves in the world and their ability to develop an enduring community. Although there is evidence to suggest that the residents of the jungle lead marginal lives in various ways, Child's protection of them and the town's ongoing differentiation of them from their transient, run-of-the-mill hobo counterparts ensures their survival. But national and local trends, including the postwar development boom of the 1950s, low levels of unemployment, relatively high wages, and the GI Bill's preventative and rehabilitative influence, make the jungle's days numbered.

A Place of Their Own

Lillian Child was walking on her property one evening in the early 1900s when she witnessed local police telling some hoboes to move along. She confronted the officers, telling them that "wandering knights of the road, who don't look like criminals and can behave themselves" were welcome to set up camp on her property and invite their friends to do the same (*Santa Barbara Independent*, March 21, 1971). With this offer of refuge, the jungle was born. The men begin by assembling a group of shacks in a grove of eucalyptus trees, and Child establishes the rules: 1. No one under thirty-five, 2. No negroes, 3. No drinkers.[3] She also imposes a hierarchy on the jungle and insists that the men elect a mayor. Child visits the jungle frequently, notably at Christmastime, when she reportedly gives each man a fifty-cent piece.[4] It is clear that she wants order on the property, and the men are to keep the jungle clean and settle their own disputes. For his role in preserving order, the mayor lives in a nicer shack and is the one Child calls on when she comes to visit. In this sense, the mayor is the jungle's spokesperson and ambassador to Child and to the rest of the city.

"Childville," "Jungleville," "Hoboville," or "Shacktown," as it is alternately known, develops quite a reputation within Santa Barbara and beyond. It is known by some as a quaint local attraction[5] and by others as a symbol of social blight. The jungle's location on Vega Mar, Child's famed seaside estate, the "star of the sea," makes its existence that much more intriguing. The size of the jungle ranges from a high of sixty shacks in 1941 to a low of three in 1962, and the rest of the waterfront develops around it to include several luxury resorts. The 400-room Mar Monte Hotel is the first of its kind built in the East Beach area. A newspaper account that hangs in the lobby describes the hotel as having "many unique features," including imported draperies and a tiled bath in every room (*Morning Press*, June 11, 1931). Opened in 1931, the Mar Monte helps solidify the link between luxury tourism and the Santa Barbara Waterfront that is one of its signature and enduring features.

Conflict over the jungle begins when guests of the Mar Monte complain that they can see the men cooking, bathing, and washing clothes from their balconies, an early juxtaposition of luxury and penury that contributes to the shock value of homeless people in paradise.[6] To appease concerned tourists and locals, Child sells the unimproved parcel of land adjacent to the Mar Monte in 1946 and supervises the relocation of the thirty or so shacks that remain in the jungle to the far side of her property, where they are better hidden. Capitulating to waterfront development is part of what preserves the jungle as a beloved, or at least tolerated, part of the city instead of labeling it a public threat, and Child's wealth allows a smooth transition that preserves an endangered community.

Police attention is partially responsible for Child's decision to relocate the jungle, as city authorities threaten to impose tax assessments on the shacks. To avoid this, Child requires the men to find building materials at the dump rather than risk being taxed for new dwellings. In addition, and because one jungle resident threatens to file a claim of "squatter's rights" on the land, Child requires the men to vacate their shacks for twenty-four hours, at least once a year, so that her ownership of the property is not jeopardized. Despite her protection of the men, when she dies in 1951, there is no explicit provision for them in her will or in the documents that deed the property to the Santa Barbara Foundation. As a result, when the estate is turned over to the city, there is considerable debate about what to do with the jungle's residents, who find themselves without a home of their own.[7]

Many people in town feel the need to honor Child's unwritten wish that the men of the jungle, now far fewer in number, should be provided for. Others bitterly oppose assistance, calling the jungle unsightly and unsanitary. The men of the jungle participate in this debate in local newspapers, offering thanks and tolerance in the face of hostility, calling Santa Barbara the "little city with a big heart." Yet they are prepared for potential eviction and are willing to leave the jungle if the town so decides. Part of the decision about what to do with the men relies on distinguishing them from younger, more mobile hoboes who are just passing through and who are seen as a drain on local resources.

The Bookman

The Bookman lives in the jungle in the early 1940s, when it is at its most populous point. Still visible from the Mar Monte Hotel, the jungle is a collection of tumble-down shacks tucked in amid a lush grove of eucalyptus trees. In comparison with the mayor, the Bookman is a member of the group, holding no special status. The letters he writes are addressed to a man named Cecil, a private citizen and hobo enthusiast, who lives in Oakland, California. The letters are dated from 1941 to 1943, with the final two letters coming from Los Angeles, where the Bookman has moved to seek restaurant work. The Bookman writes to Cecil because of an article that they plan to release on life in the jungle, which he thinks can lead to a substantial cash payout. In addition to the letters themselves, he includes fifty-five pages of notes on the details of jungle life, including shack construction, food prices and preparation, war and family, work, health, climate, scavenging at the local dump, and details on the men, their nicknames and their personalities.[8] He also describes the philosophy of the men and the specific strategies they use to get along with limited means. His exploration of exchanges fundamental to life

Santa Barbara Historical Museum

A possible Bookman.

in the jungle emphasizes the cooperative and domestic nature of what he sometimes refers to as "the colony."

The Bookman's early letters hammer out the details of his agreement to write an article with Cecil on life in the jungle. Always interested in a fair trade, the Bookman agrees to take notes on his preferred topics: "But one thing I insist on, or else no soap—It's got to be a 50-50 deal on whatever we get. That's final, whether we get $10 or $1,000." He estimates their take at "anywhere from $150 to $700" but notes that "money in any large amount will not do me any good." Although he is interested in surviving, the Bookman is not interested in accumulating large amounts of money. And as his notes attest, the jungle depends on a system of barter rather than cash payment[9] for needed goods and supplies.

In his letters, the Bookman writes about personal matters, including his friendship with Cecil, his worry over his sons and the war, his medical condition, things he needs or has saved for Cecil, and his future plans. Cecil visits the jungle some time before January 27, 1941, and in his first letter on record, the Bookman confesses: "I enjoyed your visit so damned much that I felt lonesome as hell after you left." Part of this has to do with the weather. Between January and March 1941, the rain makes it difficult for the men and for the country overall, as it is the third-wettest winter in history (Mattice 1941). Constant rain means that the dump, the main source of wood and supplies for the men, is virtually inaccessible, "a sea of mud." It also means that the men have to keep their fires going almost constantly to battle the cold and the damp.

As a result, morale in the jungle is at an all-time low, and hunger and want set in. Even a mulligan stew, which consists of any and all available meat and vegetables, "everything you have except you don't put in the coffee pot or the axe," proves to be a challenge. The Bookman notes that this small comfort is an unusual luxury for the men that winter, as the ingredients are rarely all on hand at the same time—"ipso facto: no mulligan." His first winter in the jungle has the Bookman in unusually low spirits: "I was caught flat footed + for the first time in my life I really got discouraged." This is partially due to the lack of firewood and food: "I lived nearly two weeks on 20 cents and some flour." But the fellowship of the men and being among a group of people in the same situation is a comfort, and the Bookman describes this feeling: "We were all in the same boat. I was one of a few, amen." His spirits return with the sunshine, and by the next time he writes, several weeks later, he offers Cecil some camping supplies he thinks he can use.

The positive side to the hardship of inclement weather is that the men are forced to rely on one another for survival, as the dump produces no goods, the men have no work, and their need for resources increases with more time spent in their shacks:

> Unable to get any junk; steady rain preventing any sort of activity, it became practically necessary for the community to assist each other. None had too much; some had nothing, but a system of barter developed whereby the luckier ones swapped with those less fortunate. Some had plenty of flour, beans, corn meal etc. and traded with others for oil, candles, wood, onions, etc. By this method and by being on strictly reduced rations, the colony came through fairly well through the wettest season in the memory of old time residents.

It isn't only inclement weather that encourages the men to help each other and swap items that will benefit them individually. In fact, swapping goods is such a common practice that the Bookman includes several pages on "the fine art of swapping," detailed later in this chapter.

Setting Up House

The first order of business to set up camp in the jungle is finding items to build with. The Bookman calls this "promoting" and offers meticulous detail on what items he obtains, where and how he obtains them, and what other men do to procure necessities. The main source of wood and goods for the men of the jungle is the dump, and they go there frequently to find materials with which to construct their shacks and outfit them inside. The men compete with and sell to licensed junk dealers, and "about 12 or 14 men, paying a city license of $16.00 per year, work over the dump all day, gathering rags, bottles, brass, copper, iron, aluminum, etc., which they sell each night to a wholesale junk dealer who calls their [*sic*] daily." Other men have "small incomes or pensions to get by on," and still others are the more typical "itinerants on the move" who camp at the edge of the dump about a mile from the jungle. The Bookman estimates that ten to forty of these men, "these drifters, on cold nights and rainy days, corral all the available wood, sometimes creating a

Santa Barbara Historical Museum

Setting up house.

scarcity for the regulars." Given the crude structure of most jungle stoves, "without dampers or fire controls," the men of the jungle burn quite a lot of wood, particularly during the rainy season. This fleeting comparison between jungle residents and transients shows the sense of entitlement and accumulation that go with residency versus the mobility and recklessness characteristic of the hobo lifestyle.

The Bookman finds everything from wood and cardboard to kitchen supplies, including "enamel cups and plates, knives, forks, spoons, frying pans, coffee pots, stew pots, a pancake turner, can opener, and paring knife" at the dump. In several of his letters, he emphasizes the quality of the items he promotes, comparing them with what an average American household discards: "A great many housewives, afflicted with traditional American carelessness, accidentally throw away items that are still good." He goes on to list the kitchenware items he obtains from the dump as well as the items he uses to outfit his shack. He offers to save several things for Cecil, including camping supplies and kitchenware, with the assurance that they are all "top quality." Overall, the men of the jungle gain anywhere between

Jungle entrance.

60 cents and $1.00 per week scavenging from the dump and are proud of their ability to survive on limited means. The Bookman boasts that "no housewife, however clever a bargainer she may be, can beat these men when it comes to stretching the weekly budget." The domestic life of the jungle is about thrift, and upholding this in comparison with typical, wasteful American households and housewives is a form of identity work through which the Bookman builds his own self-esteem and notes the accomplishments of the men as exemplary. Of course, this contrast also shows an understanding that the men are crossing over into territory typically considered the domain of women, of housewives. To make this palatable, he notes that the men are offering an important corrective to overaccumulation by picking up what women discard.

When the Bookman first arrives in the jungle on October 10, 1940, he is in poor health and anticipating winter, so he makes repeated trips to the dump in the wee hours of the morning, when no one else is "promoting," to find basic necessities. He describes moving into the jungle and finding a shack to occupy: "It had nothing except the bed and a broken-down table . . . In two months I was all

Santa Barbara Historical Museum

Cardboard shack.

set, but I had to do some tall promoting . . . by the tenth of December I had it so completely outfitted that it was the envy of some who had been here two or more years." This is the first of two shacks the Bookman occupies during his time in the jungle. He is particularly proud to have the rare comforts of a wooden floor and a pitched roof. The shack itself is "9 x 7 feet, with a narrow door. Height is 7-1/2 feet, allowing plenty of clearance, a factor lots of these huts failed to account for." There is also an attached kitchen, and the Bookman's stove is "a Ford model T gas tank, the plug taken out + the hole enlarged," a creative use for discarded automobile parts. Once his shack is outfitted, the Bookman reduces his trips to the dump to three times a week, primarily for wood.

Because the men find their construction materials at the dump, the size and comfort of the shacks is limited. They "build without levels or squares, no tools except a dull saw and a one-clawed hammer, using old nails bent or twisted," and it's a wonder they hold up at all. Windows are particularly hard to come by, as "decent sized pieces of glass are hard to find." As a result, and because the jungle is not wired for electricity, many men go to sleep when the sun goes down. Lamps are also hard to find, although the Bookman has two, including "a R.R. caboose lamp . . . in perfect working order." He uses discarded automobile headlights to let in natural light and preserve warmth. His walls, ceiling, and roof are made of layers of cardboard, with "curtain material from shade rollers" in between. Surprisingly weather resistant, the only challenges are keeping out the insects and the damp. To store his extra items, the Bookman builds a storeroom on the side of his shack, where he also keeps his washtub, dishpans, axes, and so on. The goods he accumulates in his storeroom and the meticulous care with which he organizes and describes his shack show his appreciation for domesticity. The jungle's permanence allows the Bookman to become adept at the fine art of swapping and avoid welfare institutions or being dependent on aid or alms. His ability to provide for himself, assist other men, and offer goods to his friend Cecil is a source of pride. In this way, the Bookman remains in control, a skilled participant in the jungle's system of barter and exchange.

The Fine Art of Swapping

According to the Bookman, "It's in a place like this that the art of swapping reaches its highest peak, owing to scarcity of money. By means of honest barter I have secured a number of things I wanted." But not all residents are wise to the art of swapping, either because they are newcomers or because they try to cheat the person they swap with. In either case, the Bookman is ready. He describes one resident called "Hoosegow Paddy," who gets drunk and then tries to swap items for wood. In one instance, he offers the Bookman half a gallon of kerosene that is 75 percent water. The Bookman says nothing to him, and later learns that this is "an old trick of Paddy's." The next time Paddy asks the Bookman to swap wood for kerosene, he gives him a generous share of wood, but "it was soaked with creosote, + if anything can burn like hell + smell worse, it hasn't been invented. It will run you out from the odor. The following day Paddy was wild + wanted to know what in hell I had given him. I said it ought to burn just as good as kerosene + water, so he shut up."

Other swaps are more fruitful for the Bookman. He discusses needing a wheelbarrow to cart items back and forth from the dump, which most men do "burro fashion" on their backs. "Cockney Al has a pretty good wheel barrow, but he never uses it himself, being too lazy to promote." Seeing his opportunity, the Bookman asks to borrow the wheelbarrow and the Cockney "said he'd smash it before he would loan it to me or anyone else." "Dirty Shirt Al" then buys the wheelbarrow for 50 cents and sells it to Scotty the shoemaker for groceries. Scotty also wants to buy a pair of bicycle tires, but the Bookman beats him to it, gets the tires, and takes them into his storeroom and waits. Two days later, "I sent word to Scotty that I had the wheels. He came to see me at once, but I had to tell him that while I was very sorry, the only way he could get them was to swap me the wheelbarrow for the pair. He growled but agreed. The look on Cockney Al's face when he saw me with his former possession was lovely to witness. He had a lot to learn about the fine art of diplomacy, and the technique of swapping."

The second time he needs a wheelbarrow, the Bookman says he "swapped with a 'Jungle Bum,'" noting that there are several in the jungle "who beg from other stiffs. I nailed him by swapping 40 cents worth of food + tobacco for his wheelbarrow." In his estimation, the Jungle Bum is distinct from the rest of the men, a "tramp who lives off hoboes" and therefore deserves what he gets. The fine art of swapping is contingent on one's identity and reputation in the jungle, and it involves adhering to the principles of reciprocity and accountability on which the community depends. A jungle resident can just as easily be paid back for bad behavior or a bad swap as he can for good behavior or a good swap, and those seen as dishonest, or not part of the jungle community, can be subject to retaliation or unfair practice. Some jungle residents are also possessive about their belongings and are not inclined to swap with others.

Jungle residents who lack diplomacy or who are not adept at the art of swapping often lose out, and those who are generous in swapping with others reap the benefits. The Bookman describes assisting a man known as "Crippled Joe, a former soldier who suffered a stroke of paralysis while in the army." Joe is anxious to repair one wall of his shack before the rainy season but has only one hand to do the work. The Bookman helps him rebuild the wall and notes that "he tried to pay me for it, but we don't do things that way here. Money is scarce + we help each other anytime we are able." After learning the reciprocal nature of assistance in the jungle, Joe finds a way to pay the Bookman back: "When bad weather set in + my own trouble kept me confined, I got mine unexpectedly. Many a time I have wakened from an afternoon nap to find a couple of eggs on my table or a slice of ham, or a dish of macaroni and cheese, for which Joe was famous." In a place like the jungle, getting one's comeuppance is something the men can count on. Newcomers who do not know the rules of the jungle are susceptible to bad trades, bad goods, and bad information. This underscores the importance of developing one's reputation in the jungle community as someone others can count on.

Although the men of the jungle are more mobile than those who settle in town, they are able to accumulate things, enjoy the rewards of residency, and sometimes cheat outsiders. The Bookman writes about needing a long-handled shovel "to dig a garbage pit + . . . spade up a small garden." Knowing that these shovels are scarce, the Bookman strategizes. He knows that one of the shacks has a shovel and a new resident has just moved in, so he pays the man a visit.

> That evening, just before dark I dropped around by the fellow's place + saw the shovel in back before I went to where he sat. "This your place?" I asked. "Yes," he answered. "Well," I said, "did you find a shovel here when you came; one with a small bit of copper wire on the handle? Someone here borrowed mine one rainy night to dig a ditch to keep out the water + he didn't return it." "There was a shovel here" he said "when I took this place but I don't know whose it is." "Mine had this wire I spoke of" I told him. "Let's see it." We looked at it and sure enough there was a piece of wire around the handle. "Take it" he said "It's not mine anyhow." I did but it must have been a mere coincidence that I noticed that bit of wire as I came around his shack to see him.

Then, in a moment of guilt and perhaps repentance, he writes, "God hates a liar."

From swapping to scavenging, the Bookman's ability to procure the necessities of domestic life extends to food purchase and preparation. Most of the purchasing is either inexpensive or involves relying on handouts from local merchants. Some are known for their generosity: "If you take a paper bag with you + go to the side door of the S.P. Milling Co., they will give you free about 5# of lima beans," "take a nickel or a dime, generally the nickel, into Larco's Wholesale Fish Co., and you won't be able to carry the amount away that will be given to you." Other merchants offer damaged goods for a reduced price: "At Johnsons Eggery, where eggs are candled, they sell you blood-specked eggs at sliding scales, according to the market, 15 eggs for 10c." Still others require the men to "dime up" or offer a dime to the "butcher or vegetable man . . . to see what they can do for you." In most cases, the Bookman notes, "If there are not too many hitting them up in succession, they will as a rule give you quite a bit." Strategizing about when and how to ask for things makes the Bookman an adept navigator of social situations, applying makeshift strategies to meet basic needs instead of relying on welfare or participating in the formal economy.

One of the most important parts of swapping and scavenging in the jungle and going to town for resources is the ability to read people. The personalities of the men in the jungle, their nicknames, and the relationships between residents are the focus of several sets of the Bookman's notes. He lists the nicknames of the men, includes a brief description of each, and offers generalizations that attempt to put the men into context as a social category. In general, he thinks that the men who stay in the jungle in the long term, the "permanent population," are difficult to characterize—"a mixture of ignorant + wise; indifferent and ambitious; lazy or active. The average age is 50 to 55, with a few around 60 and 4 or 5 at the age of 75–80." The men are admittedly older than the transient population, and their personalities and social characteristics are harder to pin down.

Identity and Community in the Jungle

After about a year in the jungle, the Bookman describes the winter of 1941 as hosting "all the hobo freaks along the coast route." He spends time writing about the "Highclimber," the "Poet," and "Sailor Shorty," three men who get into trouble in town and are familiar to local authorities and police, who escalate punishment in an effort to run them out. The Bookman calls the Highclimber "one of the great unwashed" and says he "gets full of cheap wine + starts bumming along the main stem, State St. The first time the cops grabbed him he got 10 days in the can; the second time he got 20 days, and the third time a month. He's been out now for a while + is scared for the judge threatened to give him a floater if he got picked up again." But the Bookman notes that drinkers like the Highclimber are actually "isolated cases and they are mostly drifters, not all of them belong here." Several of the men simply have odd habits, coupled with drinking, which make them undesirable:

> The "Poet" was erratic . . . He wrote sentimental trash that he
> called poetry and tried to peddle it from house to house. He got

nowhere fast, and the police invited him to go elsewhere, or else. He went.

"Sailor Shorty" has the next shack to me + he is sure a case. He is a little shrimp, but a hustling fool. Up before daylight, up + down the beach for miles, looking for bottles, iron, etc. Then around through alleys, searching for junk . . . Promptly he goes uptown + gets a gallon of wine. Then he locks himself in his shack + begins to sing. As a singer he would make a good shoe maker, but he doesn't know that.

All of these so-called hobo freaks have problematic interactions with housed citizens and police, who eventually force them to leave Santa Barbara. Even with the jungle to retreat to, unless the men remain isolated and segregated within its boundaries, adhering to behavioral standards of decency in town and the rules of the jungle in private, they are targeted for arrest or urged to move on or move out.

The jungle also has regulars who are notorious for the poor condition of their shacks or the grungy way they keep themselves. Dirty Shirt Al is described as "a young fellow, working sometimes, as a day laborer for a local contractor. He came here last fall and is still wearing the same shirt he had when he came. It has never been in water." Another jungle resident, the "Crippled Mex," has what the Bookman calls "useless trash" littering the floor of his shack and the yard outside. These men are considered unkempt, but there are others who are seen as mean-spirited. Two such men are the "Vulture" and "Chicken Charlie." Aptly named, the Vulture is described as looking like "the vulture personified. His only answer to a greeting is a surly grunt + undoubtedly he hates himself." Chicken Charlie is so named because of the roosters that he keeps as pets. One of the oldest residents in the jungle, Chicken Charlie is "the most universally hated," as he is responsible for "the yearly exodus from the estate for 24 hours on account of his crack about getting squatter's rights." Although Charlie is described as mean, the Bookman admits that he is also intelligent, locating his dump "right against several huge eucalyptus trees + the fellows couldn't burn him out without damaging them." Remaining in the jungle, despite any personality deficits or interpersonal conflicts, protects the men from being run out of town or punished for nuisance offenses and fosters their sense of community and acceptance.

The Bookman compares the men of the jungle to carpenters, mechanics, and architects, noting that they have none of their skills, and "every one would give a real mechanic hysterical fits." Although

Santa Barbara Historical Museum

Eucalyptus protection.

they may rival the American housewife in terms of thrift and clean-
liness, they admittedly fail when it comes to achieving acceptable
standards of masculine success and achievement. The most they can
do is survive and maintain their autonomy, key features of life in the
jungle and of masculinity in this era. Because of his declining health,
the Bookman anticipates that Cecil will tell him to move indoors and
tells him to "save it. I don't want to depend on anyone else as long as
I can spit." Although they may not be able to surpass settled men at
careers, the men of the jungle will not be reduced to childlike
dependence. As he witnesses various tragedies befall the men, some
because of drunkenness and some a result of old age or infirmity, the
Bookman waxes philosophical, realizing their lost potential: "Just
part of the vast army of drifters, fashioned of the same clay that con-
stitutes the structure of our codfish aristocracy, they probably once
had dreams + aspirations that perhaps circumstances and environment barred them from attaining."

Going It Alone

Many people question the men's ability to work, suggesting gainful
employment as a way out of homelessness. In an article in the local
newspaper in 1941, an estimated eighty to 100 men are served nightly
at the Salvation Army shelter. These men are said to be fit for employment or military service but do not choose either one. The older men
are said to have settled down to receive old age pensions, and one
local writer claims that the transient problem is a "young man's problem" now. The Bookman concedes that though there is work available
for the men, the terms of employment are often exploitative, and he
gives two examples of "generosity by the exploiters of the down-and-
outers." The first is of a farmer who arrived in the jungle, looking for
men to pick peas. The men left at 5:30 a.m. and did not return until
7:30 that night. They were given 81 cents for the day. The second is of
a job driving, loading, and unloading a truck of manure to a location
fifty miles away from the jungle. The pay for this job was a mere
$1.00. With employment opportunities like these, particularly for
older men with illnesses and infirmities, promoting is easier, safer,

Santa Barbara Historical Museum

Steering the ship.

and pays better. Despite these obvious examples of worker exploitation and the men's rejection of or inability to compete in the formal labor market, the town is still invested in distinguishing the men from hoboes, emphasizing their current employment in the local newspaper.

After the Bookman survives two winters in the jungle, he leaves Santa Barbara to seek restaurant work in Los Angeles. By December 1942, "defense work is plentiful," but because the Bookman lacks his birth certificate, he cannot get hired, so he turns to restaurant work. But he confesses that he cannot manage it because of his poor health: "I fainted twice in 6 weeks." This still undiagnosed illness leaves him "discouraged, cynical, depressed," but there is little he can do. His condition renders him "weak as a cat." Some restaurants, he notes, are also closed because of a wartime lack of basic staple foods. Yet even through illness in the jungle, the Bookman works to "promote" basic materials for his shack and for swapping, and the other men take care of him. It is his ability to survive that shows the grit needed to manage the physical toll of life on the move.

Surprisingly, the Bookman mentions actual violence only once, noting his readiness to defend himself when a "drunk Mexican" drove off the freeway and crashed into his shack. Startled out of a sound sleep, he says, "I was ready to give battle." It is this pugilistic sense of masculinity that we see becoming a more instrumental part of jungle life later in the century. It is also a central part of how the Bookman values himself. Rather than depending on others, he goes it alone, struggling to establish employment and build his own makeshift shelter, enduring bad health and bad weather but beholden to no one except the men of the jungle, relying on physical strength, the strength of his character, and the rules of reciprocity.

The Bookman eventually locates his two sons in Dutch Harbor, Alaska, and by the time he writes his last letter in 1943, he is in correspondence with one of them. He mentions this to Cecil. "Heard from the kid in Alaska. He's O.K. + trying as usual to get news to me past the censor." This is one of the few explicit references to World War II, along with some notes about the scarcity of specific foods and the increase in prices for commodity goods. The Bookman worries about whether his sons, who are in military service, are in immediate danger, when their term of service will be over, and when he will see them again. Although he notes that a soldier's pay is nothing to write home about, he also hopes that they can eventually produce "some coin of the realm," noting that he is a good father who was "liberal with them." His letters show that his sons discussed setting up a pension for him that they would pay into to cover basic needs. But the uncertainty about when they would be free to do so leaves the Bookman wondering when help will arrive.

In one of his final letters to Cecil, he writes that he finally saw a doctor and knows what his medical condition is. He never names it but says it is not contagious and speculates that it was caused by a period of undernourishment, worry over his sons, and taking care of his wife. He only mentions having a wife in one other letter, when he responds to Cecil's confession of restlessness: "Your reference to a desire to hit the road once in awhile is like it was with me in the first 10 years I was married. My wife would notice the wandering look in my eyes and would say 'well, go ahead for a month or so and get it out of your system and then come back and settle down. I would and I did." This brief window into the Bookman's family shows how deeply they are embedded in his past, present, and his very sense of wandering and returning in the future.

The Bookman and the jungle in the 1940s show how spatial permanence can affect the social and geographic mobility of the men and their sense of self and relationships with others. Because the Bookman has the jungle to retreat to, he can rest and recover, rather than continuing to move in search of casual labor. He establishes ties with family and friends and becomes part of the jungle community, perhaps not a mayor but still a member, and eventually moves on to seek low-wage, sporadic employment. His age, which he never says explicitly except to say he is over 50, and his physical condition prevent him from taking full-time work, and he waits for some relief from his sons, instead of going "on the dole." The Bookman's story also shows how the jungle facilitates identity work, accumulation, and fellowship among the men, and a broader sense of measured acceptance among local citizens. The jungle mayor, described below, serves during a time of controversy for the jungle, about ten years after the Bookman's residency.

Edward Anderson: Jungle Mayor

In 1964, Edward Anderson writes a short story entitled "The Saga of the Little Gray Sparrow." In it, a young sparrow becomes discontented with barnyard life and goes out into the world to explore. After

Edward Anderson, jungle mayor, 1951–1958.

many adventures, old age sets in and the sparrow is near death, but he is pleased to know that after his death, his feathers will be used to make a new nest. Even in death, even for a sparrow, the two qualities of restlessness and the desire to be useful are a clear focus of life for men in the jungle and are central to the role of jungle mayor. Jungle mayors are elected arbiters of disputes and serve as ambassadors between residents and the rest of Santa Barbara. They assign shacks to newcomers and hold the respect of jungle residents. Mayors are generally seen as men with slightly more status than the rest, and this is reflected in their dwelling place: an old gardener's shack with a Spanish tiled roof. As Anderson puts it, "This roof costs more than the whole camp put together. But this has always been the mayor's place here" (*Santa Barbara News Press,* November 29, 1953).

Another theme in "The Saga of the Little Gray Sparrow" is "either you can or you can't," a simple truth the sparrow realizes when he tries to do things he is not able to do, like float on the water or sing like a thrush. This sense of being limited by one's abilities or upbringing or current age or infirmity is something the men of the jungle understand, and both the Bookman and Anderson focus on in their writing. Anderson's age and health limit his tenure as mayor and eventually force him to leave the jungle for apartment living. To illustrate how Anderson is able to work around his limitations, one of his projects as mayor is to improve the makeshift privy that the men use as a bathroom. To do this, Anderson enlists the help of three new-comers he describes as "Railroad maintenance men from Montana. They were young and husky while the rest of us were old and more or less decrepit." They dug the men a privy, and Anderson notes that "it almost created a revolt when I went around with my hat collecting enough nickels, dimes and quarters to buy the boys a case of beer to keep them 'lubricated' while doing the hard work." The revolt died down when the men saw the results: "The real pacifier was the privy itself." This is just one of the mayor's "public works" projects that improves life in the jungle.

Like the Bookman, Anderson is proud of his ability to get things done and to survive on limited means, calling himself "inquisitive not acquisitive." He is a more prolific writer than other mayors, although several of them write in to the local paper over the years, particularly when the opinion of the men of the jungle is called for. Anderson's letters appear frequently in the *Santa Barbara News Press*, and he acts as "scribe" for the men, even after he moves out of the jungle. He uses the role of mayor to express the men's gratitude for the charitable donations they receive during the holidays and to smooth their relationship with town residents. After a particularly bountiful Christmas, Anderson writes a short article describing each donation in detail and concludes by saying "for us, Santa resides in the hearts and minds of the wonderful people who thought and acted so kindly toward us this Christmas . . . With a full heart we say: Bless you All and Thank you All!" (*Santa Barbara News Press,* December 28, 1956). He signs every letter "the old men of . . . Jungleville/the Child Estate," and his thanks eventually catch the eye of a local businessman and lead to substantial improvements for the men.

Anderson's tenure in the jungle occurs at a key moment in its history because it is at this point that the future of the jungle and its existence in the midst of paradise is at its most contentious. Anderson is a former security guard in Santa Barbara, and he earns $25 per month from Social Security. He lives in the jungle from June 1951 to

December 1958, when poor health forces him to move temporarily into town. He returns to the jungle after his illness but declines the role of mayor because of his poor health and the possibility of hospitalization. Yet he remains involved with the jungle, and his opinion is still valued by the men. Anderson is originally elected mayor just two months before Child's death, and he describes meeting her during her last visit to the jungle, "a grand little lady . . . and not just a chip of New England granite but a diamond, emerald cut, four square with the world." Most of the men share this sentiment, and one resident writes, "She always sticks up for us." Despite her protection of the men throughout her life, Child's omission of the men in her will brings the jungle into controversy.

Trouble with the Jungle

In 1952, the year after Lillian Child's death, what to do with the jungle and its residents becomes the topic of many letters, articles, and op-eds in the local paper. These arguments highlight the issues of exchangeable spaces and stigmatized identities that are intrinsic to the debate over the proper place for homeless people. Because there is no official provision for the men in Child's will, the town must figure out what to do with the unwritten moral obligation to provide for them after her death. Some town residents, including a former police officer, characterize the men of the jungle as polite and respectful, justifying their use of what is now public property. "I wonder if you have space enough to publish the opinion of a woman who for 15 years was engaged in work which brought me in contact with . . . the Jungle . . . I was a member of the City Police Department from 1933 to 1948 . . . I can truthfully say that I was never treated with anything but respect by the men" (*Santa Barbara News Press,* November 21, 1953). Other residents write stinging critiques of the jungle, targeting the moral deficiency of its occupants, including a former neighbor, who writes

> I have more than a passing interest in and knowledge of this property and . . . when I lived across the tracks from this jungle . . . Our police department was continually called upon to pick up some member of this group whose favorite beverage was cheap wine.
> If there are among these men ones who need to be cared for, why not put them where they will receive proper care and require the others to live on their pensions in places fit for human habitation.

What a farce it would be to allow that hobo jungle to continue in a beautiful city park which will certainly require large sums of money to maintain.

In fairness to all, this decision should be lifted out of the sentimental tide it has always been allowed to float on and be brought down to earth. (*Santa Barbara News Press*, November 21, 1953)

The opinion of this writer sets off a debate in the community, culminating in a series of letters in the local paper with the heading, "Jungleville Hurt by Criticism; Community Clean and Well-Run." One letter says that the view expressed above "proposes to liquidate a charming and notably democratic landmark. At the same time she would make state wards of a score or more proud and rugged individualists who are living the life of their choice . . . Let them drink the wine of their choice in their own community" (*Santa Barbara News Press*, November 21, 1953). For this writer, threatening the protected freedoms of the men in the jungle is tantamount to threatening freedom everywhere.

Given his role as ambassador, the jungle mayor is the one responsible for speaking up for the men of Jungleville and responding to the claim that they are unruly and need policing. Acting mayor John McCarthy, filling in during Anderson's medical absence, writes, "Her statement that the police had to be called so often here to arrest drunks is without foundation as there has been only one man arrested here in the camp in three years. As to the sanitary conditions—not being women, we are not expert housekeepers, but we try and keep our huts as clean as possible inside and out." And then, knowing that pity can be the greatest insult, he writes: "Through the years of insecurity we have learned the value of tolerance and we wish (the author) the best of health and luck through her declining years" (*Santa Barbara News Press*, November 21, 1953). In this brief response, the mayor excuses the men for attempting to do work that is seen as a woman's domain. He also distances the men of the jungle from stereotypes associated with transients. Excusing their cobbled-together domesticity as something not in their nature to do or do well reaffirms the neediness of the men and valorizes their attempts to keep house.

This flurry of articles prompts a second response by the original author, in which she assures readers that she is not "confused" about the jungle or its residents, and she reveals the reason for her condemnation: "We tried to have our frontage zoned for business" and "were

Santa Barbara Historical Museum

Keeping the jungle clean.

refused . . . 'nothing must be done to make the entrance of Santa Barbara unsightly,' yet across the road, in plain view of this same frontage, this group of shacks, utterly devoid of sanitation, without any regard for zoning laws enforced on the taxpayers, was thriving and has continued to be allowed to exist" (*Santa Barbara News Press,* November 29, 1953). The frustration this writer expresses, that hoboes can live in the jungle, but that she cannot open a business, resonates with the struggles between rich and poor for years to come. With so many people vying for a piece of the waterfront pie, the rich wonder why the poor should be allowed to get access to it for free, and thus they begrudge them even limited, charitable access. The exclusivity of the Santa Barbara Waterfront becomes an increasingly guarded commodity, with the rich protecting what they feel the poor are encroaching on—their right to paradise.

These articles raise several questions: Should Santa Barbara abide by Child's wish that the men of the jungle be protected? Does the jungle community cause trouble for the city, or is it "clean and well run?" And most important, why do the men choose the jungle

over other available accommodations? One article offers a response
to the last question:

> They like the idea of policing their own "community." They have
> their "mayor." They have their rules and regulations. They would
> rather put up with the inconveniences and privations of their shacks
> than with the enforced routine of institutional care . . . They attach
> little importance to many of the things that organized majorities
> consider essential for the care of people who cannot support them-
> selves according to accepted standards. (*Santa Barbara News
> Press*, November 21, 1953)

This response calls to mind Anderson's little sparrow and the simple truth in the story that "either you can or you can't." For many of
the men, it is the inability to reach accepted standards that brings the
creation of this protected, alternative community into full relief. When
you can't fit in, what do you do? Do you give up or fight to maintain
what you see as important, the one thing you can control? The same
article expresses this quandary: "Some might still earn better quarters.
Some could take advantage of public provision for their care. Some,
their histories reveal, might live with relatives, if they chose to sacrifice what they consider independence" (*Santa Barbara News Press,*
November 21, 1953). Sacrificing independence for better accommodations, for many of the men, means admitting defeat, and this is seen as
too high a price. For their cobbled-together domesticity, they can be
forgiven. Their age and limited mobility make them palatable, if not
sympathetic characters, and by staying in the jungle, they remain free
to choose their own community and keep their dignity.

It is this sense of protection and entitlement to choice that Child
provided and that the men of the jungle embraced. And Child's death
does not change their perception: keeping their independence when
all other choices are exhausted or inadequate is paramount. Yet the
buck eventually stops with sanitation, particularly after the city
learns of the mayor's privy. Although city officials refuse to find or
build permanent housing for the men, they will not sanction the existence of what has become a group of squatters. In the decade following Child's death, the men of the jungle wait patiently for the debate
to die down, showing their quiet sense of entitlement to the land and
hoping that the exclusivity of the community in terms of age and
self-governance makes them palatable if not somewhat powerful. As
one former mayor warns, "Don't forget that we still have a lot of

friends around town" (*Santa Barbara News Press,* October 14, 1962). Another jungle resident suggests that saving the men is the reason Child donated the land to the Santa Barbara Foundation in the first place. The mayor serves an instrumental role in this debate as he comes to represent the needs and concerns of the men and preserve their spatial permanence.

Provisions and Prominence

As a testimony to the jungle's local prominence and Mayor Anderson's influential role in preserving it, in 1955 local businessman Alex Hyde reads Anderson's letter of thanks for Christmas dinner in the local paper and writes him a letter in return. He describes himself as "just an old Medicine Man who helped my father start the Mentholatum business back in the 'gay 90s.'" Following the exchange of letters, Hyde visits the jungle and meets with Anderson to see how he can assist the men further. Their conversation leads to the construction of a utility building, which Anderson originally conceives of and

Santa Barbara Historical Museum

Slated for improvement.

designs. Money for the building is raised through the *Santa Barbara News Press*, underscoring the appreciation of this task as a community effort, although a large number of donors remain "anonymous." Local police chief Noah "Stormy" Cloud adds further legitimacy to the utility building by enlisting the support of the Cavalier's interracial teenage boys club to build it, for which he wins "Man of the Year."[10] He also champions the view that the men of the jungle are different from other hoboes, justifying his involvement with the project. He writes: "These unfortunate men are worthy of a helping hand from Santa Barbara . . . They have always been orderly, self-governing and co-operative with the police. Reports that they are drunken and disorderly are not true. Hobos elsewhere in town are troublemakers, but not the residents of Jungleville." Yet the building comes with a measured, conditional acceptance. As the local paper states, "The residents of Jungleville must be made to understand that the city is not committing itself in any way by permitting construction of the building and the city would retain permanent ownership" (*Santa Barbara News Press,* October 14, 1955).

Although they have no official claim on the jungle, the men remain in their shacks, have access to proper sanitary facilities, and enjoy a small indoor recreation room. Park Superintendent Finlay MacKenzie notes that by the time the land is developed, the majority of the men will have passed away or be getting assistance from local welfare authorities. For his part, current jungle mayor John Craver says that the jungle will accept no new residents, given the city's ultimate plans to create a park or zoo on the property. By 1963, with only three full-time residents left and the Santa Barbara Zoo reaching its final stages of construction, three cottages from the original Mar Monte Hotel are moved onto adjacent public property for the remaining men. One of the men dies, one leaves Santa Barbara, and the third settles in town after briefly living in one of the cottages. Eventually, the utility building itself is appropriated for use in the new city zoo, opened in 1963, and the jungle temporarily fades out of existence.[11]

As a public figure and ambassador, Anderson and other mayors make the jungle palatable for Santa Barbara. They explain the men's activities and outlook, justify the jungle's existence and culture, and argue to preserve a place of their own. Anderson is in his seventies and in poor health by the time he settles in the jungle and is well beyond the adventures he experienced as a younger man.

Unlike the Bookman, who worries about surviving life in the jungle and often considers moving on, Anderson always has his eye on settled life in Santa Barbara and remains the jungle's ambassador. Even after securing housing, he continues to negotiate with city officials to see that the men are well taken care of and that some official record of the jungle is preserved for posterity. In fact, he is approached by the Santa Barbara Foundation, owners of the Child Estate, to write an informal history of the jungle, part of which appears in the *Santa Barbara News Press*. He also contributes two abundantly stocked scrapbooks of letters, clippings, photographs, and mementos to the Santa Barbara Historical Society, which are a partial foundation for this chapter.

The jungle diminishes in size and importance after Child's death and with the waning of the main stem and hoboing in general by the mid-1950s. Anderson is also in poor health by this time, although he never mentions it explicitly, and in 1958, he moves into an apartment in town. Even after he moves indoors, Anderson remains an avid follower of local news and events, and when officials decide to turn the Child Estate into a public park, he is the first to contribute. Each donor receives a key that opens particular doors throughout the park and Anderson lovingly tapes his into his scrapbook. He also gives money to the Children's Opera, the Santa Barbara Scholarship Foundation, the Santa Barbara Historical Society, and the Dollars for Democrats Campaign and saves all correspondences.

In a letter to the editor of the *Santa Barbara News Press*, Anderson encourages others to contribute to the Santa Barbara Scholarship Foundation, saying, "My own education is of do-it-yourself variety and as such came out much like Swiss cheese with some awful big holes in it and sliced too thin." Interested in helping others learn from his mistakes, or learn in general, and in making sure his life is somehow useful, Anderson writes poems about life on the road.

"Go? Went—Gone"

*It's the spring moon
Is the tramp's moon,
Sliver of new moon luring on
From its high trail
Where the clouds sail
Slowly into the setting sun*

Follow the south wind
Follow the north wind
Or the free wind blowing west?
As the wind blows
So the tramp goes—
And the winding road is best.

Although he clearly knows restlessness, Anderson differentiates between the men of the jungle and those who do not work or settle. Because they are less mobile, are integrated within the community, and are able to live on protected property, the men of the jungle are able to scavenge from the local dump and from local merchants, and they can pursue part-time, sporadic employment. This supplements the meager pensions some of them live on and further distinguishes them from tramps and hoboes as a group worthy of protection.

By 1953, Child's mansion has fallen into disrepair. City officials allow a fraternity from the University of California, Santa Barbara to briefly occupy the property, and the fraternity brothers cause significant damage to the mansion. They are also rumored to have shot at and otherwise harassed jungle residents. With repairs estimated to cost more than the mansion is worth, and no proposed use for it, the city sets it ablaze. Citizens complain about the burning of this public landmark, saying it sets a bad precedent for such an otherwise "well-balanced community." Anderson writes to the *News Press* to pay his respects to the mansion. He writes, "In this once-large house had lived a big-hearted little lady, who in depression days befriended many friendless and homeless men—some drifters, with her permission, anchored and built shacks. Two of these old timers still live in the present Shack-town—one in his high seventies and the other . . . is 88, well on towards 89" (*Santa Barbara News Press*, July 10, 1959). The burning of the Vega Mar mansion clears the way for the zoo's development, which will forever transform the Child Estate and the Santa Barbara Waterfront.

Lillian Child: Kindness or Justice?

Lillian Brown arrived in Santa Barbara in 1906, after marrying John Howard Beale and spending her honeymoon in Europe. The daughter of a wealthy New York banker, she entertains on the estate, adding glamour to the local society pages. She is widowed in 1914, and after a prolonged and painful struggle with Beale's relatives over owner-ship of the estate, she remarries in 1921, becoming Lillian Child. For the next decade or so, the Childs hold social gatherings that bring Vega Mar back into vogue as a jewel of Santa Barbara's social scene in the roaring twenties. Lillian Child is widowed again in 1936, dur-ing the waning years of the Great Depression, and the party is over. She finds herself alone, twice widowed, and the sole proprietor of the vast but lonely Child Estate. Perhaps she merely sees the men of the jungle as a worthy distraction.

In a small town in the early 1900s, Child raises eyebrows by pro-tecting and nurturing the jungle and its residents. As one local writer comments: "Newcomers . . . are apt to be mystified at the sight of a tall fine-looking woman, impeccably turned out, visiting a market—in the background, waiting to carry her bundles, a man obviously not the usual kind of servant" (*Santa Barbara News Press,* October 16, 1946). Child's wealth excuses her eccentricity, as owning prime waterfront real estate makes her a powerful decisionmaker, yet peo-ple still wonder what inspires her to provide for the men. Many think she simply has a good heart or that she is a kind and sympathetic per-son. Child contests this as a mere stereotype, saying, "Kind? I never think of it as kind." She simply watches as the railroad tracks that border her property bring ever-increasing loads of hoboes along with cargo and as men with no place to go are run out of town.

Child's decision to sell a parcel of her estate to the Mar Monte Hotel in 1946, to protect tourists from the sight of the men, incites rumors that the jungle is closing down. Child responds: "Nothing of the kind! They are simply moving to the other side of my land . . . Now go along and don't bother me anymore. Who says these poor men are being chased away? I go down every morning to see how they're getting on with their moving. They have 15 shacks up already" (*Santa Barbara News Press,* October 16, 1946). The men respect her, move when she wants them to, and for the most part, adhere to her rules. They describe her as "a real lady." Octogenarian Alexander Graham, one of the original jungle inhabitants, comments that "she was mighty good to us" but "she had quite a temper and if anyone got out of line, she was quick to tell them, and that was just as well for the rest of us" (*Santa Barbara News Press,* November 29, 1953). The discipline she offers, hands off as it is, sets the standard for appearance and behav-ior in the jungle, keeping it off police radar. In her own words, Child says: "I tell them, 'I don't care what you do as long as you put the fires out and turn off the water.' I say, 'Don't put your houses too close together; otherwise there will be no room for a vegetable garden'" (*Santa Barbara News Press,* October 14, 1962).

Whether she makes daily visits to the jungle or only sporadic ones is anyone's guess, as she makes frequent trips to her other homes in New York and Europe. The Bookman mentions Child very briefly, saying that she is "in the East at the present" but "is due home soon; when she is here she visits the boys quite often and any time one of them does a bit of work for her it's a dollar." Others comment that she is always there to hand out half dollars at Christmastime. The Bookman's view of the Vega Mar mansion is of a "big, castle-like red stone building, with a large turreted tower . . . partially hid by a grove of eucalyptus," and he elaborates only on the servants and staff and the fact that Child is a widow. Long-term residents of the jungle are loath to give the Bookman information, as he says, "It's hard as hell to get authentic dope about the place." And, in fact, neither the estate nor Child is mentioned again in his letters. Mayor Anderson meets Child just once, in August 1951, two weeks before her death. She makes what he calls a "tour of inspection," noting that it was her last. Then Mayor Sam Curry "guided her among the shacks" and introduced Anderson as "a newcomer."

On the morning of Lillian Child's death, the men solemnly clean their shacks and the common areas of the jungle. Without her patronage, it is only a matter of years before the jungle fades into memory, only to rise again years later with a different population and a different relationship with the local community. For men in the jungle in the 1940s and 1950s, the support of Lillian Child lends them the mantle of legitimacy, a place of their own, and a sanctuary that protects them from complete dependence, harm, or persecution, or the need to rely on others not so forgiving of their circumstances. Although they are always beholden to her, she never makes them prove it, and as a result they keep their dignity, and some even feel power in the unique nature of the jungle, a perspective they share in newspapers, letters, and the friendships they forge. The rules Child imposes keep things orderly and exclusive, lending the men of the jungle an identity apart from the men on the move. Establishing a system of self-governance and an elected mayor also allows the men to be decisionmakers, calling in police or fire only when necessary. Perhaps this begins, ever so subtly, the distinction between settlers and residents versus a transient population, a distinction that will become more important in later years.

The End of an Era

The Bookman and the jungle mayor are similar because of their inability to work as able-bodied, younger hoboes can, and because of their stationary and protected status on the Child Estate. Yet they hold different positions within the jungle community and within Santa Barbara society. Both of them have consistent and enduring social ties with housed citizens either locally or elsewhere and are not isolated, or at least not isolated all their lives. Given the admittedly limited evidence of the two men's history, it seems that Anderson has more experience with wandering and transience than the Bookman, as he does so consistently and from an early age. Anderson also has more enduring social ties with Santa Barbara residents, some of whom are powerful decisionmakers. Both men are restless, frustrated by their own limitations, and want to be useful and to rely on themselves instead of on others in reciprocal rather than dependent relationships. Although living in the jungle takes substantial physical and emotional work to survive the seasons, procure necessities, and negotiate with one's fellows, it isn't work that brings them monetary benefit or prestige. The most they can hope for is some degree of comfort and to keep providing for themselves rather than relying on welfare institutions for housing.

The Bookman, the jungle mayor, and residents of the jungle in the 1940s and 1950s are considered less trouble than their younger, more transient counterparts. The Bookman distinguishes the men of the jungle from other wanderers who prey on people, including jungle bums (tramps who live off hobos), scissorbills (a farmer or greenhorn of the road), and bindlestiffs (hobo carrying a grub sack and blanket roll). Although these types overlap, being stationary and building residences, albeit shacks, lends the men a certain degree of legitimacy. It also allows them to accumulate things and to build a sense of pride over their domestic abilities. The Bookman compares the men to the average housewife several times to prove how much they are able to stretch their budgets and how diligently they clean their shacks. Although many jungle residents break the rules by drinking or by being younger than allowed or by being transients, they still endear themselves to the local community. In addition to the characteristics that distinguish them from other hoboes, many of them have or establish roots in Santa Barbara. Because they manage to garner favor with one of its most prestigious and wealthy widows and several other prominent citizens, including police and business owners, they hold a unique protected status and create a local legacy that endures far into the future.

In part because of the people who support them, the men of the jungle feel a sense of entitlement to live simply, on borrowed land and borrowed time, until they can find adequate housing or decide to move on. But there is no question that even a ten-shack jungle simply would not be allowed to flourish with city funds in a public park. It never attains that level of community acceptance. Without a critical mass of homeless people, as there was during the Depression and will be again in the 1980s, the jungle is not needed and not relevant. But the limitations of the men in the old jungle mean that they do not rankle local authorities enough to force them to move on. While Lillian Child is protecting the men, they in turn feel obligated to abide by her unwritten behavioral code, at least for the most part. In this sense and during this time period, the jungle flourishes and eventually dies out as the numbers dwindle, and perhaps the men know their remaining days are limited.

In larger relief, hobo jungles represent a makeshift domesticity, cobbled together from what scraps men can scavenge. Always located near or in train yards, they are subject to regulation not only by local police but also by railroad authorities, a problem that Santa Barbara jungle residents can, for the most part, avoid. The Santa Barbara jungle is a far more stable, permanent form of jungle for a group of men with organized roles and responsibilities, in part imposed by Child. Her plan is brilliant in its simplicity: she lets them govern themselves and sees this as a natural right rather than something that leaves them beholden to her. She does not require, as shelters will later in the century, any disclosure of personal information, relinquishing of any personal items, or admission of moral culpability. She refers to the men of the jungle as "friends," and the men refer to themselves as harmless "oldsters" who do not draw negative attention.

The next time the jungle rises to prominence in Santa Barbara is in the 1980s, when homelessness emerges as a nationwide social problem of emergency proportions. As is detailed in the following chapter, the 1980s jungle holds a far different place within the heart of the community than it did earlier in the century. Changing demographics as well as a sense of moral and political crisis infuse the reaction to the 1980s jungle with a sense of panic and threat. This urgent social climate also gives 1980s jungle residents a feeling of empowerment far different from the jungle of the 1940s and 1950s.

3

Power and Protest:
1980s

Tracking changes that occur within the unsheltered homeless population from the 1940s to the 1980s is a challenge, in part because numeric and demographic estimates do not begin on a national level until 2005, when point-in-time (PIT) counts become a requirement for federal funding. But the 1980s also begin the complicated process of establishing definitions of homelessness, delineating policies that dictate how and to whom resources are allocated, with the government interested in narrowing definitions and advocates wanting to expand them (Burt 2016, 50). Of course, unsheltered homelessness is the most difficult category to define, and communities are often left using inconsistent, haphazard methods to estimate overall need (Gabbard et al. 2007).

One of the most useful distinctions that arises in the 1980s, as a way of understanding this new and diverse population of people without shelter, is between "old" and "new" forms of homelessness (Hoch and Slayton 1989; Rossi 1989) (see Table 3.1). People experiencing homelessness in the 1980s are in the "new" category, meaning that their demographics reflect greater diversity and a growing polarization between those with resources and those without. The prevalence of unsheltered homeless people in city spaces is perhaps the most poignant signal of crisis. This decade also reflects a shift in public perception, as homelessness is understood as a social problem with structural causes. Charles Hoch and Robert Slayton (1989) show

Table 3.1 Old and New Homelessness

	Old Homelessness 1920s–1960s	New Homelessness 1980s and Beyond
Population characteristics	Single men, pensioners	Women, children/younger people, overrepresentation of minority groups
Occupation of city spaces	Concentrated in skid-row and SRO housing	More widely dispersed, more people without shelter of any kind
Public perception	Deserving, blameworthy An individual problem Alcoholics or "transients"	Undeserving, innocent A social problem Defined/separated by a hierarchy of needs

that reactions to homeless people are split between pitying some as unwitting victims of social forces beyond their control and thinking of them as undeserving, and blaming others seen as causing their homelessness and deserving of its consequences. Ironically, the undeserving are offered better shelters and better programs, and those seen as flawed by addiction or bad character are left on the street, as if this might help them.

The distinction between street people and the rest of the homeless population reflects the confusion surrounding homelessness in this era. The visible presence of unsheltered homeless people in Santa Barbara and the nation in the 1980s ignites sustained public controversy, with a federal solution materializing only at the end of the decade. With an obvious crisis at hand, who gets assistance and how they get it are key policy decisions resting on complicated, shifting definitions, and only a vague idea of the magnitude of the problem. Larger policy decisions, such as increasing taxes to pay for social services, offering universal housing vouchers, or making the right to shelter a mandate, are only considered years later, after the initial shock wears off (DiFazio 2006). Instead, policy responses in the 1980s focus on managing an immediate crisis, with shelters offering the bare minimum of subsistence, and the ladder to housing fraught with pitfalls and setbacks that make reaching the top elusive. It is perhaps no wonder that the service model developed in the 1980s replicates the same frenzied scramble for scarce resources that keeps unsheltered homeless people in emergency mode.

In the 1980s, Santa Barbara becomes a divided space, with home-less street people clustering in the public parks along Cabrillo Boule-vard, the still-undeveloped jungle area, near the landmark Moreton Bay Fig Tree—thought to be the oldest fig tree in the United States—in the railroad depot west of State Street, with military veterans living in makeshift bunkers on "TV hill" (*Santa Barbara Independent,* Jan-uary 14, 1988). They also occupy the steps of centrally located City Hall. Its wide, well-lit porch becomes a resting place for homeless people at night and a site for social protest during the day, to the hor-ror of city officials (*Santa Barbara Independent,* January 14, 1988). The homeless are in these makeshift locations, in part, because of the local decline in single room occupancy (SRO) units, which see a 31 percent reduction from 1975 to 1985 (Rosenthal 1994). Local news-papers decry the loss of 268 rooms overall, formerly in small twenty-to thirty-person facilities, centrally located in the downtown area (*Santa Barbara Independent,* December 10, 1987).

In their place, actor Fess Parker's luxurious Red Lion Inn, later renamed the Doubletree Hotel, is built in 1986 with a layout befitting Santa Barbara's cultivated image of paradise. Other hotels and luxury accommodations proliferate in the 1980s, with apartment and condo-minium complexes mixed in with private homes along East Beach. The Interstate 101 Freeway and railroad run through the center of town, effectively cutting off lower from upper State Street, as an underpass is not built until 1991. But in the 1980s, and even despite the burgeoning tourist market, much of the area between Cabrillo Boulevard and the railroad is still undeveloped and cut off from the rest of the city. Perhaps this is where the tension over the jungle arises: although slow, deliberate growth with a focus on luxury and preservation is Santa Barbara's signature style, when street people begin claiming undeveloped areas, paradise has a problem.

The New Jungle

By the 1980s, the Santa Barbara jungle is simply "an overgrown area near the beach" (Rosenthal 1994, 9), a stone's throw away from the old jungle. There are only a few semipermanent structures there, but dwellings are mostly tents, lean-tos, and bedrolls in small groupings around a central fire. Writer and activist Peter Marin frequents the jungle during this time period and characterizes it in the following way, reminiscent of the insights shared by Jackson Underwood in his study of homeless camps in Los Angeles (1993):

> It was city-owned but largely forgotten. Though it lay right on the boulevard running along the sea's edge, and right across from a much-frequented beach, it was so overgrown, so guarded and hidden by thick brush, high bushes and drooping trees that most townspeople walked right by without realizing it was there . . . It's as if while everything else was being bought and sold and built upon and utilized, these few tracts, one here, one there, were by various accidents and quirks left untouched, just *there*. (Marin 1988)

Santa Barbara's new jungle is in the middle of public space, on prime waterfront property. The sense of separate adjacency that characterized skid row and the old jungle is replaced by a thinly veiled barrier between homeless and housed, and the fear that street people will make it manifest.

In the 1980s, in part because of the legacy of the old jungle, homeless people feel entitled to claim this new, smaller, and more fragmented camping area near the beach and the aforementioned makeshift areas in undeveloped parts of the city. They do not need or want anyone giving them permission to do so, and they enjoy the sense of freedom and to be, as Marin intimates, in the wild. Yes, the jungle is a dangerous place where bad things happen. There are fights, deaths, depression, and addiction, with jungle leaders often at the center of the controversy (*Santa Barbara News Press*, December 8, 1988; January 7, 1989; January 14, 1989). But why does Santa Barbara, with all the hatred aimed at homeless people in the 1980s, care if they hurt one another or themselves? Is it the value of waterfront property that is of issue, even if no one is using it? Is it the city's public image? Is it the temerity of homeless people to think they are entitled to this, or any piece of paradise? Perhaps the legacy of the old jungle leaves Santa Barbara with mixed feelings. Perhaps some feel a lingering fondness for the fabled old men of the jungle who were seen as different from the hobo rabble and more settled and acceptable than people expected. Perhaps the city still feels an obligation to protect people who are unsheltered, as long as they adhere to spatial and behavioral rules and norms.

Pressure to get homeless people off State Street escalates in the early 1980s, when city documents show the categorical distinctions between deserving and undeserving in full effect. In 1983, the Task

Force on Lower State Street Problems—a group composed of members of the City Redevelopment Agency; Department of Social Services; Human Services Commission; Old Town Merchant's Association; Committee on Crime, Alcohol, Vagrancy, Etc.; homeless service providers; the county alcoholism administrator; and City Police Task Force—releases a summary report detailing the "Problems of transience and alcohol/drug abuse." In it, one solution is to "relocate and disperse 'street people' to a controlled environment for either processing or travel out of the area for rehabilitation . . . Warehouse problem cases" or "use an existing facility or create a village out of city limits area and transport transients there . . . Isolate bad people, create containment area." How "bad people" are defined remains unclear, and ironically, "transience" is now seen as something to be encouraged through a "get out of town approach" as an alternative to jail.

Business owners, particularly on lower State Street, view homeless people as a sickness, a literal "plague" to customers (*Santa Barbara News Press,* September 5, 1982), arguing that they should be quarantined or eliminated. As one business owner says, homelessness is an individual problem of a worthless group of people he views as expendable: "I hope you do get sick, I hope you die!!" (*Santa Barbara Independent,* May 26, 1988). In 1988, armed with signatures from approximately eighty other business owners, State Street merchants plead with Mayor Sheila Lodge to curb public drinking, panhandling, and "street crimes" they say have reached "epidemic" proportions (*Santa Barbara News Press,* February 9, 1988). They also encourage the city to implement police patrols to remove homeless people and make shopping fun again (*Santa Barbara News Press,* February 22, 1988).

Despite the increased fervor for criminalization measures, the cost of policing is an impediment, particularly when there are difficult proof procedures, as in the case of sleeping and camping offenses. In 1984, Rosenthal releases a report indicating that 956 people have been arrested in Santa Barbara for crimes related to homelessness from December 1982 to November 1983, costing the city over $100,000 and foreshadowing the argument that homeless people should be housed because it saves money spent on policing and emergency services (Culhane, Park, and Metraux 2011). As local sources report, the city issued 774 sleeping and camping citations in 1984, 481 in 1985, and 241 in the first two months of 1986 (*Santa Barbara News Press,* March 27, 1986). The drop in numbers is explained both by the effectiveness of fighting these citations, many of which are overturned, and the effectiveness of citations in ridding the city of homeless people who do not fight them.

Hostility toward homeless people manifests itself through business complaints and criminalization measures, including increased fines or jail time for nuisance offenses, and in highly publicized vigilantism against homeless people, targeting street people in particular as the scourge to be eliminated. The split between categories of homeless people deemed worthy of assistance and those seen as a waste of time frames the distinction between deserving and undeserving that shapes social services and policing. With their presence on city streets becoming a problem, many people experiencing homelessness and living unsheltered in the 1980s feel a sense of indignation that coincides with a national social movement.

Protest and Street People

The 1980s are a particularly tumultuous time as Santa Barbara and the nation struggle to understand and manage the presence of a large and diverse population of homeless people in public places, and several competing portraits emerge. One is of the rootless wanderer, initially popularized in academic literature via the theory of disaffiliation. Homeless people are understood as disconnected, without productive social ties, as not part of the team (Bahr 1973). One author reflects the confusion many feel about who the "new homeless" are: "There is not even agreement on what to call these people. They are hoboes, it seems, if they are at a distance . . . if the distance is great enough, they may be called Knights of the Road. But if they are close enough where their boozy breaths can be smelled, they are winos. Somewhere in between are tramps and vagabonds and bums" (*Santa Barbara News Press,* March 29, 1979). Whatever the label, "these people" cause problems because of their appearance and behavior, and many think they should be forced to move on or move out, for the good of the city, despite the stress such mobility causes (Carr 1994). Others see them as individuals and families struggling to make ends meet, understanding that many work, many don't drink, and even when they do, bad behavior is a result of untenable circumstances. One homeless woman, choosing to remain anonymous, explains this dichotomy in personal terms as "a curious social stigma attached to the down-and-out, that we are unworthy, incapable, dirty, unmotivated bums" (*Santa Barbara Independent,* March 17, 1988).

The upshot of this polarized view of homeless people is that it separates them into categories and assigns presumed social and individual characteristics. Judging the underlying moral worth of some people over others offers a confusing system of stratification that dictates how services are meted out. Certain categories of people are provided for, but inevitably, those living in the jungle are not considered worthy of assistance. Part of this has to do with the overlapping social categories that they fit into: male, single, transient, alcoholic, "street people" who deserve what they get. Although there are women in the jungle, kicking them out is simply collateral damage, and if they want to be sheltered, there are more local options available to them.[1] There are also children in the jungle in the 1980s, but like the women, they are comparatively few in number.[2]

Rob Rosenthal's book *Homeless in Paradise* (1994) chronicles the rise of homelessness in the 1980s in the midst of Santa Barbara's opulence. The striking contrast reflected in the title also belies the antagonism between homeless people and the city's more powerful, influential citizens, as business owners complain that homeless people

Anonymous

A child in the jungle.

are a nuisance that won't go away and homeless people counter that they are trying to survive while being run out of town. One of Rosenthal's primary findings is that agency and efficacy are among the most powerful tools for combating the stigma associated with homelessness, and even for escaping it entirely, although this last piece is less convincing, as several of the most prominent people in his book are still homeless in Santa Barbara by the year 2000. But homeless people in the 1980s feel that they can stand up to business owners and demand their rights. As photographer Kevin McKiernan, whose photographs are featured in this chapter, explains, "homeless protest influenced tourism, showed power . . . they were able to speak out and got a burst of confidence that frightened the city more than anything else." Street people view themselves as the agents of change and feel responsible to other homeless people to stand up for what they believe in, even stepping up to run emergency homeless shelters. How does the jungle foster this sense of agency and serve as a catalyst site for organized resistance that joins with homeless social protest in the 1980s?

Exactly when the jungle reemerges after its demise in the 1960s is unclear, but jungle raids begin to make headlines in the late 1970s and throughout the 1980s (*Santa Barbara News Press,* January 7 and 14, 1989), and Rosenthal estimates that hundreds are displaced by police sweeps designed to clear the jungle of homeless inhabitants. But the jungle is only a peripheral part of his book and inhabitants are considered a category of homeless referred to as "street people." The complete list includes "wingnuts, kids, transitory workers, skidders, and Latino families," separated on the basis of demographics as well as the resources they access and people they spend their time with (Rosenthal 1994, 48). These are an analyst's rather than a member's categories, in the sense that they come from an outsider rather than from homeless people themselves. Terms such as *street people* are coined by the city and used to justify a raft of new enforcement measures including sleeping and camping and increasing penalties for other nuisance offenses (*Santa Barbara News Press,* May 5, 1988).

As Cresswell (2001) points out, how homeless people are defined has important legal implications. In this case, those designated as "street people" are separated and regulated based on assumptions about who they are and what they deserve, specifically relating to behavior and public space. Separating homeless people into categories on the basis of age, race, ability, or moral worth and rewarding or punishing them accordingly simplifies both the problem and the solution. The result is confusing, identity-specific services that assist portions of the population deemed most sympathetic or most costly if left unassisted and punishing or removing the rest.

In the 1980s, the two primary struggles that pit homeless people and advocates against city officials, housed citizens, and business owners are the right to sleep and the right to vote. Homeless people are adamant that they should not be denied these two basic rights, which are fundamental to survival and citizenship. Because there is no adequate shelter for the growing homeless population, sleeping in public is common and inevitable, and homeless people are cited repeatedly and often endure brief jail stays for this and other nuisance offenses. At least in the legal sense, the metaphors of the yo-yo, the revolving door, and the leaf blower (Roberts 2004) aptly characterize the cycle that homeless people find themselves trapped in and which hinders their ultimate escape from homelessness (Rosenthal 1994). Moving back and forth between jail, the street, and the emergency shelter keeps homeless people de-centered, off balance, and further from developing long-term plans or solutions. If this is part of what characterizes "street people," it is a category developed and sustained through policing and through the cat-and-mouse game of regulation and resistance.

Sleeping and Voting

In an effort to rid Santa Barbara of the unsightly presence of homeless people in public places, the city begins an ugly, drawn-out war over the right to sleep. This struggle gains national attention and is the subject of a doctoral dissertation (Haggstrom 1994), a book (Rosenthal 1994), several lawsuits, and articles in the local and national press. Unlike the jungle that existed earlier in the century, this one offers no permanent protection, as it is on public property, and unlike the men of the old jungle, those living in the 1980s jungle do not stay in their place literally or figuratively. They are younger and more diverse, they drink in public, wield large knives, and feel entitled to rights and spaces and to argue for them either alone or with advocates (*Santa Barbara News Press,* December 20, 1988). They move around the city and continue to return to and, in a sense, claim certain city areas in protest or as living spaces. They also do not accept the idea that they are "beyond . . . usefulness" and instead say they are looking for work, have fallen on hard times, and deserve shelter (Rosenthal 1994, 100), or at least the right to sleep unsheltered without citation.

Despite these obvious temporal and spatial differences, the 1980s jungle also fosters a sense of kinship and community. People who live in the jungle, the more numerous and diverse "new homeless," take care of each other. They fight for each other literally and symbolically and see themselves as bonded not only through the everyday struggle for survival but also through the struggle to be seen as worthy of the right to sleep in the undeveloped areas of a city they consider home. Like the men of the jungle of old, they also have powerful friends who go to bat for them to gain basic rights and privileges, which they cannot secure for themselves. The victories they win empower them to feel entitled to city spaces and embolden them to take further action. The sleeping and voting controversies are led by several jungle leaders, introduced below, who head organizations founded by and for homeless people, reinforcing their sense of agency and social mobility, or at least the idea that change is possible.

The legal champion for homeless rights in this era is the Legal Defense Center (LDC), which later merges with the Committee for Social Justice, composed of lawyers Willard Hastings, former public defender Glen Mowrer, and author and activist Peter Marin. The LDC works to protect the jungle and the right to sleep there. As shown elsewhere, the proof procedure for sleeping and camping in makeshift locations relies on evidence of a crime (Wakin 2008). Is it the act of sleeping itself, the presence of a bedroll or other camping supplies, or merely looking homeless that is punishable? To ban sleeping, a biological necessity, means treating homelessness as a status and not a condition. The experience of this, for homeless people in the 1980s, is that they are committing a crime merely by existing, not to mention other behavioral or nuisance offenses, or even the actual crimes some do commit. This is problematic because law enforcement ideally focuses on something one does rather than who one is.

As the battle wages on, the city pushes unsheltered homeless people farther and farther out into marginal zones, suggesting that even their comfort is a threat. Mayor Sheila Lodge, completely fed up with this prominent, ugly problem in her city, suggests that "undeveloped city property is available to the desperate, as are sidewalks, so long as the sleeper doesn't interfere with foot traffic"

(*Santa Barbara Independent,* March 22, 1990). Despite the indifference expressed by city officials, the jungle in the 1980s has two things going for it: critical mass and hope. People experiencing homelessness are numerous and diverse enough to confuse business owners and citizens who characterize the situation as an individual problem and are outraged enough to engage in protest activities with housed activists. The threat of chaos is part of the jungle's power— that it might sully the attraction of an otherwise pristine beach town and cause a loss of tourist revenue. The protests in favor of the right to sleep and vote underscore this threat.

Jungle Leaders

James Magruder is startled out of a sound sleep, wrapped in dead leaves and newspapers, among the roots of the Fig Tree. Without skipping a beat, he reaches for an empty forty-ounce bottle, breaks its bottom off on the ground, and is ready for battle. James is known as an "enforcer," a "regulator," a tough guy in the jungle. He is charismatic enough to have friends and followers but too used to

Santa Barbara City Council, 1986.

street life, too addicted, too damaged by past experiences to ever make it out. James is the most charismatic, most pugilistic jungle leader. He has a small group of loyal followers, mostly men, who along with their dogs occupy the jungle for the central years of protest, from the early to late 1980s.

James grew up in the Santa Barbara area but left home to live on the streets beginning in the 1970s. People fear and respect him because of his willingness to enforce street justice and to fight for his friends and other homeless people who are unable to fight for themselves. People also love James. He is handsome, energetic, and seemingly without limits. He leads protest marches, falls in love, gets married, then breaks up with a woman he meets in the jungle (*Santa Barbara Independent,* June 15, 1989), and is someone others want to watch and follow.[3] James is also, in Rosenthal's terms, a "street person," meaning that he lives primarily on the street, has difficulty accessing work or benefits, incurs many citations for sleeping and various other nuisance offenses, and seeks out only the most basic emergency services. Yet he is not cut off entirely from housed citizens, he does not lack a social network, and he is in touch with family members, who live locally and offer various kinds of support.

Nancy McCradie and Bob Hanson are also longtime residents of Santa Barbara and one of the few couples to emerge as homeless leaders. They live in an RV that Nancy's parents helped her purchase and are raising Nancy's son from a previous, abusive marriage and eventually a daughter they have together, born in 1984. They do not sleep in the jungle full time, as Nancy owns an RV and Bob owns various vehicles of his own throughout their relationship. Both of them are articulate, employed, and able to work with housed citizens as well as people who live in the jungle. They are leaders of protest and social-movement activities throughout the 1980s and beyond. In comparison with James, Nancy and Bob are more focused, and some describe them as more self-serving. They eventually fall into the familiar mode of working on behalf of homeless people rather than building consensus among them (Rosenthal 1994). Yet people follow them because they help bridge the gaps between street people and housed citizens, and they speak the language necessary to get things done. They are also resented on this basis, and some think they are not "real" homeless people. Their prominence and the controversy that surrounds them also emphasizes the hierarchy among homeless people related to housing solutions and resources.

Nancy and Bob deserve special mention because their activism in the 1980s earns Bob his nickname "Protest Bob" and makes both of them recognized homeless leaders. Their activities are frequently covered in the newspaper, as they lead marches and sit-ins, and Bob in particular is notorious for his willingness to challenge laws or policies deemed unjust for targeting homeless people. In the late 1980s, they lead a march to the nation's capital to raise awareness for homeless rights. Nancy says: "I've learned firsthand that the American people care about homelessness and want to do something about it" (*Santa Barbara News Press,* November 8, 1988). This feeling never leaves them, and both continue to organize on behalf of homeless people long after the 1980s. Bob repeatedly runs for city council and for mayor in Santa Barbara, but he is criticized for lacking direction and for his sporadic drinking, which bonds him with other jungle residents but prevents him from being taken seriously by city officials. In a 1989 summary of mayoral candidates, the quote next to Bob's name reads: "The bankers and developers own this town" (*Santa Barbara Independent,* October 26, 1989).

And then there are quieter jungle leaders. One of these is Edwin. Like James, Bob, and Nancy, Edwin is also a street person in his thirties, and he lives between the jungle and the Fig Tree. He is the first person elected president of the Homeless People's Association (HPA), a collective grassroots organization founded by and for homeless people, and it is this role that gives him the name everyone calls him from that point on, "Prez Ed." People have confidence in his leadership because he listens and he tries to build consensus. His involvement with the HPA is born out of frustration at being harassed for activities related to being homeless, many of which he has managed to do for years undisturbed. But the interesting thing about Prez Ed and what distinguishes him from Nancy and Bob or James is that he stays out of the local limelight. There are very few mentions of him in the newspaper, and his name appears only once in a published source (Haggstrom 1994). The one photograph of him is in a calendar produced to benefit the family shelter, Transition House, in which he sits comfortably in his jungle among the few possessions that make up his home.

Prez Ed's main attempt at organizing is trying to win homeless people the right to vote. Along with other HPA members, being denied this basic right is something he considers unconscionable.

Prez Ed.

According to law in the 1980s, people without an address cannot vote, so homeless people citing the Fig Tree as their address are denied. In response, Prez Ed decides to change this by organizing HPA members to set up a small information table at the Fig Tree and to work with local advocates on the legal side of this and other issues related to the criminalization of people experiencing homelessness. Prez Ed is less charismatic than James and a less organized or contentious presence than Nancy and Bob. He is uncomfortable around housed people, and when the HPA merges with the Coalition to End Hunger and Homelessness (known locally as just "the Coalition"), a broader-based group of homeless people and advocates, he declines most meetings as he continues to quietly argue for better treatment and provisions for homeless people. But Prez Ed gradually starts to lose his connections with advocates and city officials, and he simply does not translate in housed company, so he retreats further into the jungle.

Advocates and Affiliates

Prez Ed's HPA is the one organization founded and run by street people, with Nancy McCradie largely responsible for its long-term endurance. Beginning in 1982, in addition to advocating for the right to vote, one of its main goals is to force the city to repeal the anti-sleeping ordinance passed in 1979. This ordinance is an emergency measure that was introduced, passed, and put into effect all on the same day. It is a reaction to what Santa Barbara feels is an immediate crisis, as greater numbers of people appear in public and are cited for camping during this time. To fight citation, homeless people argue that they are not camping, merely sleeping, which is not a violation. Changing the anti-camping ordinance to an anti-sleeping ordinance means that citations can be upheld without the burden of proof that camping requires (a bedroll, camping supplies, and so forth). The HPA lobbies City Hall to repeal the anti-sleeping ordinance and to provide some form of shelter for people without.

The HPA also sets up the aforementioned information booth at the Fig Tree to inform people about the ordinance and other issues related to homelessness in Santa Barbara. This results in ongoing clashes with the police and business community, which attempt to regulate the HPA's hours of operation, the number of people staffing the booth, and allowable behavior. In order to remain a public presence at the Fig Tree, the HPA starts to distance itself from street people, despite the fact that they are its staple members. When local business owners complain that there is public drinking at the booth, the HPA denies association with the drinkers: "That's not us." This is a familiar dynamic among homeless groups (Rosenthal 1994, 104). To get any privileges, you must gain categorical distance, a separation between good and bad or acceptable/unacceptable people and behaviors. If the city objects to drinking, the HPA says "we" don't drink. If the city says we support veterans, the HPA raises US flags around its encampments. Embracing the acceptable in terms of people or behavior is a form of compromise that reinforces marginalization. By distancing themselves from behaviors they obviously engage in, the HPA reinforces the distinction between us and them, making drinking a personal rather than a public issue and one that needs punishment and regulation rather than simple privacy.

While the national outcry against homelessness builds, the HPA continues to focus its energy on the ongoing local protest against the anti-sleeping and anti-camping laws and the right to vote. In October 1984, Prez Ed works with Protest Bob and other HPA members to install a mailbox at the Fig Tree. Using a coupon from a local hardware store, they purchase and install four mailboxes, one by one. Every time the city removes one mailbox, another one appears in its place. Years later, Prez Ed describes this as "a mind fuck," and then adds, "It was beautiful." Yet when homeless people attempt to register to vote using the Fig Tree as their address, the county refuses to accept their registration forms. Although they are legal citizens and many are long-term residents, lacking a fixed address means that they cannot enjoy their constitutional rights and privileges.

One month after the mailbox incident, HPA members begin a voting rights protest on Highway 101, which runs through the center of town with four working traffic lights impeding its flow. Six men holding signs on the island between the northbound and southbound lanes, one of them reading "Homeless people need shelter and love," move out onto the highway when the light turns red. How the protest actually begins is unclear, but the men block traffic and make national news in the process. By themselves, these protests are empowering for Prez Ed, Protest Bob, and the HPA, yet they do little more than raise awareness, gain media attention, and annoy police. The HPA also protests regularly at City Hall and the city council offices, and members are seen as disruptive, disorderly, and generally unpleasant. Despite attempts to convince people that they are ordinary, decent citizens, even other homeless people see them as separate from the group that the city negotiates with. This polarization only increases as the struggle wears on.

Good Cops and Bad Cops

Kit Tremaine is a modern-day Lillian Child, a friend to homeless people. Instead of property, she provides funding to assist with legal advocacy and shelter. Through her generosity, Nancy McCradie, Rob Rosenthal, and other Santa Barbara activists go to Chicago to attend the founding convention of the National Coalition for the Homeless. She also funds Willard Hastings, from the Legal Defense Center, to represent homeless people and to pursue various forms of litigation. The trip to Chicago eventually results in the formation of the Santa Barbara Homeless Coalition, which is intended to combine existing

Kevin McKiernan

Protest, Highway 101, Santa Barbara, November 3, 1984.

organizations of homeless people and advocates. The Coalition is composed of more than just the street people of the HPA. It also welcomes members of the Single Parent Alliance, a group of mostly women with children, and homeless and housed advocates. Many HPA members do not merge well with the Coalition and continue their own, separate forms of activism and protest, and the division between acceptable and unacceptable groups continues to widen.

In 1984 and 1985, the highly publicized murders of two "transient" men, Kenneth Burr and Michael Stephenson, shine a national spotlight on the issue of homelessness in Santa Barbara. Burr is shot once in the head while sleeping in the jungle, and his murder is never solved. Arrests and citations for homeless people increase after this, as does fear in the jungle, and a local man, not convicted of the murder yet claiming credit for it, posts a flyer warning other "Tree people . . . You are not welcome here. I will make life difficult for you as I did for Mr. Burr." Within months of this incident, Stephenson is stabbed to death by military prep students and during the attack is reported to have said, "Oh no, my friend, oh no," which becomes a local rallying cry for homeless rights. These horrific murders, along with Santa Barbara's draconian anti-sleeping, anti-camping ordinance become the subject of a Doonesbury cartoon series and attract national attention (Rosenthal 1994). Despite the idea that jungle residents are seen as people to be feared, they are in fact the victims of unruly citizens who object to and are willing to fight violently against their existence.[4]

Despite these tragic murders and the growing dichotomy between deserving and undeserving, in a few notable cases, people living in the jungle participate in shelter solutions, with jungle leaders James Magruder and Prez Ed running a temporary emergency shelter in the winter of 1987. This gives them a sense of inclusion, at least the feeling that they are part of the solution, and it challenges the good-bad dichotomy that both Rosenthal (1994) and Haggstrom (1994) describe as central to understanding homelessness in this era. This dichotomy describes those on the "good" side as those willing and able to negotiate with the city council, so perhaps even James and Prez Ed would not make the grade. But at first, the good cops are business owners interested in preserving the pristine quality and exchangeability of Santa Barbara's public spaces and members of the Santa Barbara Homeless Coalition, and the members of the HPA are the bad cops.

All of this changes when national homeless advocate Mitch Snyder comes to town, threatening mass protest and suggesting that in Santa Barbara, "there is a special kind of hatred against the homeless" (*Santa Barbara News Press*, January 19, 1989). In a speech on the steps of City Hall, Snyder references President Reagan, whose ranch is nearby, saying, "What he has done, he has not done alone. He was elected by a society that is abandoning democracy. It is based on never-ending competition, individualism and greed" (*Santa Barbara News Press,* January 19, 1989). Snyder threatens to return to Santa Barbara if the city does not repeal the anti-sleeping, anti-camping ordinance: "We will bring thousands of homeless people to Santa Barbara to go to sleep and go to jail repeatedly until we break the backs of your dirty little laws" (Haggstrom 1994, 379). Although the ordinance is never repealed, some compromises are made, and the city is at least willing to negotiate with members of the Coalition rather than brave a new tide of unruly homeless people and the shame of media attention.

After Snyder's visit, the Coalition becomes the good cop and the city is willing to negotiate. Street people, Snyder, and the HPA are lumped together as bad cops. This distinction is based on a feeling of common ground with the Coalition that city leaders do not feel with the HPA. Being able to talk with clean, sober, well-spoken academics and professionals proves to be far easier for city officials than to meet with dirty, disheveled, drunk, or belligerent members of the HPA or to manage Snyder's threats. The petulance that inspires James Magruder's friends is seen as embarrassing and annoying at city council meetings.

Behind the scenes, Will Hastings also gains ground arguing against the anti-sleeping, anti-camping law. The primary argument he uses is that it infringes on the right to travel, once again upholding mobility and consumption as citizen's rights. Santa Barbara Municipal Court judge Frank Ochoa finds the ban against sleeping unconstitutional, overly broad, and designed to target transients. "If this ordinance is applied equally, the infant sleeping in the carriage on State Street is committing a criminal act" (Walker 1985). His decision is later overturned. Although sleeping and camping are still considered offenses, these actions give the HPA a renewed sense of purpose. Rather than incurring a fine for violating the city's anti-sleeping, anti-camping ordinance, homeless people instead ask for a jury trial and for representation by a public defender. Because of the time and expense this costs the city, a majority of these cases are dismissed. But the controversy over sleeping and camping stretches on, succeeding only in putting a temporary damper on increased ticketing for these offenses.

Using the carrot-and-stick mentality, some conditional sleeping and camping is allowed in undeveloped city areas at the same time that enforcement is stepped up around State Street, the city's main commercial thoroughfare. The city also attempts to provide for some segments of the homeless population, but not those it calls "street people," or "Fig Tree types."[5] As a result of this targeting, other homeless people feel the need to separate from this group. A twenty-two-year-old woman, homeless in Santa Barbara for over a year, writes, "One thing I ask is not to stereotype all homeless as long haired, non-shaven dirty alcoholics and junkies. Some of us are just trying to survive" (*Santa Barbara Independent,* July 14, 1988). Yet the city invokes exactly this distinction to justify punishing "transients." Although it is incorrect to assume that most street people are transients, their presumed mobility is used as a weapon by the city, and police develop tools to target those who are seen as nonresidents, noncitizens, or simply drifters passing through. These tools are also used against jungle leaders such as James, Nancy and Bob, and Prez

Ed, all of whom are repeatedly cited for sleeping and camping offenses and all of whom were born and raised locally. In January 1984, a group of four police officers led by Lieutenant Charles Baker, known as "the Baker Boys," boast having made 10,696 arrests in the prior year, 15 percent of which are classified as "transient" arrests. They develop a lasting reputation and become a permanent fixture on the police force. Known as the transient detail, their aggressive attitude toward homeless people draws charges of police brutality (*Santa Barbara News Press,* February 15, 1989).

Although the right to sleep is never fully granted, homeless people win the right to vote in December 1985, in a California appeals court case.[6] The fight for homeless rights also galvanizes around several highly publicized incidents, among them the aforementioned murders and Mitch Snyder's visit to Santa Barbara. Although the success of the HPA is, on its own, a measured victory, setting up the information booth, protesting the anti-sleeping, anti-camping ordinance, and winning the right to vote all empower homeless people to pursue other forms of protest. In November 1984, the HPA and others hold a march to then President Ronald Reagan's ranch in Refugio

Homeless advocate James Magruder, November 6, 1984.

Canyon, to raise awareness for homeless rights. James is so enthusiastic on the day of the march that he climbs a telephone pole in protest, holding a sign that reads, "Homeless can't vote in USA," which makes national news and underscores the idea that change is both possible and inevitable.

Sleepless in Santa Barbara

The growing distinction between acceptable categories of homeless people and those who should be moved on and moved out informs the development of emergency shelters as well as enforcement measures. In April 1986, Santa Barbara opens Transition House, its first family shelter, with a thirty-five-bed capacity and rigid rules and restrictions. The only other shelter is the Salvation Army, which has the same number of beds and similar conditions. In December of the same year, the city contributes $50,000 to make Transition House a permanent family shelter. In addition, the County Health Department assigns a nurse to provide medical outreach at shelters, using the argument that emergency room care is simply too expensive. County general relief worker Ken Williams organizes the social work community to offer increased outreach and services to sheltered and unsheltered alike and remains a powerful advocate for homeless people for years to come. These measures highlight the city's desire to offer limited assistance to families and to prevent the most serious health risks, save tax dollars, help the undeserving, contain immediate threats, and isolate or regulate the rest. Reintegration in the sense of education, employment, and rejoining the community are simply off the table in an era when even sleeping is considered a crime.

In addition to criminalization strategies, other emergency measures are implemented to provide an immediate solution to the problem of shelter and keep homeless people off the streets. The first is the opening of Casa de la Raza, a nonprofit community center, for a three-month period for thirty people in January 1987, a particularly cold winter. Prez Ed and James agree to run the shelter, which is without showers or food. They are not paid but are trained by the Red Cross and put in charge of their peers (*Santa Barbara Independent*, January 28, 1987). The Catholic Rescue Mission also opens, allowing limited shelter stays, and is located next to the city's sewage treatment plant, which the HPA protests. In July 1987, Governor George

Deukmejian passes an emergency measure allowing the use of National Guard armories as temporary shelters, open when the temperature drops below 50°F if it is raining, and 40°F if it is not. Given these specific restrictions, homeless people unable to tell the exact temperature do not know whether they can access the armory. Despite complications like these, armories continue to operate as shelters well into the 1990s, but many are mere warehouses without social services and are often located far from city centers. As a testimony to their inadequacy, the Santa Barbara Armory makes local headlines in 1988 because it is without heat that winter (*Santa Barbara News Press,* November 23, 1988; December 1, 1988).

Together, these solutions house a small fraction of the population in the barest of accommodations with confusing regulations and minimal resources. None of the solutions make an attempt to permanently house people experiencing homelessness or to offer rehabilitation or detoxification beyond joining a twelve-step program. Public health nurse Linda Harris, who works with homeless people in shelters and on the streets and in jungles, says, "We punish women for being alcoholics and drug addicts; we take their kids away, but we don't give them any treatment" (*Santa Barbara Independent,* February 16, 1989). And every time some gains are made, more action is taken against street people and against the jungle in particular.

In fact, in 1987, days before the opening of Fess Parker's Red Lion Inn, the jungle is razed entirely, forcing residents to disperse to other areas of the city and face dangerous conditions or regulation. A report of the incident says that "the city removed three truckloads of clothes, wood, furniture, and junk to the county dump" (*Santa Barbara Independent,* January 28, 1987). The HPA remains active, although many of its activities are gradually subsumed under the umbrella of the Santa Barbara Homeless Coalition, with graduate student Jane Haggstrom as its director. Activities of the HPA remain protest based, and they continue to hold marches and camp on the steps of City Hall to protest the bulldozing of the jungle and to fight the anti-sleeping law.

Imitation of Domestic Life

Unlike the Bookman and the jungle mayor, most of the men in the 1980s jungle do not move into mainstream housing and employment.

Anonymous

James and friends.

But some of them distinguish themselves from run-of-the-mill home-less street people by virtue of greater resources and a closer align-ment with mainstream values. They are the "good ones." Nancy and Bob are among few couples who go from living in the jungle to liv-ing in their vehicle and owning several additional vehicles they use for transportation and storage. They are also employed in mainstream jobs in or near Santa Barbara, and they raise a child together. As a result, they are the "go-to" homeless couple, and Nancy in particu-lar is frequently asked to participate on local advisory boards or to lead initiatives related to homelessness and vehicle living. Their ver-sion of domestic life is much closer to what "normal," nonhomeless, nonstigmatized people accept. Nancy and Bob may not be part of the power elite that direct Santa Barbara's future, but they offer unintended, ancillary support, as they reinforce societal norms and move further and further away from people living in the jungle in terms of needs, concerns, and experience.

For those without a vehicle to live in, the impermanence of the 1980s jungle affords less of a chance to establish a domestic environment than the jungle on the Child Estate. Being able to build and settle on land without the fear of being kicked out is not something 1980s jungle residents enjoy. Their sleeping structures are less durable and lacking in basic comforts. This makes it even more difficult to present themselves well, to interact with housed citizens, and to look and feel as if they are worth talking to. Membership in the HPA and participating in social-protest activities and in running the city's first emergency shelter gives homeless people a sense of being worthwhile, of having something to fight for, or even simply the right to fight for themselves. Aside from Nancy and Bob, the majority do not translate well among city officials or planning organizations. But perhaps this is not the intention.

Homeless people in the 1980s feel that they have a right to Santa Barbara's public spaces. Their sense of survival and resistance is based on maintaining a feeling of control, on the idea that change and even literal motion are possible, rather than feeling trapped. It is this sense of agency, expressed through protest and raising awareness that is surprising in a city in which homeless people are the victims of violent attacks, and many people openly express the view that homeless people are trash. Those who participate in the municipal structure face what Marin describes as "an odd combination of belonging and escape, of being close to, and yet free from, a world in which you have no place" (Marin 1988). The HPA reinforces this sense of inclusion as an important distinction between the Santa Barbara Homeless Coalition and the HPA, with the former group feeling only slightly less marginalized than the latter. Perhaps, as J. Sakai suggests (2014), the lure of wealth, power, and superiority is strong enough to make even homeless protesters play along, all for a chance at some semblance of acceptance and the illusion of participation.

In 1988, there is a rare case of a jungle resident, a street person, gaining permanent housing. Notorious jungle leader James Magruder has two dogs that the city impounds as a public threat (*Santa Barbara Independent,* October 1, 1987). The judge tells James that unless he has a house where he can keep the dogs, they will be euthanized.

Around this time, James inherits money from his grandfather and buys an inexpensive house in an undesirable part of town. His mortgage payments are $1,200 per month, so James invites his jungle friends to move in with him and rents to those on general relief or Supplemental Security Income (SSI). Overnight, James goes from having little to no formal responsibility to becoming a landlord in charge of household bills, from living in the jungle to having a house of his own. James and his friends fix up the house with old furniture, a black-and-white TV, but they have no stove. They eat fast food, drink all day, and sleep in their clothes in a heap in one of the bedrooms. When James misses the jungle, he piles up blankets in the backyard and sleeps with the dogs under the stars or in the midday sunlight, depending on how drunk he got the night before. There are frequent fights in the house, and eventually, drug dealers begin using the house as headquarters and in return supply heroin to whoever wants it. After this, a young woman tragically overdoses and is found dead among the blankets and bodies the next morning. Other women visit the house, but most are there to sleep with the men, drink, or use drugs, and are gone again, leaving the men to brag about their exploits or wallow in self-pity.

Gradually and inevitably, addicted and overwhelmed, James falls behind on his payments. Tenants leave without paying, dirty the house, and further jeopardize his tenure there. The electricity is eventually turned off, then the heat, and James and his friends wait for the eviction notices and police to come and send them back to the jungle. When Peter Marin asks James how he feels about returning to his old life, he says, "I don't care. I lived that way for fifteen years and I don't give a damn. I think I like it better." And then he pauses and thinks a moment and says, "Well, maybe that's a lie. Or maybe it's the truth. I can't tell. It's right on the line, I guess" (Marin 1988).

James's experience is unusual because his family's money facilitates a move indoors and because he becomes responsible for others on a scale he never experienced. The side of domesticity that James embraces is the feeling of control, comfort, and freedom, but not paying bills, and not holding others accountable. The rules of the street, he can enforce; the rules of society, not so much. But to be fair, when does he get to practice? As James suggests, the freedom he can enjoy in the jungle is far greater than it is in a house he has to maintain. Of course, James is without his own family members to support, aside from his dogs,[7] and does not have immediate health needs or concerns that might force a move indoors. He also lacks the temperament or interest in fitting in with shelter rules and schedules, beyond meals and shower times, or a bed in case of emergency. His ability to move back to the jungle depends on his ability to survive as one of its regulators, and part of this capacity comes from his physical strength.

In contrast with James, Nancy's ability to survive depends on literal mobility, on being able to escape potential abuse or to hide from predators, a constant threat for women in the jungle. It is informed by a history of abuse and the need to protect herself and her children with the safety of a locked door. Nancy lives in a vehicle because the financial burden of moving indoors would leave her with scant financial resources to cover other expenses for herself and her family. So perhaps hers is another version of domesticity and survival that offers a contrast with James and an indication of what life on the streets and in the jungle is like for women. If we can call James's version of masculinity dependent on physical prowess, threat, or willingness to fight, and if we grant that this is a staple form of being able to survive in the jungle, then Nancy and other women facing homelessness have a few options: (1) make sure you have a regulator like James protecting you, (2) take your chances with physical and sexual abuse, even from said regulator, (3) protect yourself to the best of your ability by ensuring privacy, safety, and mobility to whatever degree you can. Addiction, income, and family status inform these choices, as Nancy does not have family members who can support her move indoors, beyond the purchase of a vehicle. Her relative freedom from addiction and her stable employment mean that she can maintain her own version of domesticity and control that is resource-dependent, relying on her ability to fit in with housed society rather than on physical strength.

Prez Ed never moves indoors and remains a jungle resident well into the 2000s, camping outdoors and going inside only for meals and occasional showers. Far less is written about Prez Ed than Nancy and Bob or James. His family is from the Midwest and visits him occasionally to be sure he is eating, and to try to coax him indoors. But Prez Ed never settles for indoor life. He is an alcoholic, like James, but not a fighter, and he never feels comfortable with housed people. The 1980s are an important time for Prez Ed but not because he leaves homelessness or even because he helps win the right to vote for homeless people. His stint leading the HPA simply makes him feel worthwhile and important, as if he has something to contribute. The national debate about homelessness is perhaps what facilitates Ed's activism, but it does not get him housing and he never participates in anything other than grassroots homeless movements or volunteering at emergency shelters. Of all the homeless leaders described in this chapter, only Nancy and Bob are able to sustain a semipermanent solution to housing. After James's brief homeownership in the 1980s, neither he nor Prez Ed live indoors again.

Out in the Cold

The 1980s jungle has a few logistical features in common with the jungle of earlier decades. Both are adjacent to but separate from the mainstream, in hidden areas, across from the beach and in close proximity to newly built luxury hotels. Police try, successfully in later years, to remove the jungle from public view by conducting several raids in which people's possessions are carted away and eventually the site is bulldozed entirely. Without any assurance of protection, jungle residents scatter, only to resurface in essentially the same areas, when things cool down. Thick foliage separates the jungle from tourists, citizens, and luxury hotels, and therein lies the age-old problem: how to rid the city of any sign of poverty, of squatters and street people, without offering provisions that many fear will welcome blight, or merely offer comfort. Ironically, there has always been poverty in paradise, but its increase in volume and visibility makes it seem like a new and pressing problem threatening to take root.

The mobility that characterizes residents of the old and new jungles is similar in the sense that both communities have a host of regulars, residents of Santa Barbara who interact with the city and speak on behalf of other homeless people. But the growing division between homeless people in the 1980s means that those with greater resources, including vehicles, jobs, and education, are separated from unsheltered street people, who are seen as hypermobile, drunken deviants. The protection that Lillian Child afforded the men of the jungle of old allowed them to argue with the town at some remove. They wrote into the local paper, they dialogued with citizens willing to visit. But they knew their place, they stayed there, and they characterized themselves as "decrepit," "old," and not worth bothering with. By contrast, the young mavericks of the 1980s jungle are a threat. They occupy city areas in protest, sometimes for weeks at a time, attract wealthy and powerful advocates, and refuse to go away. Without territory or protection, they band together, wandering into the main thoroughfares of town, feeling that they can make a difference, can raise awareness, and that they are entitled to basic rights. This poses a threat to the city's sense of decorum and order, but the decision about what to do with the men of the jungle reverses over time, particularly regarding mobility.

When the jungle is a protected space, the men are encouraged to stay there and stay out of sight. Settling is rewarded. When it is a public space, inhabitants are encouraged to move on or simply keep moving to avoid sanction, and mobility is rewarded. But in the 1980s, unlike earlier decades, there are no easy transportation routes, no freight trains to jump or other ways of leaving town and staying away, which is complicated by legal trouble that often mandates staying in a particular area. There is some notion of providing for Santa Barbara residents, but no recognition that some of these are the same "street people" assumed to be transients. Behavior is also targeted differently in the 1980s, as not only drinking but sleeping and voting laws attempt to restrict biological needs and constitutional rights, eradicating the deserving, bad ones. Despite these challenges, homeless people refuse to leave town or to be erased from public record: they agitate, they work with advocates, they threaten the city with a bad reputation, damaging its tourist appeal. They even participate in running the city's first emergency shelter. And they gain rights that empower them to continue to take action.

Once the media spotlight stops shining on homelessness and the city of Santa Barbara, restrictions and regulations attempt to put homeless people back in their place, meaning prison or shelter. Those who remain on the street incur sanctions that make it more difficult to return to settled life, to think of themselves as upstanding citizens, and eventually, many stop caring. The culture of homelessness and the jungle in the 2000s shows the evolution of unsheltered homelessness since the 1980s decade of crisis. Institutional cycling creates a politics of entrenchment (Marr 2012), whereby homeless people are repeatedly cited for nuisance offenses, shuffled back and forth between jails and prisons, and between shelters and poorly resourced service agencies, which gradually remove them from any sense of agency or social change. Rather than fight for their rights, homeless people living in the jungles in later years are modern-day outlaws, either literally or figuratively in the sense of being removed, for the most part, without any sense of escape.

4

Danger and Risk:
2000s

By the year 2000, the waterfront's undeveloped spaces are dwindling as the city seeks to maximize profits from its pristine coastline. This means luxury tourism, including over forty hotels in the downtown area and an estimated $1 billion in annual tourist revenue. The preservation efforts of the early 1900s still prevent large-scale commercial development, and the city struggles to realize its original vision of paradise. As one writer puts it, "The relaxed atmosphere which characterizes Santa Barbara's waterfront and harbor is deceptive" (Conard 1982, 185) because it is engineered to be an exclusive area devoid of industry, poverty, or its poorest citizens, intrinsically linking the area's natural beauty with the ideals of wealth and entitlement. The ongoing challenge of managing homeless people in public places leads to increased criminalization as a powerful tool to contain and punish them and keep tourists going to the beaches, hotels, and restaurants. To remain in business, minimizing or eliminating homeless people, their belongings, pets, vehicles, and other possessions, is the name of the game.

For homeless people themselves, avoiding regulation means hiding in the interstices of urban areas, sleeping in vehicles, public parks, beaches, and jungles, where multiple dangers proliferate. Inevitably, people living in the jungle receive citations for nuisance offenses, including sleeping and camping, trespassing, and drinking from open containers, and they often receive multiple citations.

97

Sometimes, they blend in well with tourists and residents at venues like the farmer's market or drum circle, and sometimes not. When they manage to become part of the tourist attraction, like the man with 1,000 aliens and other memorabilia glued to his van parked along the waterfront, or the man named Mason who sang and played guitar on State Street (*Los Angeles Times,* May 13, 1993), they are grudgingly tolerated, even beloved. When they are in the wrong places, at the wrong times, doing the wrong things, they are cited repeatedly. Others have legal cases pending or are on parole or probation and must remain in Santa Barbara, and virtually all are in and out of jail to answer for minor offenses. As a result, the millennial jungle is fragmented, hidden beside the railroad tracks, on freeway on/off ramps, in parks and beaches, and in other wooded or forgotten areas throughout the city. Homeless people living in these areas are unable to leave for a myriad of reasons, not least of which is the downward spiral set off and perpetuated through criminalization.

The jungle exists in virtually the same place it always has, and I visit it with expert guides who protect me and let me in, to whatever limited extent, to their world on the margins. The railroad tracks today, along with aqueducts and waterways, serve as transportation corridors for homeless foot traffic. They are easy ways in and out of town, a valuable resource for people on the run. Outdoor living and homeless encampments are common throughout California and well documented in Ventura County to the south and Santa Cruz to the north. In a visit to Santa Cruz in 2008, a homeless couple agreed to take me to their camp in the Poganip, a park adjacent to the University of California, Santa Cruz campus, and part of a larger 1,000-acre greenbelt overlay district, which provides ample space for homeless campers. They live there with ten to twenty other people, several of whom have been there for years. On our way out of town, we walk along the railroad tracks until we start hearing voices. Drug dealers were controlling that part of the tracks, and we had to make a detour because there was no way we could pass them unmolested. New in town, clean, white, obviously not part of the community, I was a distinct liability. This is because of the harm I could do as a possible cop or informant, and because of the harm that could come to me or to my guides if they took me to a place I was not allowed to go.

Creating danger zones like this, where street justice holds sway, is in many ways just as scary and offensive as developing privatized, pristine spaces where luxury and consumption create a sense of entitlement and privilege that justifies inhumane treatment. California is infused with this ironic juxtaposition of luxury and penury (Borchard 2005; 2010), the rich controlling the city and poor people pushed to its margins. The age-old question of who public spaces belong to and who is entitled to a better, safer, cleaner quality of life, in fact to dictate its terms, is wrapped up in questions of moral worth and a separate system of access to public space. Being in the wrong place, at the wrong time, doing the wrong things depends on who decides what is right and who the offender is taken to be. Criminalization makes sure that homelessness is punishable in a way that fuses condition with status, as if homeless people have expired registration stickers that make them targets until they fix themselves.

In contrast with Santa Barbara, Santa Cruz takes what many call a "hippy-dippy," liberal stance on homeless camping and visibility in the downtown area. Although the city is not without its share of criminalization measures (National Law Center on Homelessness and Poverty and the National Coalition for the Homeless 2009), the tenor among activists suggests that camping be allowed as a choice, a matter of individual preference. There are notably fewer women who suggest this in homeless or advocacy circles, in large part because of the danger the jungle poses to the few who enter. Women, as a result, more often live in vehicles or in shelters, and when they do camp, they do so with a boyfriend or protector, risky as that may be, or they face other dangers. Santa Barbara, as elsewhere, has a greater number of shelters and services for women experiencing homelessness, and as a result, the people camping in the jungle today are still predominantly male and camp with one other person or in a group. Very few people, male or female, ever camp alone. People refer to the jungle as the area along the railroad tracks, both north and south along the ocean. Of course, the old Child Estate has long since become the Santa Barbara Zoo, but jungle camps still press against its fences.

Modern-day jungle residents use a combination of services to meet basic needs, including meals, showers, mail, clothing, medical care, and access to federal and local forms of relief. They are living in the jungle for many reasons: avoiding shelters, preserving relationships, feeding addictions, and managing legal complications. Some are there because they have aged out of foster care. As a twenty-four-year-old man camping in Santa Rosa explains, "There's nothing . . . they didn't transition me for a job experience or anything

Ricky's camp against the fence.

like that, didn't give me nothing on how's this going to work, here's a reference for this or that, they booted me straight to the street and not knowing anything, I went straight to jail." Cycling back and forth between jail and prison and enduring the racial segregation and violence typical of prison life feeds into the nihilistic struggles that take place in the jungle. When I meet this man, he is living in a tent with his girlfriend, who is six months' pregnant. When I ask her if she plans to continue camping, she tells me, "I will go to a shelter, I have to. My mom had me out in the streets but I need to have this baby and get a job and you really can't do that if you're camping out."

People living in the jungle avoid shelters because of the stigma that surrounds homelessness, meaning that most service interactions and contacts between the "normal" and the stigmatized are fraught with tension, reaffirming the feeling that homeless people are to blame for their current state and any problems they are experiencing. This is the stigma theory, which explains homelessness as something caused by personal failure and justifies doing nothing about it. Although being homeless is a collection of lived experiences, reactions to it reify poverty as an inherent quality and punish it accordingly. The stress of homelessness is magnified by criminalization and shelterization and other forms of punishment and exclusion, all of which in combination create a downward cycle, a vortex that worsens and advances all vulnerabilities, making escape increasingly elusive. The stigma of homelessness is defined and reinforced through mixed contacts, service interactions, and criminalization.

In this chapter, I examine survival and resistance in the jungle through three sets of relationships: Ricky and Edwin; Moms and Russell; and Cuba and Martin. Using interviews, field recordings, transcriptions, and field notes, I focus on how residents understand and experience the jungle and the immediate shelter environment, how they survive and resist criminalization and social stigma. I explore how jungle living intersects with shelters and other makeshift settings, even housed society, and compare its resources and risks with other alternatives. Jungle residents' experiences of space and time are used to show how mobility becomes cyclical and the ability to access basic housing and employment is eventually out of reach. The cycle of exposure to criminalization and repeat incarceration, violence, trauma, and addiction affects identity and self-esteem, making people in the jungle feel permanently separate, unable to interact with anyone but their own kind (Shaw 1930). This downward spiral ends in death or incarceration, and passing time in the jungle means waiting for the inevitable.

The Context of Shelter

The events in this chapter are set during a pivotal time in the history of homelessness in Santa Barbara because the city is building its first emergency shelter, a feat that is years in the making. So the mixed contacts that occur between shelter residents and staff and between homeless people and business owners in the neighborhood are particularly charged. Jungle residents see the shelter as an opportunity to get a meal, a shower, or a bed for the night, but they are frustrated with the slow process of completing the shelter building itself. It is constructed and open to residents in stages that leave them unsheltered for several months of the year, with sporadic closures during construction, and without consistent services, or services of any kind annually from April 1 to November 30, when the shelter is closed because of warm weather. As a result of this rocky opening, jungle residents want to be sure that shelter staff know who is really in charge and that though staff might enforce the rules of the shelter, they do not enforce the rules of the street.

The emergency shelter is a warehouse space opened in 1999, twelve years after the original provision of armories as shelters in California. It fits approximately eighty cots for men and women, and it was founded by a group of wealthy business owners interested in keeping homeless people off State Street, the most commercially lucrative and touristy part of town, the cash cow that keeps the city's affluent citizens afloat. It is located just off lower Milpas Street, State Street's less expensive, ethnic parallel, and is within walking distance to the waterfront, the old jungle, and the parks and beaches lining Cabrillo Boulevard. The shelter is located on Cacique Street, which ironically means "street of chiefs," and its opening is transformative. It has an intracity magnet effect, pulling homeless people in for needed services and concentrating them in the same central, downtown corridor where police can find and cite them easily and repeatedly. It does its job of removing visibly homeless people from State Street, but it simply redistributes them to a different area, where they are like fish in a barrel.

In 2000, Cacique Street is a well-traveled way station for people heading in and out of the beaches, parks, and jungles and going back and forth to the Rescue Mission, the Salvation Army, and other service locations across and uptown. Designed to alleviate the visual burden of homeless people, emergency shelters like the one on Cacique Street do not offer a clear path to transition out of homelessness, or even consistent access to services that meet basic needs. There is one case manager for the entire shelter, and he serves approximately eighty people per day. He keeps office hours and consults with anyone who comes in, although he lacks the tools or the drive to try to help everyone. There are other staff members who offer referral services to outside agencies, but most of such service is sporadic at best and stays that way for years to come.[1]

The beaches and parks in the immediate Cacique Street neighborhood offer comparatively better amenities, including public restrooms, public parking, a place to rest after a meal, and the nearby convenience stores offer cigarettes, cheap beer, and snacks. These locations are also freer of the critical mass of homeless people in the shelter itself, which people describe as "Babylon" or "Peyton Place" because on any given day there can be fighting, making up or breaking up, people under the influence of drugs or alcohol, or the need to call the police in for whatever reason, you name it.[2] In addition to people sleeping on the streets and in the jungles, those living in cars and RVs also line the streets leading to the shelter. Living in the millennial jungle means a great degree of overlap between various segments of the homeless population, frequent interactions with law enforcement, and decreasing chances for exit, or even interaction with mainstream society. Instead, homeless people are isolated through policy responses that target specific populations and problems rather than addressing systemic failings.

People living in the jungle avoid the shelter because, in addition to avoiding law enforcement or the drama, danger, or disease of other homeless people, they don't want to submit to authority. There is also a sense that people come into shelter because they are ready to admit that they are personally culpable or deficient, sinful or sick (Lyon-Callo 2008; Gowan 2010). The shelter system in general, in an attempt to serve homeless people, quantifies, diagnoses, and attempts to treat various forms of what are seen as personal weaknesses. It is an agent of regulation, curtailing behavior, time, and space, marking homeless people as inferior and deficient. Some of this is up front, in the marginal, industrial city areas in which shelters are located or in the rules and regulations that are a requirement for entry. But some of it is interactional and more subtly reifies the experience of homelessness as a problem of identity. People going through it are seen as failing to measure up to societal norms, and it is up to undertrained and underpaid staff to figure out why. While they do so, the clock is ticking, as length of stay requirements and meeting program goals are the keys to keeping programs funded and demonstrating success. This urgency is a feature of the larger shelter, service, and corrections industries, which focus on containing or fixing, if not eradicating, troublesome populations.

In shelter settings, focusing on curing the sickness or sinfulness of homelessness (Gowan 2010) means exacting behavioral compliance as evidence of improvement, whether or not it leads to housing, employment, or services. This leaves little room to address the underlying structural causes of homelessness and the insurmountable barriers that still prevent escape. Even if homeless "clients" are willing to humble themselves by jumping through staff-designated treatment plans and compliance hoops, there is no guarantee of a better life, a job, housing, or anything beyond basic shelter (DiFazio 2006). Resisting "treatment" is seen as evidence of denial or lack of readiness and often increases the overall "sickness" of the client and his or her time on the street. And, of course, most jungle residents will never submit to shelter or any attempt to curtail or regulate their behavior. Many are too traumatized to even think about it.

Others weigh their options. A fifty-seven-year-old man camping in Sonoma County explains, "I built a little hut in Rohnert Park and lived there for years . . . I got arrested and they took me to Atascadero, a long-term mental hospital, for ten or eleven months, and then put me on Supplemental Security Disability Income (SSDI) and I lived in a board-and-care facility with all men. It was either that, which I did for two years, or live on the streets." When I push the issue, asking him, "Do you prefer the streets?" he replies, "No, it's not that. If I had enough money, I would rent an apartment. I don't have enough money but I'd prefer that. If I don't have enough money, then I prefer the streets." Like many people who leave institutions of correction, mental hospitals, foster care, or military service, fitting into the routines of normal life is a challenge. California's housing market is also notoriously exclusive, ranking second in the nation for the highest housing wage, translating to earnings of $34.69 per hour to afford a two-bedroom rental. This means that someone making minimum wage must work 116 hours per week (National Low Income Housing Coalition 2019). People receiving Social Security or Supplemental Security Income (SSI), the former determined by earnings and the latter by need, typically make less than this and are priced out of the mainstream housing market.

Space, Time, and Mobility

Instead of space-time compression, homeless people living in today's jungles experience space-time elongation, or stretch, as they are dependent on the routines of institutions for daily necessities, policed for performing these necessities in public, and at the mercy of public transportation to shuttle them back and forth for basic goods and services. They occupy city spaces like an amoeba that extends and contracts into a city, town, or beach's empty, quiet areas, during the lonely times of day and night, ready to retreat at any sign of threat. It is not only where they are but when they are there that reflects their difference and marginality.[3] To survive means being sensitive to regulation, which restricts when and where homeless people can be and threatens to curtail their movement completely through the imprisonment that eventually comes with repeat ticketing. This means living in a state of almost constant duress, in which even freedom of motion is challenging (Goffman 2014). Research on homelessness and housing instability supports the idea that losing one's home, or changing it frequently, is detrimental to one's self-esteem and future success. Many jungle residents find themselves in a holding pattern, stuck in Santa Barbara to answer for prior offenses and attempting to avoid new charges and other consequences of housing instability.

Experiencing homelessness in paradise has a sink-or-swim quality in which fitting into a program means swimming free of the constant stress of regulation or a life in public (Carr 1994). But program space is limited and comes with exclusive entry requirements, tight timelines, and ongoing adherence to rules and regulations, and people already under duress often crack under pressure. Without a program or a way out of homelessness through housing and employment or other assistance, it is easy to sink back into the tide of people going around and around, but not out. And once you are caught up in a crowd of similarly frustrated and stigmatized people, tensions build and the cycle of addiction, poverty, criminalization, and incarceration becomes a vortex that you are drawn into, one way or another.

In Santa Barbara, simply being in public places is problematic, as people experiencing homelessness are heavily regulated by police and stigmatized by housed citizens and business owners, who effectively dictate appropriate modes of appearance, behavior, and identity through the city's municipal code and through specific ordinances targeting the visibility of homeless people as well as specific behaviors (National Law Center on Homelessness and Poverty 2013; Mitchell 2001). In the cyclical world of homelessness, repeat negative interactions with police, other homeless people, and service staff can create additional dangers and barriers to exit. People living in the jungle in the 2000s avoid public attention, but the majority are not involved in organized resistance beyond fighting tickets. The space they inhabit is refuse space—unused and forgotten but still in the shadows of tourist areas. It remains close to luxury hotels, pristine beaches, and the city zoo, and the homeless people living there go back and forth to meals, showers, and shelter programs; to the post office and check-cashing services; to the county clinic, Social Security office, and housing authority; the jail, the prison, and other service and regulatory agencies. But none of these offer a viable path out of homelessness until it is too late. And homeless people must walk or take public transportation, as the services they need to access are often far apart from one another and jail or hospital release does not take homelessness into account. This wastes time and money and is an additional source of frustration and barrier to exit.

People experiencing homelessness follow the routines and schedules of shelter and institutional life to access resources, manage health care, access benefits, and answer for criminal-justice issues. But often, transportation and service schedules are not in synch, leaving people experiencing homelessness frustrated in their efforts to get things done or stranded in the middle of the night with no place to go. Homeless people's relationship to time is also complicated because it is not equated with money. People living in the jungle do not talk about spending time, as if it is a commodity. Rather, they talk about passing time, doing time, and killing time as a chore bereft of worth or options, an uncomfortable holding pattern that is accompanied by various forms of risk and obligation. Time is spent moving back and forth between places that do not have needed services, cannot or will not provide them, or do so while treating clients themselves as though they are a waste of time. Those not seeking service linger in public places, waiting for handouts or punishment, the latter more likely than the former. If you are homeless, time is something you must have in abundance, as poorly coordinated and underresourced service provision will waste it prodigiously. Without easy access to transportation, this can mean days of waiting. This kind of space-time stretch is a regular feature of homelessness, causing people to opt out of all but the most pressing, emergency services and to lose the inclination to even keep a schedule.

Homeless people's time, like anyone's, can be boiled down to a dollar amount. But instead of this amount being a wage paid to the individual, it is seen as a one-way tax on society, making homeless people a burden that costs, and reducing the cost means permanent housing over emergency services. Of course, this approach neglects the moral and social-justice arguments for housing homeless people and reduces it to a question of money: How can we pay less for the same people and feel good about it in the process? Ironically, homeless people support thousands of service personnel through salaries and hourly wages from public and private agencies that are part of the homeless service industry (Willse 2015). Delivering shelter and housing and various kinds of case-management, public health, outreach, and specialized services are all costly, not to mention the cost of policing, and none of it would exist without homeless people.

Acknowledging and quantifying this pay-in is a needed corrective to the idea that we alone bear the financial burden of homeless people without receiving the financial benefit that comes to those addressing the problem. As race theorists similarly ask: Where would the prison and shelter industries be without poor people of color (Boothe 2007)? Understanding and quantifying this societal pay-in contests the idea that homeless people present a burdensome, one-way cost to society and suggests instead that they keep the service and shelter industry afloat. But this should not draw attention away from the moral implications of a society complacent with the idea of a perpetual homeless class.

One final constraint on time in the jungle is how long one's physical strength can hold out. Physical strength is a primary resource in the jungle, but it is constantly put to the test through the rigors of outdoor living, made more difficult with the addition of physical and mental-health issues, addiction, and disability, and other common challenges and risks, including the shadow work and day labor many use to procure sustenance. This makes people living in makeshift settings like the jungle vulnerable to injuries and illnesses that go untreated. Once homeless people lose their health and physical prowess, their position is compromised, they become vulnerable, and any resources they have, including medication and income, become more difficult to guard and protect. Women living in today's jungle, still few and far between, must also be fit enough to manage the jungle's daily exigencies and its predators. As a result, women living in the jungle are almost exclusively girlfriends of men living in the jungle, who offer them physical protection. Relatedly, they are almost always susceptible to sexual violence and harassment, whether or not they are living with someone, and must constantly manage this danger.

Identity and Resistance: Mixed Contacts

Irving Goffman describes "mixed contacts" between the stigmatized and normal as "the moments when stigmatized and normal are in the same 'social situation'" (1963, 12). Mixed contacts between homeless and housed people often inspire embarrassment and shame for people experiencing homelessness and reaffirm the pity, fear, and disgust of housed citizens, making people on both sides avoid these encounters altogether. This avoidance can have serious consequences for homeless people, as it reinforces various kinds of exclusion and mandates a different use of space, time, and communication, resulting in legal complications and negative effects on self-esteem. Sociologists have also discussed how a culture of the street reinforces the values, dress, attitudes, and behavior that clash with those found in housed society (Anderson 1999). The longer you live in the jungle, the less you translate in the normal world, until eventually you stop trying and couldn't if you wanted to. Mixed contacts reinforce the stigma of homelessness, making people feel separate and adding to the depression and addiction that often go with it. Mixed contacts have personal, social, and legal implications and are frequently what initiates the cycle of citation-warrant-arrest-repeat, a common and virtually unavoidable trap for people living in the jungle.

This cycle affects where people live, for what duration, and under what circumstances. In the three examples of "couples" or "partners" living in the jungle described below, addiction and trauma contribute to the cycle, as addiction is often the reason for citation and trauma is worsened with addictive behavior and is often an initial cause of homelessness. For the people included in this chapter, mixed contacts present a problem, as they are associated with punishment and correction, as well as degradation and disrespect. Because of the importance of mixed contacts in defining and shaping the stigma of unsheltered homelessness, in the next section I pay attention to how jungle residents manage these interactions and what consequences this has for their ability to survive and engage in resistance activities. The jungle's history in Santa Barbara, as a protected community on private land and then as a public, undeveloped site for social protest, makes questions of public space, survival, and resistance the keys to understanding its role as a galvanizing force for the homeless community.

When people living in the jungle interact with the normal world in a way that contests its authority, they are trying to prove that the concerns of the normal world are incorrect, that jungle residents are worthwhile people, and that street justice reigns supreme. It is this simple idea of resistance as contesting authority and standing up for oneself that proves fertile ground for examining how the exigencies of jungle living inform the identities and resistance activities of residents. When seeking help means relinquishing control over one's sense of self, this causes immediate resistance and negates any consideration of the long-range consequences. In other ethnographic work, homeless people enact various forms of protest (Liebow 1993; Duneier 2000) although they know it is not in their best interest to do so or that it amounts to simply blowing off steam. This can mean leaving the shelter or telling off shelter staff, regardless of the consequences or the dangers of the street if they are "86'ed" or asked to leave. There may be immediately precipitating factors like release from jail, prison, or the hospital that frustrate people desperate for services. Experiences with violence, trauma, and addiction also lead to protest and frustration. All of these circumstances, along with the regular rigors of jungle living, affect the identity and resistance strategies found among people experiencing homelessness.

Without an organized movement, or the resources for social change, as Teresa Gowan (2010, 24) illustrates, everyday forms of resistance "are just as likely to reproduce inequality as to change it." But how did people living in the jungle today fall so precipitously far from openly questioning capitalism and wage labor or participating in the organized social-protest movements of the 1980s? Why do they now seem like the culled and silent masses? The reason, in part, is that the most pervasive responses to homelessness are criminalization, shelterization, and medicalization, which suggest the proper place for homeless people is incarcerated, in shelter, or institutionalized. These responses play out in the way services are offered and in how people experiencing homelessness understand and articulate their own condition. In this chapter, I explore these overlapping responses as a way of understanding the spatial and temporal trap homeless people are enmeshed in and what they see as a way out.

Ricky and the Rules of the House

When I first met him, in 2000, Ricky was thirty-eight and I was twenty-nine. He had been living on the streets on and off since the late

Michele Wakin

Ricky.

1970s and was a leader in the protest movement in the 1980s. Ricky's camp is located just over a railroad trellis next to the city zoo. This makes him the informal gatekeeper of the jungle, always knowing who is home and who is living where, as everyone passes by his camp to get to and come back from meals and services. But Ricky is, as jungle mayor Edward Anderson once described himself, "decrepit," despite his youth. A life of alcoholism has made his nails soft, making it that much more difficult to open the pull-tab beer cans that he drinks from morning to night. The list of maladies he suffers from is also long, including fatty liver disease, sclerosis of the liver, colon cancer, hepatitis C, peritonitis, and duodenal ulcers, making him seem far older than his years and making his remaining days in the jungle both grueling and numbered. Although his camp is well-located, he is no longer a leader and cannot regulate the jungle's activities or enforce its rules.

Ricky is forthcoming about his personal life and, like the Bookman and Edward Anderson before him, keeps records that include meticulous detail on his various illnesses and significant life events. Although he never pinpoints one specific incident that causes him to become homeless, he tells me about a number of precipitating events with the common themes of trauma and addiction. Having just read Clifford Shaw's 1930 classic, *The Jack-Roller: A Delinquent Boy's Own Story,* I was exploring the idea of push-pull factors leading young men to take to the road. Ricky's troubles began when he was a junior in high school. He wanted to quit school, but his parents said that he needed to abide by the rules of the house or leave. He left and moved south to live with his uncle and work odd jobs in Kentucky and Kansas. But it was the death of his sister that he said "was when my downfall started." She and Ricky were the two middle children out of six and enjoyed a close relationship. She was twenty-three and engaged to be married when she was hit and killed by a drunk driver, and as Ricky describes, "That screwed up my emotions completely."

Ricky was born in a small town in Minnesota, where the majority of his family still lives. His mother is a retired schoolteacher, and Ricky says, "She can make anything, including cabinets. She fixes plumbing and is computer literate." His father is a retired postmaster, still fit and able to bicycle into town. Both of Ricky's parents are in good health, and he is proud of his family. It is mutual, and his mother confirms this during our first telephone conversation by saying, "Thank you for taking an interest in our Ricky, we love him a lot." But living with them for any length of time is out of the question, and has been for some time. Not abiding by the rules of the house or those of his parents, employers, or anyone else in authority is a common theme for Ricky.

Although his work history includes cutting steel and laying tile, all of his jobs have been temporary. He entered the US Air Force as a physical therapy technician in 1979 and received his associate's degree in applied physical therapy. He was honorably discharged in 1983 but says, "I got into a lot of trouble," so they didn't want him to reenlist. Ricky got married before entering the military, and his wife gave birth to a son while he was away. Despite this, just after his release from service, she served him with divorce papers. It happened while he was at work, in front of everyone. When he returned home, she told him, "I just don't want you anymore." He then left for Florida to pursue odd jobs and slipped further and further into the bottle. Peppered with a history of trauma and addiction, by the time I meet him, Ricky is clinging to the adventures he experienced in the past as a measure of self-worth.

Part of remembering his past involves trying to reassert himself as the person he was, rather than the person he is, as if his former self can cancel out his current one. Ricky casts his actions as a logical rejection of a regular, structured life. As his niece idyllically puts it, Ricky is a man "who chose to live his life outside of the conforming walls of conventional rules . . . He broke out of the conformist pattern and lived his own life." The stories Ricky tells, over and over again, are about the outdoor adventures he had as a younger, fitter man. They emphasize his independence, his maverick attitude, the desire to help others, and his physical prowess, all stereotypically masculine attributes. Considering himself a guide, tracker, and hunter, he says, "If you're hungry and you need a rabbit, give me a call." By saying this, Ricky performs a classic form of identity work in which he harks back to the times when he had a role to play deserving of respect, a counter to the obviously dire straits he is currently in. But his seemingly fanciful and repetitious stories show a clash between his past and present, a time of possibility and a time to say good-bye. This clash shows the dual nature of the jungle, as a place once known for its promises and possibilities, a place tied to employment and adventure, but one that gradually sinks into decline, as residents become either "decrepit," incarcerated, or stationary, as work dries up and possibilities dwindle.

Mixed Contacts

During my first visit to Ricky's camp, he crosses a small railroad bridge to greet me, and we walk back over to his jungle to sit down and have breakfast. I bring him a McDonald's Breakfast Supreme in exchange for the interview. It is then that I realize, to my surprise, that we are not alone. As my field notes somewhat dramatically describe: "When we got there, I saw that there actually was another guy there. He was skinny and tan with dark straight black hair. He had a funny look in his eyes, one of hunger and fear and the power to be invisible." This is the first time I meet Ricky's camp mate Edwin, who is so dirty and blends in so well with the trees and underbrush that seeing him there is a shock, particularly as I had been warned repeatedly about the dangers of the jungle.

Over the course of my visits, Edwin is there for part of the time, every time. He brings Ricky meals, goes on bottle and can runs, and goes back and forth to the corner store for beer. Along with Edwin's recycling income, which he estimates at $65 in a good week with three days on and four days off, Ricky's general relief check of about $90 per week pays for their expenses, and the local shelters and churches provide meals and other services. Although not romantically involved, proclaiming "We are hetero," Ricky and Edwin are domestic partners nonetheless. Far different from the anonymity that characterizes life in hobo jungles, Ricky and Edwin's friendship and understanding of one another goes beyond the provision of resources to worrying about and protecting each other physically, socially, and emotionally. For this reason, during one of my many visits to camp, Edwin questions the authenticity of my "friendship" with Ricky, suggesting to Ricky in what is an unusually critical moment for him that "she's just using her personality to get you to open up." Ricky disagrees with him, but it is a rare moment in which the balance of power subtly shifts: suddenly, instead of being an honored guest, I am a questionable outsider.

Edwin is warning Ricky not to trust me, protecting him from the pain of being duped into giving up personal information. But it is more than protecting themselves from legal trouble, as I'm certain there is at least some suspicion that I might be a cop or informant. Edwin is also protecting Ricky from me emotionally, so that he doesn't divulge too much and won't be left feeling dejected or exposed after I leave. Edwin calls my loyalty and integrity into question and correctly reads my "friendship" with Ricky as temporary and research based, knowing that I will eventually move on, a fact I never try to hide. In my visits to the jungle, I am always an outsider and also, potentially, an authority figure.

People living in the jungle are used to relatively upsetting and insulting "mixed contacts" with authority figures in which they are typically judged and punished. This often comes with some form of regulation or sanction targeting behavior and the use of public space, and it has long-term consequences that reinforce the cycle of marginalization, circumscribe time, and forge lasting imprints and injuries on one's self-esteem. Applying for various forms of assistance, appealing for emergency services, accessing shelter as well as shadow and mainstream forms of housing and employment, and occupying public space are all situations that involve mixed contacts between the normal and the stigmatized. Because these interactions are so frequently negative, they reaffirm a marginal status and lead to the rejection of mixed contacts altogether. This, in part, explains Edwin's skepticism about my presence in the jungle and his withdrawal from society.

These interactions alone, even without the added violence, addiction, incarceration, and mental illness that often accompany chronic street homelessness, can lead at minimum to stress and depression (Oyserman and Swim 2001). They can also lead to violent, negative reactions, and a deepening of addiction and mental illness. As one of Ricky and Edwin's friends, a man called Hopper, put it, "You can't stick a dog in a corner." Sticking already stigmatized, traumatized people in a corner, by criminalizing or demoralizing them, as many service situations and mixed contacts do, is one way of triggering or reinforcing the shame and trauma that go along with this particular stigma. The reaction is often, and not surprisingly, knee-jerk immediate. For Ricky and Edwin, this means arguing for their rights, which they did successfully in the 1980s and less successfully in the 2000s, when simply messing with authorities is a source of amusement.

Gorillas, Lollipops, and Jungle Nuts

Ricky tells me that his nickname in the jungle is "Lobo" or the "Bushman," although by the time I meet him, everyone just calls him Ricky. In the 1980s, he was an authority figure, an "enforcer" in the jungle, someone who made the rules and made sure everyone abided by them. Ricky managed the first winter shelter in 1988, for which he received a commendation from the city council. He describes an incident in which he narrowly averted trouble when a shelter guest brandished a knife. Ricky watched a staff member challenge the man, trying to take his knife away. Sensing danger, Ricky went over and closed the knife, gave it back to the man, and told him to come back when he could be less violent, "the next day even." Then he fired the staff member. Understanding and respecting the feelings of people living on the street is, in this story, essential to offering service. It is also his physical prowess that keeps Ricky in charge, but by 2000, he is 38 years old, and things have changed.

One of the first signs that Ricky is losing his grip on being an enforcer is that his friends do not listen to him when he tells them

James and Brandy.

how to behave in his jungle. He can no longer enforce the rules of his house. James Magruder, the 1980s leader who still lives in the jungle with his partner, Hopper, visits Ricky and Edwin frequently, and during one of these visits, they bring their dog, Brandy, to camp, and Ricky gets upset because the dog walks on his sleeping area, getting dust all over everything. Ricky yells at them but they pay no attention to him, and instead of leaving, Hopper tells a story of a man who was threatening him. He says, "If someone goes after me, I have backup," and he smiles at James, "Magruder is my left-hand gorilla right here," and then looking at Ricky, he laughs and says, "You're my left hand lollipop." Despite Ricky's attempts to uphold his former glories and adventures, his friends know that he is past his prime, a lollipop. This makes him particularly vulnerable to violence, threat, and theft. In fact, Ricky complains that James recently slapped him and that he knows he is still at risk. Like the Bookman before him, but for very different reasons, Ricky is also "weak as a cat."

Despite their current obstacles and challenges, Ricky and Edwin enjoy talking about the 1980s as the good old days, during which they fought for and won the right to vote and ran the city's first emergency shelter by and for homeless people. Edwin tells me that he also volunteered to prepare meals for the local Salvation Army and he did so regularly in the 1980s, describing in detail a meal that he was most proud of: egg rolls. Because of his dedication, he says, "They eventually let me sleep inside and gave me some money here and there," but it never amounted to formal employment. In one visit to camp, I bring an article about the sleeping and voting controversy and specifically ask about Prez Ed, wondering what happened to the former jungle organizer. "That's me," Edwin replies with a smile, and I am a bit surprised. "So *you* are Prez Ed, *the* Prez Ed?" I ask him, and both he and Ricky laugh proudly. "I didn't think you were ready to know yet," Ricky tells me as his reason for keeping this secret.

While they win some important victories in the 1980s, and each has a role to play, their current lives offer few chances for mixed contacts that allow them any sort of status. Ricky has a former employer who serves as his payee, both he and Edwin are in touch with their families, and both access the emergency shelter, Salvation Army, and churches like the Open Bible that offer a weekly meal. But these interactions are fraught with unequal power and with shame. The other form of mixed contact that occurs more frequently is with police. Unlike in the 1980s, interaction with law enforcement is more one-sided, individualized, limited to immediate action, and lacking a critical mass of homeless protesters or advocates. This is problematic, as Ricky and Edwin receive frequent tickets for trespassing and for drinking from open containers, and their inability to pay makes them both subject to repeat arrest.[4] This is particularly true on "warrant Friday," when police use outstanding tickets as a way of "cleaning up" the jungle in high tourist areas or high traffic times, before outdoor festivals such as Fiesta or Solstice, or the opening of a luxury hotel like Fess Parker's Red Lion Inn (later renamed the Santa Barbara Beachfront Hilton Resort). As a result, most of the resistance Ricky and Edwin enact is designed to frustrate authorities and amuse themselves, but it never puts a dent in the ticketing.

Instead of organized protest, Ricky and Edwin imagine incidents in which they can turn the balance of power, get the upper hand, and laugh at the police. Of the numerous incidents, past and present, enacted and imagined, that Ricky describes, most involve tricking police who come to issue him open container tickets. In one instance, Ricky tells me that he plans to fill an empty beer can with water, arrange his bed to look as if he is sleeping, and when the officer goes to wake him, he will be across the bridge with a full beer, laughing at the officer. He also plans, but never lives to pursue, the possibility of deeding the small easement their jungle is located on to Edwin, using the claim of squatter's rights. Criminalization is the main thing he imagines protesting, and his plans emphasize how important the jungle itself is for Ricky, along with upholding his sense of justice and his mutually protective relationship with Edwin.

Most of Ricky's resistance, however mirthful, is in the past, and even his mixed contacts are now limited. He describes a time in the late 1980s when the sleeping-and-camping issue was on the calendar to be discussed at a city council meeting. Ricky arrived and signed up to speak during the time for public comment. Instead of saying anything, he approached the council table, reached into his pocket, and placed a Brazil nut in front of each city councilor. When he finished, he returned to the podium and proclaimed, "You have just been given the Jungle Nut Award," presumably because their actions in policing the jungle were considered "nuts" by those living there. Ricky tells this story repeatedly, and it brings him a laugh every time, illustrating what many jungle residents feel: that they cannot truly change their situation, so they may as well enjoy the process of proving the normals wrong, even if they are merely giving themselves a laugh in the process. It is an upbeat response to a catch-22 situation in which flight is not possible and fighting is futile, unless you are fighting each other. It also shows that most city councilors, business owners, and other normals are seen as being against homeless people and ready to criminalize them for minor offenses. Even advocates are not truly seen as friends of homeless people because of the multiple conditions and restrictions that go with assistance and, as Edwin points out, many of us are "two-faced," outsiders, and not in it for the long haul.

In an open meeting of the Santa Barbara Homeless Coalition, the group serving as "landlords" of the new emergency shelter, James Magruder's partner, Hopper, arrives drunk and proceeds to weigh in on the conversation. They are discussing policing in the neighborhood and how to reduce the impact of the shelter on area businesses. Hopper tells them he has been homeless his whole life and the cops know him. He says he has never done anything wrong but they still give him open container or camping tickets, suggesting that the concerns of people on the street, like himself, are relevant to the conversation on policing. A neighborhood business owner interrupts him and asks, "You say you've been homeless your whole life?" and Hopper nods affirmatively. "Well, what's wrong with you?" Hopper says, "Nothing, this is what I chose," and the man says, "Well then, why come here and complain?" and Hopper tells him that he wakes up to a picture of the sky that he doesn't even have to pay for, hinting that he enjoys paradise for free, naturally and without pretense. But everyone is clearly uncomfortable with his presence and do not understand what he is saying, so the shelter director offers to talk further with Hopper in her office, to avoid the pain of this highly charged mixed contact.

It is rare for men living in the jungle to interact with housed people in a context that is not service or regulation driven. In the situations described above, Ricky and Hopper don't really hope to change the minds of the people they talk to. Ricky, as always, wants to be in charge, to be the one to label someone else for a change. Hopper, easily appeased, also wants to be part of the conversation. Their actions are performed to amuse themselves and their friends and to make a subtle but enduring point about the pretense of normal life and the benefits of living in the jungle. But the pressure of mixed contacts like these, a one-shot deal to express yourself in a group of well-heeled haters, means that jungle residents often show up drunk, sabotaging themselves before they even get started. Validating the life of the jungle through bad behavior and jovial protest reaffirms its marginal status, and jungle residents are seen in the eyes of the housed community as childlike drunks who need discipline and punishment.

When he is finally awarded SSI in June 2000, Ricky leaves to return to his family in Minnesota. He is frustrated with the rigors of travel and the expense, and he misses the jungle and Edwin. Ricky and I exchange letters and he calls when he is able to, either from his parents' house or from a pay phone near the forest, where he camps in a tent. Ricky has an outstanding warrant in Minnesota, so in July, when he is feeling strong enough, he leaves for Wisconsin, where he remains. His calls and letters warn me not to go into the Santa Barbara jungle alone and to tell his friends, except for Edwin who knows the truth, that he is on vacation because he fears that his SSI will be terminated if they discover he has moved out of state. Ricky manages a combination of camping and living with family to survive the winter and when the weather breaks, he plans to head back to Santa Barbara. He never makes it. His mother sends me a card marked "In memory 1962–2001," and it reads: "He lived as he had to and made our lives richer for knowing him, helping anyone he could but being unable (and he tried) to help himself."

Russell and Moms

Moms is the first person to make me feel welcome in the emergency shelter. Her philosophy about people is that "you have to take everyone who comes in that door on the same level, no matter what they smell like." So the fact that I am conducting research is different but not daunting for her, and every time I walk into the shelter, she remembers my name and shouts it out in her booming voice so I know where to find her. Russell and Moms camp down the tracks from Ricky and Edwin. Two months into knowing Moms, she tells me that she needs to have major surgery on her neck. She is in the hospital for only two days and has a titanium plate inserted between two vertebrae to keep them from rubbing together. With no place else to recover, she returns to the jungle and within one week, she collapses on the railroad tracks and is rushed back to the same hospital. Upon her second release, she is unable to return to the jungle and everything changes, especially her relationship with Russell.

Russell is Moms's camp mate. He is six feet, one inch, white, with a husky, athletic build. He wears his hair shaved or short with a trimmed goatee and always looks clean and presentable, not homeless. He keeps a small day-pack of essentials, which he carries back and forth from the jungle to the shelter, where he receives meals and some respite from the midday heat. Russell is Moms's companion and protector, whom she calls "the son of my heart." As Russell is not nearly as forthcoming as Ricky, talking to him takes patience and time. He only reveals information when he is ready, not because I ask him, and of course I answer as many questions as I ask. All I know about Russell's family, for example, is that his mother wrote him a letter that Moms said "would freeze your heart." Russell also told me that he has no tattoos because he made a promise to his mother and kept it. But I never ask him about her further or about his childhood because I don't think it would go over well, but even more important is the principle that people in the jungle don't poke each other's wounds unless they're looking for trouble.[5]

Moms takes care of Russell in whatever ways she can, proudly making sure that he is eating properly and has basic necessities. She is about twenty years older than he is, although she looks far older, and is heavy set, with a cane she uses to plod from one point to another. Before and after surgery, she looks ungainly walking down the street, making Moms and Russell an odd couple. Although they are always together, there are often one or two others who camp with them, and despite some speculation, their relationship is officially platonic. Sandy is their closest friend, blonde and heavy set but fitter and younger than Moms. She is the most constant of their companions, which both eases and causes tension, as Moms has an increasingly harder time keeping up with them. Sandy also has a boyfriend who is in prison, due to be released in two months, but she rarely talks about him until just before his release. Prior to Moms's illness, the trio of Sandy, Moms, and Russell live peacefully in the jungle.

When Moms gets out of the hospital for the second time, no one is willing to help her find a medical bed: not the shelter's case manager and not the Salvation Army, at least not at first. Instead, I assist her in finding a motel in Oxnard, about thirty minutes away from Santa Barbara, where she can convalesce. The Committee for Social Justice pays for the room, and I drive her back and forth and talk with her daily to make sure she is okay and has everything she needs. Her first concern is always Russell. While she is away, Russell and Sandy become romantically involved. Although Moms wants Sandy and Russell to visit her, they both develop colds and cannot risk her health, even if they did have transportation, which they don't. So Moms is isolated in Oxnard, alone for the first time in forever, away from her friends, and she begins to panic, fearing that she's lost her place with Russell, her only place in the world. Although Moms's relationship with Russell is an instrumental one for both of them, like most jungle relationships, it is short-lived and riddled with sudden, immediate, and traumatic losses.

The fulfillment of domestic needs in relationships like Ricky and Edwin's, Moms and Russell's, is part of what binds people in the jungle, as a companion will help you survive when no one else will and will accept you and care for you in the process. Can everyone expect this even from their "home," from their family, or from the agencies paid to serve them? What are the consequences of the sudden, traumatic loss of such a close, against-all-odds companion? It is hard to tell, because people don't mourn their losses in the jungle—they are simply too many, too deep, and too often to cry over. You just move on and try to survive. But losing these instrumental relationships, for both Edwin and Russell, makes them vulnerable. Once Moms cannot watch things, Russell begins to give in to himself and his demons of addiction and violence, and then his former cell mate gets out of jail. From there, it is only a matter of time before he returns to prison.

Walking Away

After some resistance, the Salvation Army accepts Moms into a medical bed and once she is settled in, she takes the bus or the Easy Lift van across town to the shelter, wheezing and coughing all the way there, as if she should rest and stop smoking but can't or won't. She is there to get her mail and to check up on Russell. Moms is furious that Russell and Sandy are closer, and she confronts them immediately on the day she returns. They are standing in front of Johnny's, a lunch place, when Moms arrives, hopping mad and accusing Sandy of taking Russell away from her. Russell, now Sandy's protector, yells at Moms to stop picking on Sandy. This obviously upsets her, and Moms accuses them of abandoning her, saying that Peter Marin and the Committee for Social Justice are the only ones doing anything for her. This sets Russell off, and he asks, "Who was there for you when you collapsed on the tracks?" Moms has no answer to this question but is still seething, and then he deals the final blow, saying, "I can walk away from you any time I want to." Moms hears this and snaps completely, smashing her walking stick into pieces against the stone fence. From then on, she is a shadow of her former self. It is a matter of months before she is found dead in a chair in the shelter, but by then Russell is long gone.

In this exchange, Moms blames Russell for his ineptitude with things like driving long distances and finding money for motel rooms, official business of the normal world, while Russell reminds her that he was there for her when she really needed him in the jungle, where no one from the normal world even visits. In the aftermath of Moms's release, everyone's attitude toward her changes: shelter staff consider her a liability, her former friends don't understand why she can't just accept that things have changed and move on, and even those with the most patience for her, like Sandy and Russell, eventually tire out. Physical strength and stamina are part of the jungle's currency, and once people can no longer survive its rigors, they die or move to hospice care, or another place of last resort, and their friends and companions are forced to move on. But fitting into a "normal" life is not easy for someone so far removed. In her fight with Russell, Moms begins to realize how important her connections to the normal world are and that these are things he cannot help her with. But Russell's counterpunch reminds her that before she needed the normal world, he was there for her, protecting her in every way he could, something no one will ever do for her again.

Once Moms can't live in the jungle, Russell and Sandy continue to grow closer, although Sandy still pines for her boyfriend, soon to be released from prison. Moms thinks Sandy is naïve and childlike and that she will believe anything Russell or other men tell her. Yet there is a fondness between Russell and Sandy that briefly calms and settles both of them. Once, when he develops a cold, Sandy buys him a card and has everyone at the shelter sign it to make him feel better. She also says that Russell appreciates the things she does for him and that this is really a first for her. Just prior to her boyfriend's release, Sandy buys a new bicycle that Russell finds for her, and she repays the favor by buying crack to smoke with him. This dashes Sandy's hopes of getting a motel room upon her boyfriend's release, as her money is gone, and the episode begins a one-way, addictive streak for both of them.

At about the same time, Russell's former cell mate, Brett, returns to the neighborhood after serving a two-year sentence for narcotics. Russell starts calling Brett his partner, his backup, his second in command. Russell's crack use also begins to escalate, fueled by Brett's return, and he develops a nervous habit of combing his facial hair obsessively, as if he can't stop doing it. Sandy becomes increasingly despondent after her boyfriend is released from prison and does not spend time with her. She feels she is losing him, and her crack use increases. One day during lunch, I ask Sandy why she isn't eating. She tells me that the top plate of her partial denture is rubbing against her gums, and she pulls her lip up to show me a scary-looking gray hole. "I don't want to be a crack whore," she says, but then shrugs, as if to say, "If the shoe fits . . ." I remind her that her SSI claim is still pending and that maybe this would be a way to get off the streets. She does exactly this when she is awarded SSI and parks her RV on quiet streets in the industrial area. She reunites with a different former boyfriend, also recently released from prison, and stops visiting Russell or the jungle at all.

Along with increased crack use, Russell and his gang, which consists of Brett, James (who looks like a cross between Russell and Brett), and a guy everyone calls "Elf" because of his comparatively short stature, begin drinking daily. After lunch at the shelter, they sit on the patio to cool off and by 2:00 or 3:00 p.m. announce that it is "beer thirty" and retreat to the jungle. A woman named Judy is now Russell's girlfriend. She is white, thin, and has a voice and skin that remind me of rust. Judy is also a chronic alcoholic, with paranoid tendencies, and begins living in the jungle with the group sometime after Sandy moves into her RV. Judy and Cassie are the only women staying in the jungle. Cassie is small and wiry, and everyone says she is "51/50," shorthand for the section of the California Welfare Code that authorizes involuntary confinement for people who are considered a danger to themselves or others. Cassie is my exact build and age, and she is an anomaly in the jungle, acting with the wild abandon usually reserved for men (Wardhaugh 1999, 103). One day I drive over to the shelter with a trunk full of lightly used clothes to give to Cassie, and she is so excited to try on a black dress that she boldly takes off her shirt with nothing underneath to see how it fit.

Going the Distance

My first and only visit to Russell's camp feels like the saddest day in the world. One of my primary informants just left the area for good, and even fieldwork feels disappointing. It is also my birthday, and California without family or friends and the clash of happy sunshine makes the day seem particularly lonely. Russell and the gang (Brett, Judy, Cassie, and Elf) are leaving the shelter as it closes down, and I walk with them to the Texaco station so they can buy beer. I wait just outside the door after they pay, ready to say good-bye, and see Russell waiting, motioning for me to come with them. "I'll walk you back when you're ready to go," he says, maybe sensing my fear. But they know it is my birthday, so this invitation is like a gift I can't refuse. Judy and Cassie leave to go to the Rescue Mission to take showers but plan to return to camp afterward, and I don't know what to expect. I think we might just hang out at the park and wait for them, but instead Russell, Brett, Elf, and I walk down the tracks for about ten minutes after passing Ricky's camp, so this one is much more remote and is actually two separate sleeping areas. The first is a clearing among the bamboo with a tarp for a lean-to and a tent in the center. There is a small path leading to the second area, which has a small tent, sleeping bags, and a tarp. This is Russell's camp.

Cassie and Brett sleep in the large tent in the outer camp with Elf under a separate tarp, and Judy sleeps between Russell and James, who is already there when we arrive. Russell gives me an official welcome to camp and greets James, who grins at us with surprised delight. I sit next to Russell and Brett, wondering nervously when Judy and Cassie will return and watching how quickly they are drinking their beers. I feel Brett staring at me with hunger and curiosity. We never talked before today, and he says he has his BA degree and wants to go back to graduate school. I don't believe him but I act like I do. Judy and Cassie finally return, and Judy and Russell start playing with each other, pulling off little bamboo sticks and hitting each other with them, joking about playing with bigger sticks later on. I don't want to interrupt them, as their horseplay is clearly escalating, but I am getting increasingly uncomfortable and nervous about returning down the tracks alone with Russell. I feel better when Cassie comes out of her tent and sits with us, and then everyone starts to get hungry. There is no food at the shelter and the Rescue Mission is closed, so Brett and Russell decide to go dumpster diving.

James stays behind to light a fire and I walk back along the tracks with everyone, listening to Brett and Russell kick rocks forcefully into them the whole way, a noisy business—clang! clang! clang!—interrupting the silent darkness. We get to my car and park by the Texaco station so they can go to the dumpsters behind Trader Joe's. "I thought that was locked up," I say, and Russell replies that someone gave him the key before leaving town. My heart sinks for a moment, and I'm thinking of Ricky, who intended to leave his key for Edwin. Judy stays in the car with me, stepping out to the Texaco for more beer, and Cassie leaves to talk with some friends in a van parked close by. Russell and Brett return with a package of bratwurst and I drive them to get firewood from an art studio bungalow by the ball field where they leave discarded wooden pallets. They go to work on the pallets immediately, smashing them like drunken teenagers in oversized work boots, enjoying the destruction. They put the wood in my trunk and I drive them to the trackside, with no intention of returning to camp. "So you're not ready to go the distance," Russell wagers, and I lie, telling him that I have no supplies, badly hiding my fear.

Was this fear justified? Perhaps. I'll never know, but I got the feeling that smiles and good tempers would wear off quickly with more alcohol and other drugs, and with whatever visitors happened to come by. This was surely the case at Ricky's camp, and Russell's camp was isolated. Whatever happened there could not be seen or heard from the outside. Also, and most important, women are considered easy prey in the jungle, where physical size and prowess reign. As another informant once explained, "If you have a cookie and everyone wants it, sooner or later they're going to try and get it." Women are almost never in the jungle alone and the men they stay with are almost always their boyfriends, lovers, or temporary partners or protectors. Women in the jungle are also frequent victims of violence and abuse, even from their companions. It wasn't so much what anyone said or did to threaten me, it was being around a group that was about to lose focus, and I feared getting caught in the fray. Not easily scared, after this trip to the jungle I sat shivering, unable to sleep, thinking about all that I witnessed and wondering: How had the jungle come to this?

White

I did not realize that Moms and Russell were white supremacists until Moms and I were in my car driving to a hamburger place. She insisted on taking me to lunch for helping her find somewhere to recover in Oxnard. We took off in my car, and I switched on my favorite R&B radio station. Out of nowhere, Moms said, "Wow, Michele, I didn't realize you like N—— music." Russell let his feelings show more subtly and slowly and always related to something or someone specific. Describing himself as a "white separatist," he justifies it by saying, "I don't want genocide or anything." And he coexists peacefully with the "border brothers" who also camp in the jungle, learning several phrases in Spanish and saying "it's a matter of respect." Russell is thirty-five and has been in trouble with law enforcement for the last eleven years, and his racism is at least partially fueled by prison life. But, as with so many things that seem to go with living in the jungle (addiction, mental illness, trauma), it's hard to tell which comes first. Russell only talks about prison when I am with him for several hours and when I manage to remain quiet.

During one of these times, he tells me that in one of the prisons he did time in, "The warden when I was in prison was black and all of her relatives worked there. I told them I was a white separatist so they taunted me relentlessly." As he tells it, Russell taunts them back, and they beat him senseless. One of their favorite things to do with him is get him in a choke hold and make him pass out and let him fall to the floor. Then when he comes to, he is on the floor in the middle of a beating. At the same prison, he describes the "shark tank," which is a "cage that you can just fit in standing." Guards poke you with sticks through holes in the cage and you wriggle hopelessly to avoid them. Serving time for narcotics, his favorite story takes place in the infirmary. It is how he spent his New Year's Eve in the year 2000, and it involves a fight and a standoff. Russell makes a bet with another inmate that he can get through the steel bars of his cell in eight blows with his metal bed. His cell mate bets that it will take at least fifteen, if not twenty. It takes eight. Once he is out of his cell, Russell proceeds to assault the guards who come to subdue him. With their knees on his head, back, and shoulders, they eventually send in an exterminating squad to douse him in pepper spray, soaking him completely while he lies trapped on the floor.

After this incident, the guards offer to let him stay in the infirmary because his release date is so close, but Russell chooses to "go back and give 'em hell for the rest of my time." As Jack Black once wrote, when he was put into a straitjacket while in prison, he was so infuriated with this treatment that he "vowed I'd never make another friend or do another kindly act . . . I turned on society for my revenge" (Black 1926, 198). Perhaps this sentiment resonates with Russell, who is in administrative segregation for much of his last stint on the inside. Administrative segregation, he explains,

> is like segregated housing, there's no movement. You're in a cell pretty much, um, 24/7, you got your exercise, you got two, some institutions have three days. You get exercise yard for 2/3 hours once or twice a week. It's a pain in the butt, but it's part of the routine. It's all in-cell feeding, no day room, maybe a library book once a week. Most of the time you're just—how you're communicating with everybody is through kites and fishing lines.

He describes going before a "shoe review," which is a board that decides if you need to stay in administrative segregation or if you're ready to go back on the main line or receive counseling, a psych evaluation, or something else. He objects to how they talk about him during the review and confesses, "I went off on one of the counselors" who took his cell mate's side, believing that Russell did all the things he was accused of doing. So they gave him a psych evaluation and moved him from one state prison to another, trying different medications in an attempt to subdue him.

Russell gets into trouble in prison, but he also has a role there. One day at the shelter, in a discussion about prison life, a man who was recently released says that when something happens in the prison yard, you don't do anything. Russell gently corrects him, saying, "Yes I do, I regulate." The man laughs and says, "No you don't, you're a house mouse," and without shifting his tone at all, Russell says, "No, I'm a regulator, I ain't no house mouse, I'm a yard regulator. I hear war, huh? Head up? Let's go play. I wanna see what's happenin', what are we doing? I used to live for that." I don't understand the role of a regulator, but on another day, Russell explains it. "Sometimes, there is so much tension in the yard, you can feel it. Something is going to happen. Then someone gives you a sign to keep the person you're talking to busy." So Russell distracts the target while someone else comes up to stick them with a homemade weapon. "Then," he says, "you just move tables and pretend it didn't happen, move on with your day."

The reason Russell is in Santa Barbara is that he keeps getting "yanked back from Colorado" for legal trouble in California. So while the prison deeds and demons continue to follow him, Russell is also not free to leave, to mend fences with family, to go home and find himself. He lives in the jungle, where trauma and violence visit daily, feeding into addiction and a vicious cycle of violence-arrest-release-repeat, and the cycle turns into a vortex that he is drawn into. People in the immediate neighborhood, including shelter staff and other homeless people, fear him and give him a wide berth. Even when he begins to drink and take drugs and goes back to his old, violent, racist ways, no one intervenes, and the jungle slowly pulls him in.

Jungle Vortex

One day I arrive at the shelter and something is different. There is a shiny new Fleetwood parked in the driveway and a small, thin white man in a suit is making his way into the shelter. He looks wealthy, delicate, and out of place, his bald head shining through his thinning hair like a bird's egg. Then I remember that it is the day they are announcing the opening of the shelter's new kitchen, and the man in the Fleetwood is one of the primary donors. Russell is there, too, lingering in the background, but something is wrong. He seems agitated, is combing his goatee constantly, nervously waiting, ready to pounce. It is about 4:00 p.m., and he has been waiting all day for a man he calls a "little wetback, paisa dude" to leave the shelter. It looks like it is finally going to happen, and Russell gives Brett a "heads up" and they follow him out. The kitchen ceremony is also coming to a close, and the man in the Fleetwood is returning to his car.

Russell says he saw the man, this "paisa" (paisano or "homeboy" from Mexico) lurking around his stuff and then noticed that his organizer and a necklace were missing. So he waits until the man decides to leave, knowing that he can get into more trouble if he fights on shelter property. The man eventually walks out of the shelter with his shopping cart full of things, and Russell stalks him until he gets halfway down the driveway and then jumps on him and starts punching him and tearing at his backpack. The man screams a high-pitched scream, and I think for a second that Russell is going to kill him. Russell rips open the man's bag and finds his things inside, but he continues to throw punches, as if confirmation of the theft gives him a new sense of rage. The police arrive, and everyone stands around not knowing what to do but glad that the fight is over. The man in the Fleetwood makes a smooth and hasty exit, and Russell heads inside to cool off.

The conversation after the fight focuses on two things: the fact that Russell found his belongings on the man, and whether or not Russell was wrong to attack him. In the moments after the fight, Russell feels justified in what he did, but he is still searching for confirmation. He says to me and a social worker named Candace, "I wasn't wrong, was I?" and neither one of us tell him he was. I say, somewhat surprised, "The cops aren't even saying that," and Candace thanks him for keeping his cool but then warns him, "If the guy needed stitches, it would be an automatic felony against *you.*" Russell, calmed by our responses, goes on to ask her about a job she was going to arrange for him, and she puts him off because of the obvious, immediate tension. Of course, now there won't be any job. When the police question the man that Russell attacked, he is still bleeding and is very upset, "I lost control of my stuff," he says with a heavy accent, suggesting that Russell planted his things on the man. "That's too complicated," the officer tells him. "They went through my stuff, they have no right," the man yells. The officer tells him that they did have the right to go through his things, "because stealing is wrong. God says it's wrong."

In the aftermath of this incident, there is a lot of speculation about whether or not Russell did plant his things on the man, to stir up a war with the paisas. But Russell's version of street justice wins for the moment, as no one challenges him. Although I have a camera with me, I don't record the fight at all, for fear of violent repercussion. Despite the confusing aftermath of the fight, one thing is certain: although Russell may feel validated in the moment, with his former cell mate—his "celly"—by his side, one day the paisas will catch Russell alone, and then he will pay. The next morning, he meets with the shelter director to debrief after the fight. But everyone fears Russell at this point and does not want to incite his wrath further with punitive action. So he continues down a one-way path, and as he does, instead of cycling around but not out of paradise, he is sucked down, along with the others in his crew, into a vortex of destruction that leads him back to prison.

Cuba and Martin

Ricky and Russell share a distrust of people in positions of authority, but they know they need to engage with them and maintain relationships with them to survive: to get meals and mail at the shelter, to get an SSI check, to navigate sleeping and camping tickets, to get medical assistance, and so on. For Martin, and for many others like him who are camping in the jungle, their undocumented status shapes all interaction with authority, meaning that they have access to the referral services through the emergency shelter but no access to SSI, SSDI, general relief, or other federal or state relief. It also means that interactions with law enforcement are more dangerous, as many fear deportation and will do anything to avoid it. The police know this and use it to issue multiple citations in order to meet their monthly quotas. There is also a language barrier, as many of the men do not speak English, and many people, including the police, do not speak Spanish, and the stigma of homelessness and undocumented status means that they are a hidden and vulnerable population. As the story of Russell demonstrates, people refer to the men, and they refer to each other, as "paisas," particularly a group of young men, described below, who camp in the jungle.

It takes a longer time for me to get to know Cuba and Martin for the three simple reasons that (1) I am white, (2) I am a woman, and (3) I appear to be a person in authority. Because the Santa Barbara Police Force, Tactical Patrol Unit, also known as "the transient detail," or "the Baker Boys," uses confidential reliable informants (CRIs) to pursue alleged crimes that occur at La Barda (the local labor line where mostly undocumented workers wait for day labor), and because most CRIs are white, English speakers, my presence there is at least confusing and at most a potential threat. In addition, women among the men at the labor line are there because they are in a relationship with one or more of the men or because they are family members, and very few women sleep in the jungle. The paisas' jungle is just down the railroad tracks from Russell's camp between the railroad tracks and the Bird Refuge, close to the old jungle of the 1940s.

Cuba and Martin share a camp close by, but they are older and have been in Santa Barbara for longer than many of the men, contributing to their decision to camp separately. The paisas' camp is larger, and it hosts a younger population of men from Mexico and Central and South America. They are notorious drinkers who also use other drugs, such as methamphetamine and crack. This behavior breeds a sense of lawlessness and violence that sometimes spills over into Russell's camp, or vice versa, another reason that Cuba and Martin prefer to stay away. Martin is a striking six foot, one inch tall, a good foot taller than most of the men at La Barda. Everyone calls him *tres patines* because he is missing two toes from torture he endured in a Mexican prison. Day labor is harder for him to come by, and he is easy to recognize, meaning that he has to keep his nose clean to avoid getting cited.

This is relatively easy for Martin, as living with Cuba is far more peaceful than living in a group. Cuba is also a US citizen with access to benefits that cover basic expenses, at over $600 per month. He has a bicycle with a tow-behind on the back that he uses to store his possessions and the bottles and cans he recycles. Cuba and Martin are slow, sporadic drinkers, not as consistent as Ricky and Edwin, smoking marijuana and drinking several beers per day, depending on income. Their routine is to walk from the jungle to their recycling route, where they have several steady customers who save bottles and cans for them. After a few hours of recycling, they eat lunch at the shelter or at *la lonchera,* the lunch truck parked alongside the labor line, where they talk and smoke, and eventually return to the shelter for dinner, if it's available, or cook at the grills next to the picnic tables by the volleyball nets on East Beach, across from the old jungle.

I finally learn Cuba's real name after we have known each other for months. We were in the shelter and someone asked me who I was talking to and I said, "Cuba." He said, "That's not my name," as if I should have known all along. Never having had a nickname myself and realizing that he never called me anything, either, I asked him, "Well, what's my name?" and he smiled and said, "I don't' know," so we laughed and introduced ourselves and shook hands. Everyone laughed with us. Cuba is older than Martin, and his pale, delicate skin, gentle manner, and slim build make him look a bit like a woman, a fact not lost on his friends at La Barda, who jokingly call him *malecon.*

Most of the paisas, also called "border brothers," are from Mexico, Honduras, and El Salvador, so Cuba is something of an anomaly. Even though he speaks Spanish, he is always different and stays slightly apart. Martin is the same, so they make perfect companions. Cuba arrived in the United States on a homemade float, which he made and launched so he could leave the island that gave him his nickname. Neither one of them talks much about the families and lives they left behind. Unlike Ricky, who relives his past frequently, the pain of what Russell, Martin, and Cuba have left behind makes it hard for them to talk about. The first time I meet Martin is in the shelter parking lot where many people park their vehicles during the day. I see a textbook on family medicine in English in the back of an RV and wonder who it belongs to, so I ask. It is Martin's. "El lea todo (he reads everything)," Cuba tells me, but reading is just a distraction, as he cannot not take classes or work legally in the United States.

La Barda and La Migra

The day-labor line called "La Barda" is in the immediate shelter neighborhood, just down the street from the Rescue Mission, where seventy-five to 100 men wait for trucks to pass by and pick them up for work. The conditions of seeking and accepting work are physically challenging and often lead to injury. Without access to health insurance or workmen's compensation, any injury means a loss of income and perhaps a loss of employment for good (Valenzuela et al. 2006). Most jobs pay close to minimum wage and can lead to weeklong or monthlong labor, particularly for the bigger, younger, fitter men. It is an option many engage in sporadically, along with recycling and drug dealing, and relying on shelter meals and services, to meet their daily needs.

La Barda is a place of limited and dangerous opportunity, and Cuba and Martin are not likely to get chosen for work, when younger, fitter men are available. The work is both difficult and disposable, meaning that when the conditions of one job are substandard, it can be better to leave it, rather than risk one's person or pride. But in cases when men get work through referrals, leaving the job can be risky. For example, when someone is chosen for a job and is asked to get other men to work with him, if you are known as a good worker, you are more likely to be chosen. Cuba is more likely to get picked up than Martin but is less likely to stay with a job in which the employer is seen as unfair or unkind. Perhaps this is because he has income to fall back on, or perhaps it is a reflection of the transient, disposable nature of the work. In any case, Cuba tells a story of being chosen to work moving dirt with four other men. The man who hires them gets angry with Cuba and yells at him for not putting the dirt in the right place. Cuba tells him, "if you don't like the work, forget it," and he leaves. This makes him a liability for the one who referred him for work, so he is less likely to get referrals in the future.[6]

Looking for work at La Barda is risky and looking Mexican while at or near La Barda is also risky. It is a legally sanctioned waiting and solicitation area that exists on a public street, marked by two signs indicating where it is legal to wait. It is just down the street from the Rescue Mission and within walking distance of the emergency shelter and the jungle. In order to get work with the first cars that arrive, the men typically, in this line and elsewhere, "swarm" any vehicles that they think could be employers, often leading to injury before securing work (Valenzuela 1999). They also step off the curb and outside the legal area in order to be the first ones to greet potential employers. Once they do so, they are breaking the law and can be cited for solicitation in a public right of way, an offense that carries a $320 fine, making it prohibitively expensive for most of the men and leading to ongoing legal trouble. In addition, police conduct sting operations in which they pose as potential employers and cite any men who step off the curb to secure work (Wakin 2008).[7] CRIs also frequent La Barda to report on criminal activity. But because many CRIs are also trying to avoid criminal charges of their own, the information they provide is often inaccurate.

Men like Cuba and Martin, who are waiting at the line more than they are seeking employment, are vulnerable to citation simply for being outside the official solicitation points. In one case, Martin reports being cited while he is sitting in the shade alongside the labor line, with no intention of seeking work that day. Translated from Spanish, he says: "The officer arrived and said, 'I'm giving you a ticket.' I said, 'Why, if I'm sitting in the shade, not asking for work?'" Martin tells the officer that he thought discrimination was illegal in the United States and later confides that this officer in particular, along with one other, comes to the line at least twice a week to give the men citations regardless of what they are doing. On the day Martin is cited, the two other men he is sitting with also receive citations and are equally upset about it. One of them tells me that he asked the officer why he is getting a citation ("Por que?"), when he was not soliciting work. The officer takes out his *placa,* or badge, points at it and says, "That's why," meaning that the man is getting cited regardless of what he is doing and the officer's status and authority is enough of an excuse for citation.

When men at the labor line are cited and want to contest the citation, they must appear in court. The fear of "La Migra," and the poverty of the men at La Barda, means that most citations go to warrant. Although the police department has complaint forms, the men rarely feel entitled to contest unfair treatment. They simply hide and wait and hope their health, strength, and luck hold out. In rare cases, men will contest poor treatment on the job, particularly nonpayment. For this, they need to appeal to the labor commission and document their case. But few men have any official paperwork for jobs they receive through La Barda. In fact, in the one case I record of a man pursuing nonpayment, he presents a handwritten piece of paper with the hours he worked and the wages he is owed to the labor commission. Without a phone or address, continuing to pursue this case means showing up randomly at a busy office to see if they can assist him, so the case goes nowhere.

El Caso

The legal entanglements that are so often a feature of life in the jungle and at La Barda can be difficult to avoid, particularly when they target who one is rather than what one is doing. In Martin's case, once his citation goes to warrant, he can be picked up, fined, put in jail, and possibly deported. Although jail stays for outstanding warrants are usually finite and do not typically involve deportation, they do two things to undermine the stability Martin and Cuba have established in the jungle. First, jail stays mean the potential loss of possessions and contacts. People move on when you are not around. Although men like Cuba and Martin, as well as Ricky and Edwin, will wait for one another, it is hard to manage life in the jungle alone. The loss of one's possessions and the inability to maintain one's recycling routine are setbacks that make survival and reintegration into the jungle that much more difficult and further distance residents from the mainstream. They are also more vulnerable to outside threats without a partner around, and there is the emotional loss of one's daily companion, a relationship that can be both instrumental and irreplaceable. The sad truth about relationships in the jungle is that, whether the connection is real or not, they are almost always temporary.

Even one interaction with law enforcement can affect one's chances for reintegration or exit. Frequent interactions with law enforcement can also foster mutual hatred and distrust between the men and the police, a common phenomenon with highly segregated, stigmatized, and disenfranchised populations. Once you are on police radar, anything you do is subject to additional scrutiny and attention. When you can be cited for merely sitting in the shade and do nothing to contest it, it is easy to be drawn into the cycle of citation-arrest-warrant-repeat, and cases of resistance are swiftly crushed, particularly when they are making progress. When Martin is cited for sitting in the shade at the labor line, he appeals to the Committee for Social Justice along with the two other men who were cited. The committee is pursuing cases of overzealous police enforcement of the labor line, including two officers making repeat arrests and writing different municipal code charges for the same violation, yelling at and intimidating the men, and writing appearance dates for the next morning. The last example is a simple error, but one that causes wasted time and confusion.

When Martin and the two other men appear in court, a lawyer from the Committee for Social Justice represents them, and I give expert testimony, as I am conducting research at La Barda. Each of the men is asked to testify as to his whereabouts and actions at the time of citation. A translator is present, as most of the men are Spanish speakers, so the case is slow moving. The primary issue in the case is whether it is legal to be sitting down outside the officially marked labor line area or whether men can be issued citations because it is presumed they are seeking work if they are in the area. As the case drags on, the commissioner asks the police officer who cited the men and is finished with his testimony if he wants to leave, which officers frequently do in these cases, then find out the decision later. This particular officer elects to stay and says he "wants to find out how this one turns out." Because Martin did not have tools with him and the other men did, they were considered as seeking or soliciting work, and only Martin's citation is overturned. When this happens, the officer smiles at Martin and stares at him, memorizing his face. It is a matter of months before this officer finds him again. Yet for the moment, Martin feels happy, as though justice has been done.

For the next several weeks, things are quiet. Martin and Cuba avoid the labor line and spend more of their time cooking meals at the picnic tables beside the beach and across from the city zoo. Weekdays there are quiet and shaded, and the grill and table setup is ideal for men in the jungle. But Martin and Cuba are conspicuous, both because of Martin's height and slight limp and the tow-behind Cuba uses to haul recycling materials back and forth. They are also in the same basic area every day and are on bikes or on foot, so they are easy to spot, stop, and cite. Within two months after Martin's case, Cuba receives a citation for his tow-behind, the first he has ever received for this, and they are both cited for illegal camping during a sweep of the jungle.

For Cuba, this is a setback. He has to find a new way to haul his recycling take and figure out what to do about his ticket. For Martin, it is a different story. When he does not pay the citation, it goes to warrant and he is brought to jail and offered a deal. If he agrees to leave town voluntarily, he will be transported to a reintegration program in Mexico, where he can learn a trade and live with minimal supervision, but he can never return to the United States. If he stays, they threaten to make his life a living hell. When they present him with these alternatives, Martin is beside himself. He considers staying and moving to San Francisco but isn't sure he'd ever actually get there, even if he pays for bus fare, which he cannot afford. The last time I hear from him, Martin is living in Mexico, in a program, and doing well. But I never see Cuba again and even on repeat visits, no one has seen him.

Los Casos

Cases in which men are cited for looking for work are numerous, but very few are brought to trial. In addition to separate accounting systems for shadow work, meaning that arrangements are often made via word-of-mouth without anything written, the language and cultural barriers between the men of the labor line and the criminal justice system are numerous. The fear of deportation and victimization at the hands of police is overwhelming, making many men avoid law enforcement altogether by not paying citations and letting their tickets go to warrant. In the few cases that do go to trial, the men are required to testify about their whereabouts on the morning of the citation, and since few speak fluent English, a translator is usually present.

As an expert witness in trials in which men contest citations for violating Municipal Code Ordinance 9.140.020 (pedestrian solicitation outside labor line), I typically interview the men before the trial to see what their testimony will consist of. I also interview them after the trial to see how they thought it went. Juan Rene was one of the men given repeat citations by the same officer but insisted that he was not soliciting work and instead was returning from work he completed. The prosecuting attorney asks him where he was dropped off, and he replies, "At the coffee shop next to Trader Joe's." This gives the prosecuting attorney and the commissioner pause, as both are locals and neither is familiar with a café in this plaza.

It is, in fact, a very small no-name bakery with two tiny tables and one glass case. There is no sign announcing its presence, and I never knew it existed either, amid the Starbucks and other fancy coffee places that the town is famous for. This one sells weak cinnamon coffee and homemade Mexican pastries. No white people besides me are ever there when I arrive. The prosecution's ignorance of this small shop, catering to an invisible population, makes Juan Rene look guilty, as if he is fabricating his story. He also fumbles over the details of who had his things and why he needed to get them at the labor line. He tells me later that he had trouble following the translator because he listened to the questions in English and then did not always follow the direction of the questioning in Spanish. In one case, he answers "yes" to a question he earlier answered "no" to, and the prosecutor has to confirm which answer is correct. Although he is telling the truth, after these blunders no one believes him.

Without a lesson in cultural competence, to explain the parts of town where marginal people go, their whereabouts are always a problem. Any accounting procedure is tainted by the multiple strikes against men who are homeless and undocumented and who have received a citation they must answer for. Getting the men to talk with me required several repetitions of the human subjects' informed consent that outlines my explicit lack of involvement with law enforcement. It also involved working closely with Martin, Cuba, and other men and women whom I trusted, to explain why I was interested in talking with them, to tell them where to find me, and to assist with translation. The fact that I had an office in the local Salvation Army helped convince them that at least I was not a police officer. And though this work addressed some specific cases of wrongful citation, it put only a small, temporary dent in the injustices visited upon the men of the labor line, as they are still targets for law enforcement.

A Recipe for Disaster

As it was in the 1980s, the jungle in the new millennium is a public but hidden setting where people go because they have no other options. Santa Barbara is still without a year-round shelter, and without one, street living is a forced choice for those without resources, including employment or other income, as well as the paperwork needed to establish various forms of assistance, fit into a program, or apply for Section 8 or rental housing. Living unsheltered is common throughout California and lasts well into the 2000s, even reaching crisis proportions in some areas. Protest in today's jungle is muted, a far cry from the organized resistance of earlier times. Instead, residents find themselves with limited means through which to avoid or contest ongoing legal trouble for nuisance crimes associated with sleeping outdoors. They have criminal records, mental and physical health issues, and histories of institutional care, trauma, and addiction, either before or soon after they start living in the jungle.

In fact, many people are relegated to the jungle because of ongoing legal trouble, including outstanding warrants and terms of probation and parole for more serious offenses, meaning that they cannot leave even if they want to. They also cannot linger in public or shelter settings for fear of citations and rearrest, and are therefore stuck in the jungle, waiting for trouble to find them. The ongoing legislation of public space relegates homeless people to the most hidden and precarious locations like the jungle. It circumscribes their time, as homeless people must always answer to organizations, service providers, and authorities who want to "sweep" them away, particularly when they are in lucrative areas or when there are events or complaints. And of course, if you are like Martin and are on "police radar" and are undocumented, you are easy to sweep away permanently.

In order to fit back into society, people living in the jungle need to earn enough money through employment to compete in the rental market or use SSI or SSDI or a Section 8 housing voucher to afford a basic efficiency apartment. But having a place to live does not mean, for example, that Ricky would stop drinking or that Russell would stop being violent or stop being a racist, but who knows? One thing is clear: the jungle is no place for anyone. Like prison, it makes violent people more violent, depressed people more depressed, sick people sicker, addicts even more addicted, and of course, jail and prison are very much a part of life in the jungle, contributing to the trauma, violence, addiction, and depression even further. Amid all of this, interactionally, homeless people move further and further away from the mainstream and become exhausted with the rules, routines, and stigma associated with shelter settings.

Beyond legal trouble, perhaps the most significant toll that the jungle takes is on identity, on self-esteem, on one's ability to interact with others. This is probably the hardest feature of jungle life: the broken spirit. Despite the resistance activities of other homeless groups or the individualized activities performed and merely talked about by Ricky and Edwin, Moms and Russell, Cuba and Martin, there is really nothing that puts a dent in the idea that these are throw-away people except their relationships with each other and their strength and resilience. But even these forms of resistance are not enough, as no one in this chapter lasts long after this writing, either alive or on the outside. They are laughed at, feared, and even appeased in public settings, but they are rarely listened to, rarely asked their opinions, rarely respected or able to fit in with normals.

Jungle residents do not have the power or leverage with which to argue for increased rights and privileges. Even the threat of chaos so prevalent in the 1980s has mostly been neutralized by the early

2000s, although small group and individual protests, like Martin's case, occasionally boil to the surface before being crushed. And there is always disagreement about which needs and rights are most important, and for whom, so most people focus on their own immediate needs. As Prez Ed describes, today's jungle is everyone for themselves and is based on competition for scarce resources. There is a shrinking, threatened sense of community in the face of advanced polarization, leaving people in the jungle fighting one another instead of the causes or consequences of radical inequality.

Along with the decline in affordability in the mainstream rental market and an increasingly inaccessible employment market, even a minimum wage job is not enough to secure basic housing. There is also a social drop-off that people living in the jungle experience. Informed by the pain of mixed contacts and the triple threat of stigmatization, shelterization, and criminalization, people living in the jungle are less interested in or able to participate in routines or group activities. Other research has documented what increasing time on the streets does for people's appearance, interactional strategies, cultural understandings and preferences, and ability to cope. It is this trauma- and injury-induced withdrawal from society that makes it that much more difficult to reintegrate. Couple this with extreme marginalization, ongoing exposure to violence and loss, addiction, mental and physical health risks, and other forms of trauma, including incarceration, and you have a recipe for disaster.

Surprisingly, this disaster serves a distinct purpose for society. It upholds a growing service and shelter industry and a thriving prison industrial complex. When we look toward solutions, these things hang in the balance. Perhaps the failure to address the root causes of homelessness shows the magnitude of the problem. But perhaps it also raises the question: Are we truly invested in solving it? In the next chapter, I examine strategies to improve the lives of people living unsheltered through classes, employment, and other forms of makeshift housing. Under discussion are the barriers involved in providing resources to improve individual well-being and quality of life and the growing polarization that divides and threatens homeless people nationwide.

5

A Hierarchy
of Makeshifts

Understanding how the jungle fits into a hierarchy of makeshift settings means exploring how homeless people prioritize their needs and resources and the various exigencies they face. Of course, if you are homeless, resources are limited and needs are varied, but the jungle, in comparison with other makeshift settings, leaves residents at greater risk of experiencing the dangers of the streets, and this takes a toll on self-esteem and the ability to exit. Understanding chronic homelessness begins with tracking numerical and demographic trends, a task still fraught with pitfalls that include: the timing of the point-in-time (PIT) count on a single night in winter, the uneven count methodology across regions, and the complicated policy definitions put into practice by variously trained volunteers and advocates. Counting people who are living unsheltered is important because it is tied to federal funding, because the unsheltered population seems to be growing in certain areas, with an increase of over 13,000 people in California in 2017 (National Law Center on Homelessness and Poverty 2017; Annual Homeless Assessment Report 2017), and because unsheltered homeless people are more likely to be at risk of chronic homelessness or death.

In simplest terms, chronic homelessness is either a sustained, one-year period of homelessness or multiple bouts with it, say, four times a year. Whether it is continuous or sporadic, it is accompanied by one or more conditions that make daily living or employment a challenge, including mental illness, substance use disorders, physical disabilities, or other medical conditions. Current data show that 69.3 percent of the chronic homeless population is unsheltered, with over 41 percent of all chronically homeless people nationwide living in California (United States Department of Housing and Urban Development 2007; Annual Homeless Assessment Report 2017; National Alliance to End Homelessness 2018). Understanding these trends makes reintegration strategies that much more important, as they focus on replacing the routines of work and daily interaction with improving conditions and quality of life, rather than isolation and punishment.

Situating the jungle within a range of makeshift living arrangements shows differing degrees of social isolation that is both a by-product of urban policy and a preferred alternative to shelter. Chris Herring's (2014) discussion of West Coast encampments focuses on larger camps of fifty or more people that endure for a year or more across the Pacific Coast (National Coalition for the Homeless 2010). Understanding the structure of encampments as both policy and preference driven is a way of contesting the idea that they are either zones of exclusion or of resistance or that homeless people and authorities are necessarily at cross-purposes. Instead, regulation and resistance converge, and communities adapt in various ways to each other's presence. Of course, this adaptation is neither universal nor benevolent (Herring and Lutz 2015). In fact, the emergence of homeless tent cities is still hotly contested, but the ones that persist and proliferate draw attention to a crisis in managing homeless people: shelters, streets, and prisons are dangerous and costly alternatives inspired by inefficient policy decisions. If homeless people can be better, more cheaply housed in tent cities and if this is the solution they prefer, given the alternatives, then there is a momentary convergence between homeless people and advocates, as there was in the 1980s with the push to create more emergency shelters.

Some cities allow encampments to flourish in particular areas and ramp up enforcement in others. Encampments such as Dignity Village in Portland, Oregon, achieve legalization, permanence, even tiny houses, all of which protect residents from what people living on the streets or in shelters face (Wright 1997; Heben 2014). Tiny houses also present a sustainable, affordable alternative to mainstream homeownership, showing the similar themes of thrift, sustainability, and protest, which resonate with homeless people. In still other areas, existing encampments are co-opted and run by local state entities as outdoor shelters with varying degrees of self-governance. Despite the differences among the camps, residents across all of them underscore "the moral resources and sense of purpose" that the camps offer, as well as a focus on inter- and intracommunity safety (Herring 2014, 293). Of course, this safety comes with a price, as rules and regulations, including community participation, are par for the course in most permanent, sanctioned camps.

Heben's (2014) research records thirty-nine sanctioned and unsanctioned tent cities from 2009 to 2014, with the majority clustered on the East and West Coasts. The organizational structure among the camps varies, as do the number and demographics of people living there, their relationship with the local community, and their overall goals. Some who use the camps are grassroots and survival focused, camping where they can, moving often, hoping to remain undetected, whereas others work with nonprofits and municipalities to secure legal rights to a long-term camp. Still others are involved in the practice of sustainable living embodied in the tiny-house movement and other environmentally conscious solutions to housing, for example, ecovillages. Similar to Herring's research, Heben also finds that the camps that endure tend to mirror the structure and rules of shelter life.

If outdoor encampments can be co-opted and turned into shelters, have they really achieved their goal? In previous research running a parking program for people living in their vehicles (Wakin 2014), I learned firsthand that appeasing local authorities often involves compromises that shelterize makeshifts, imposing rules and regulations that contrast with their organic development and resident needs for safety, community, and a sense of purpose and control. The increasing tendency to shelterize makeshifts makes them more acceptable to local communities, but the danger is that they reproduce the rigidity found in most shelters, as well as the loss of community (Dordick 1997). Is the alternative to this self-governed camps, affordable housing, geodesic domes, or another kind of compromise? Is it filling an immediate need or challenging inequality as the underlying cause of homelessness?

Survival and resistance blend together in tent cities, and people living there protest the cruel and unusual punishment of being criminalized for offenses relating to survival (National Law Center on Homelessness and Poverty 2013). As Heben's research shows, while self-governed, illegal encampments focus on a sense of respite, rehabilitation, and community, occupying public space makes their existence precarious. Self-governed sites are easily disbanded, threatening overall stability and long-term viability. Longer-term sites allow for larger, more permanent structures and groups, and they are typically sanctioned, with rigid rules and regulations as conditions for use. NIMBYism (not in my backyard) affects the creation and sanctioning of legal encampments, often forsaking proximity to other services, or to transportation, in the name of keeping the peace. The farther encampments are removed from the mainstream, the more they become marginal spaces for discarded people. Given the contested nature of tent cities, it is surprising that anyone would actually choose them as a means of protest and even more surprising when they gain national attention.

The Occupy movement presents a strange convergence of "normal" people protesting by living in tents in public areas—the same places that typically roust out the homeless from their tent cities. The irony of this is not lost on Heben (2014) or other researchers. Protesting the gross accumulation of wealth by the 1 percent, the movement's use of public space makes and then breaks its longevity. But the sense of community it inspires, along with a critique of radical inequality and a sense of safety in numbers, overlaps with homeless tent cities. Despite these similarities, one of the main differences between Occupy's tent cities and homeless ones is the public response. Like so many offenses that homeless people are cited for—sleeping, leaning, asking for money—when housed people commit them, they are not offenses. Doing things in the name of survival is a problem for a group of people considered marginal, not to mention resistance and protest. For this reason, there was often tension between homeless campers and nonhomeless occupiers.

When homeless people slept in the same park and attempted to eat the same food donations as the occupiers in downtown El Paso, many in the latter group became uncomfortable (Smith, Castañeda, and Heyman 2012). Organizers of the Occupy Wall Street (OWS) movement in New York City had to confront the fact that homeless people are an even better example of the detrimental effects of capitalism and inequality than many protesters, yet homeless people still felt like outsiders. The us-them mentality that so tightly governs access to resources was keenly felt in El Paso and other OWS encampments. Homeless people were seen as detracting from resources, like community donations of goods and food, and perhaps weakening the overall message, at least at first. But when homeless people were integrated into the movement, at least in this particular encampment in El Paso, everything changed. Formerly seen as outsiders, once they were integrated into the camp and the movement overall, the sense of community, of having a role and a purpose, was keenly felt, even leading at least one person to transition to housing (Smith, Castañeda, and Heyman 2012).

Partnerships between housed advocates and people experiencing homelessness are critical in fostering greater acceptance and understanding, easing mixed contacts, and arguing for increased rights and privileges. In research on homeless social movement organizations (SMOs), Daniel Cress and David Snow (1996) examine the resources needed for mobilization and collective action and weigh the importance of externally versus internally derived resources to sustain SMO activity. Not surprisingly, they find that most homeless SMOs depend on external support. Yet resource dependence does not always mean that advocates co-opt or shape SMO action. In fact, the very act of organization building is, in their view, "a necessary substitute for the absence of everyday connections in order for the mobilization of disruption to occur" (Cress and Snow 1996, 1106).

It is the absence of everyday connections that characterizes life in today's jungle, and this separation builds over time so that reconnecting is that much more difficult (Udelsman 2011). But perhaps that is the point. Over time, the Santa Barbara jungle goes from being a protected encampment on private property to a symbol of national poverty and unrest to a fragmented hiding place for the criminalized and excluded. It is the fear of unruly people interfering with tourism and creating a sense of unrest that is the impetus for much of the criminalization that happens locally, as well as the creation of the city's first emergency shelter. Despite the overlap between the jungle and other local solutions to housing, which include shelters, vehicles, and the streets, the jungle is seen as the bottom of the barrel. Its population is still almost exclusively male, and largely consists of people now called the chronic homeless. Given the odds stacked against people living in the jungle, how do their survival and resistance strategies compare with those in other makeshifts, and how successful are such strategies in getting people off the streets?

Comparing jungle living with recreational vehicle (RV) living is a way of developing a hierarchy of makeshift settings and examining the effects on people living in them, as related to protest and resistance. It is a way of understanding what kind of place the jungle has become, how its meaning has changed over time, moving away from a sense of sanctuary, the danger and adventure of hopping freights, or the promise of employment to a place of respite, violence, and addiction. What are the resources and risks that the jungle offers in comparison with other makeshift settings such as vehicles, and how do these impact self-esteem and the capacity to challenge the idea that homeless people are worthless and culpable? Does the good-bad distinction still place people living in the jungle at the bottom of the ladder, or are all homeless people now in the "bad" category, meaning that they are seen as deserving, as culpable, and as punishable for their offenses? Possible answers to these questions are explored in this chapter using other makeshift settings to compare with the jungle and evaluate the sense of agency among its inhabitants.

Paradise Revisited

By the time I return to Santa Barbara in 2016,[1] having not been there since 2008, the most obvious change to the waterfront area is the addition of Chase Palm Park, stretching along Cabrillo Boulevard from Garden Street to Calle Cesar Chavez, with a large carousel in the middle. Many of the untamed, undeveloped areas now have pavilions and fences, keeping them regulated, pristine, and marked for tourism and consumption. The shelter is still going strong, but it too seems to be sanitized, without the usual collection of residential vehicles parked in the neighborhood or the usual throng of people waiting outside. Homeless people can still be seen sleeping in the corners of public parks, on the beaches, or in vehicles all along the area of the waterfront now known as the "Golden Triangle," but most aren't trying to draw attention. They seem quieter, more subdued than in previous years. Even the seedier side of Haley Street now boasts cool café hangouts, and homeless people are being pushed farther and farther out of town.

On this last visit to Santa Barbara, I feel different and triumphant, as if I know a secret about the city that I can still share, even as a visitor. I also return as the mother of two young daughters and feel elated to show them this small piece of paradise. It is in this frame of mind and before conducting any formal research that I walk with them from our hotel, in the early dawn on a July morning, out onto East Beach to greet the ocean. We pass the Cabrillo Pavilion, a stone's throw from Ricky's camp, where homeless people can pay $5 to take a shower. There are rows of red and yellow kayaks chained together on the beach behind the pavilion, waiting for the tourists to arrive. I look over and see two homeless people sleeping together in a large sleeping bag next to the cement barricade that marks off the pavilion area. They are rolling around and kissing, so I ignore them and keep walking.

We see three other people sleeping separately, a man and two women, sitting up and rubbing their eyes in the early morning light next to the kayaks. We plod slowly across the uneven sand and by the time we are parallel to them, about twenty-five feet away, the man is standing up. He looks at us and says, "Sorry!" I have my infant daughter strapped to my chest, and I am holding hands with my six-year-old. I feel her grip tighten as we continue walking past him. I squeeze her hand back, smile at him, and say, "You don't have to be sorry—it's okay—you're fine." He looks pleasantly surprised and says, "Well, a lady just yelled at me," and shrugs, palms to the sky. "Don't worry," I reply, "it'll be okay," and keep walking. He looks at me, grins a little and says, "Thank you," and we keep watching each other as we walk away toward the wharf and head into town. He was looking at me like Ricky used to look at me, like I am a princess who stumbled into paradise.

Hopper Climbs out of the Jungle

By the time of my last visit in 2016, almost everyone I've written about has died, gone to prison, or been forced to move on and out of town. Even indestructible James Magruder, king of the 1980s jungle, dies in 2006, at age forty-four, leaving his partner, Hopper, behind. Hopper was always the gentler one of the two, a chronic alcoholic like James but less violent and aggressive. Returning and talking to Hopper helps put the jungle into perspective as a convergence of stigmatization, shelterization, and criminalization that work as a vortex to drag people down into the jungle, where they gradually lose touch with mainstream society. For Hopper, watching James and several of his friends die lights the fire he needs to find a way out. This is a path he carves alone, amid a confusing and inadequate array of services that he navigates with life-and-death desperation.

"How did you get out? Where did you go?" I ask him, incredulous that he is sitting in front of me, more than ten years after meeting him. Although Hopper shows the signs of hard living and walks with a cane, he is obviously sober and is working as a case manager for the United Way. We meet at a coffee shop called the French Press, and when I approach him, I see that he is talking on his cell phone. "I convinced them I was suicidal so I could go to the psych ward," he tells me, after he hangs up. "Then I went to sober living for a month at the Riviera, then the Rescue Mission. They didn't want me but gave me a year to try." Even in his last, desperate attempt at sobriety, Hopper is judged and almost dismissed, as the stigma of homelessness still clings to him. In an effort to help Hopper, a spirited, energetic outreach worker named Sue, herself a recovering addict, agrees to assist him in getting off the streets, and he attends City College part-time. He also does outreach work for Alcohol, Drug, and Mental Health Services (ADMHS) and watches Sue tragically relapse and die, able to help him but not able to help herself.

Because of Hopper's time on the streets and criminal background as a homeless person regularly guilty of "illegal lodging," his health insurance (CalCare) is revoked, and other programs and forms of assistance are harder to come by. The reason for this is that many of Hopper's tickets, perhaps the majority, were left unpaid. Unpaid tickets eventually go to warrant, meaning jail time and further legal complications that can lead to arrest and loss of benefits. When Hopper finds out how much legal trouble he still faces as a result of living on the streets, he is incredulous: "How can they take away from my future?" he asks. This is the shadow of a transcended stigma that has so marked Hopper's life that he can never rid himself of it entirely, particularly its systemic confines and the toll they've taken on his sense of self. Perhaps the system suffers from compassion fatigue, too tired out with failed attempts to still harbor hope of escape. Then again, perhaps men like Hopper are engineered to feed the system, all the while being blamed for what they are costing it. Despite many obstacles, Hopper persists in his sobriety and the Rescue Mission eventually helps him sign up for Social Security and Section 8 and move into his own apartment.

In his current role as case manager, Hopper has a twenty-five-person caseload. His clients struggle like he does with memories of past and recent trauma and the rigors of sober living. His phone rings constantly while we are talking, and he finally answers it to tell the caller he is on his way, limiting our time together. It is a client who is waiting for the money and paperwork he needs to move into an apartment. "This guy will call until he reaches me, over and over and over," he says, and I empathize. "It's stressful to be a 24/7 case manager," I say, as I did the same thing running a program for people living in their vehicles for a ten-month stint in 2004–2005 (Wakin 2014). "I try to set boundaries," he tells me, "from 10:00 p.m. to 7:00 a.m., no phone calls," but the job is more than that, much more, and at random hours. It is, unfortunately, a form of torture he needs to repeat, in part to put his past into perspective. He asks me if I remember the 2003 movie *Streets of Paradise*. "I'm the last one alive out of that whole crew."[2]

"So how do you handle case managing?" I ask him. "Do you ever feel like you're getting burned out?" "I'm there right now," he tells me, "but not with the people, with the bureaucracy. But I don't want to lose hope." We meet just after the Fourth of July, which takes a lot out of Hopper, as he is in charge of arranging a barbecue and other events for people trying to get off the street and stay sober. All of this helps keep him motivated, but it's a lot to manage and he doesn't have enough help. He does it because he knows sober living is hard and that "addiction is the loneliest disease. People coming off the street need activity, or they get isolated and depressed," he says, so he provides them with a moment of safety, comfort, and hope. Despite how hard and frustrating the work can be, Hopper's solutions and perspective help with some of the most difficult cases of people whom everyone else has forgotten.

He tells me the story of a woman found eating out of garbage cans. The city wanted to have her committed, and he pointed out that he too ate out of garbage cans and is now case managing. Even though he has these insights, people don't listen to him. "The past still sticks with me," he says, and his input often gets dismissed. "I offer my point of view, they thank me and try something else, which inevitably does not work, and they come back to me." This happens all the time, as even formerly homeless voices are dismissed, degraded, disrespected, and simply ignored more frequently than not. This treatment is part of a set of exclusionary strategies designed to keep homeless people marginalized, self-doubting, system-feeders. During mixed contacts, this marginalization is dramatic, as if Hopper's transcended stigma is laid bare yet again, reminding him of how far he fell, so that even his recovery is not enough to get him respect. Homelessness is like dirt you can never wash off.

It calls to mind the distinction between undeserving victims (good people), that is, women with children, veterans,[3] people in programs, the sober, contrite, and deferent, more often white, and the deserving poor (bad people), that is, those living on the streets, the addicted and chronically homeless, who are disproportionately single men and people of color. People living in the jungle in the 1980s and beyond are almost always in the bad category, meaning that their interactions with housed people, organizations, and decision making bodies are often based on trying to obtain services, avoid legal trouble, or simply manage being treated as worthless, where the only acceptable response is to apologize and let others attempt to punish or treat you. This response reifies the experience of homelessness as an immutable part of the self, when it often is only a temporary state. Attempting to fix the self without managing the experience of homelessness first, and all of its tragic effects, is the most common yet ineffectual response. At an interactional level, during mixed contacts and service situations, homeless people are often ignored or degraded. Even though Hopper knows more about living in the jungle and on the streets than any case manager, his word is always doubted, making his sobriety, like his addiction and his life in the jungle, an uphill battle.

The fact that Hopper does persevere and survive is proof that change is possible; he resists the jungle's hold, scales its steep and slippery walls, and, to a degree, escapes. He is one of the few who actually does, but the reminders of his former life are everywhere: in the clients clamoring for his assistance, the staff workers who don't take his advice, and the memories of friends he has lost. Hopper is against-all-odds unusual because he carves his own path and it leads to reintegration rather than exclusion. What he wants, at the heart of it, is to help others, to fit in, to be a source of hope. How do we create these opportunities for everyone and not just "the good ones" or those who somehow manage to help themselves? I explore answers to this question in the section below by examining a series of classes organized for people living in the jungle and in the shelter neighborhood.

The People's Institute

This project began in 2005 because of couches. The emergency shelter, renamed "Casa Esperanza" (House of Hope), positions its couches in the entryway, like a small cluster of failure for people waiting to see a case manager, needing a respite from constant walking, or unable to stand for long periods of time. Practically, they are used as a daytime sleeping place and staff begin to resent it. One day, I witness a staff member and a homeless woman living in an RV in the neighborhood conspire to tape signs onto the heads of people resting. They read: "I've fallen and I can't get up." In a more productive vein, shelter staff also work with local advocates to offer some activities for people so that they will not just "vegetate" on the couches. The Committee for Social Justice, still the premier advocacy organization for homeless people, agrees to offer classes at the shelter to give people something to do during the day.

As their program materials indicate, the purpose of these classes is "to offer greater educational opportunities for homeless people." Offering educational opportunities that target homeless people's quality of life, as I later find out, is a lofty and unusual goal, in part because to secure funding, programs are typically prioritized if they lead to housing and/or employment, assistance in managing or breaking the cycle of addiction, reintegrating into the community after prison or military service, but not life enhancement, and not education without employment. This is ironic because for many homeless people, if they don't experience something that builds their comfort and self-esteem, and gets them interested in participating in group activities and routines, they aren't even willing to try for housing. If we have learned anything from housing first and trauma-informed care, it is that building a sense of safety and comfort is often the first step toward addressing long-term goals (Kim et. al. 2010).

The Committee's first set of ten core classes runs for eight weeks, from February 23 to April 15, 2005. The most popular classes are photography, drawing, yoga, music (two sessions), Spanish/English conversation, and dance. This first session is erratic. Clients do not show up consistently or do not always know they are part of a class even though they signed up for one, and instructors grow frustrated, as they are all volunteers, and they begin to question whether this is worth their time. Three of the classes—human rights, writing, and poetry—are discontinued before the term is out, because no one shows up. Despite these challenges and frustrations, this session reaches approximately fifty students overall, with thirty core students who attend consistently. Attendance for each of the core classes typically shows that three to five people show up for most of the sessions. Nevertheless, because of the difficulty involved in running these classes, the Committee does not plan another session.

Knowing that these classes are an important resource and having some understanding of how to run an effective set of course offerings, I assemble a board of directors composed of teachers, activists, and shelter clients to collaborate in organizing a second session. We meet monthly and receive two small grants through the Fund for Santa Barbara and the McCune Foundation to pay teachers a small stipend and cover course materials and other program expenses. To develop classes for the second session, which is split into two shorter five-week sessions, we survey the thirty initial core participants to evaluate the first set of classes and offer suggestions for the future. We also place a suggestion box at the information desk at Casa Esperanza, which yields twenty written suggestions, and hold an additional ten extended interviews with current and potential future students to explore their reactions to the classes. Students in the first session say that the courses are a success in three areas: creating an interest in future classes, having a positive effect on the student's life, and the sense of accomplishment each class inspires.

A student in the yoga class who suffers from chronic neck and back pain because of a prior injury said, "Without this class, my recovery would be impossible. This class makes me feel centered and able to go about my daily activities without so much pain." Other students write about the sense of community that classes foster: "I didn't know any of these people before, now I'm helping them with their exercises. It's nice to be able to reach out like that." The songwriting and music classes were particularly popular with students, one of whom writes, "I was accepted and nurtured to express what's in my heart, which made me feel good about myself . . . I would feel terrible before class and wonderful afterwards." Echoing these sentiments, Ed Mannon, whom everyone calls "Crazy Ed," undergoes a dramatic change through his participation in the guitar class.

Ed is a longtime resident of Santa Barbara. He is developmentally disabled and was released from Devereaux California, an advanced behavioral health facility, in the 1970s. Blessed with a wealthy family, Ed receives enough money to afford basic necessities. He lives in a milk truck on a strip of land that houses an old surf shop and is located between the freeway and the train tracks in an overgrown area that the city has temporarily forgotten about. About three years before I meet him, Ed finds a secondhand guitar and buys it, "for $20 and a bag of weed," and he never puts it down. The guitar is like his security blanket, and he gets better and better at playing it. Intelligent and opinionated, Ed is a great conversationalist. One of his hidden talents is that he is a self-taught expert on Irish folk music, a genre that is something of a rarity in Southern California. But Ed's signature feature, beyond his guitar, his musical knowledge, or his personality, is his beard. If you close your eyes and picture what comes to mind when I say "homeless person," one of the standard images is of a man with a dirty shirt, unkempt hair, a straggly beard: Ed.

Despite the fact that I enjoy talking with him, Ed is hard to be around because he rarely showers. Two weeks into the classes, I show up at the guitar class, which I am taking along with the others, and I see a man I don't recognize. This fellow is thin, older, clean-shaven with short hair and not very many teeth; and he has a boyish twinkle in his eye. Looking closer, I realize that it is Ed. "Wow, man, you look amazing," I tell him, and he sheepishly and a little flirtatiously replies, "Well, yes, thanks." Although I wonder what, specifically, inspires him to clean up, I don't push the issue until after class, letting him savor the moment. When we're finished, I finally ask, "So what happened to you, did the staff corner you again?" knowing that shelter staff occasionally gang up on him and coax him into a haircut. "Nope, Michele, you see what it is is that I'm not used to having someplace like this to be and now that I do, I just wanted to clean up for you good people."

Michele Wakin

Ed.

Ed's milk truck.

Quality of Life and Death

Taking classes and having a living space that you control are privileges for those who work, pay taxes, and see themselves as entitled to do what they want, when they want, behind a door they can lock. Homeless people pay taxes, always do some sort of work, but cannot afford an apartment, so they survive under duress, not knowing when they will be targeted for doing things central to their survival and when whatever stability they create will be disrupted. Surviving as a homeless person is an irony in which your present state shapes how your actions are interpreted and even your attempts to do what's right are taken the wrong way. Self-sufficiency, for example, is a prized trait for homeowners and breadwinners, but when otherwise homeless people purchase vehicles to live in, they are ticketed repeatedly, until they lose their vehicles or leave town. Because they are poor, they are targeted and debased, marked for removal. This is true even for working families or people with handicapped placards, usually considered sympathetic, "good ones."

Crazy Ed has never been a "good one." A fixture in the Santa Barbara homeless scene since the 1980s, Ed is one of six children. The milk truck he lives in is a stone's throw away from the old jungle and from the city's only emergency shelter. There are three or four small wooden structures in various states of disrepair on the same parcel and an old surf shop that is sometimes open, sometimes not. Ed pays a small rent to live in the milk truck and does so undisturbed until just after the shelter opening, when all signs of homeless people become a blight to the area, and both law enforcement and business owners take action. In one notorious incident, then city council member Brian Barnwell goes to the parcel with a local developer, intent on making money off the property, and is confronted by Ed and his dog, Sara.

The event is covered in the local newspaper, and I bring it to Ed to ask him what happened. Apparently, Barnwell walked onto the property because of business interests but was oblivious to the fact that people were living there. "He was on his cell phone, Michele, I was yelling at him to stop and he never looked up," Ed explained. "Sara (my dog) was getting pretty upset the closer he got." Perhaps entranced by the business prospects of this small strip of forgotten paradise, Barnwell continues on, oblivious to the threat, and Sara attacks, famously biting him on the behind. Barnwell picks up a metal lawn chair and beats Sara back with it, hitting Ed in the head several times in the process. "I had migraines for weeks, Michele, but that never made the paper." Within weeks after this incident, the parcel is bulldozed completely, just like the 1980s jungle. It is purchased for renovation and Ed is cast back out into the street, a much older man with significant limitations and vulnerabilities and no sanctuary.

He endures several years in a combination of places; a cheap, shared apartment in Carpinteria, just south of Santa Barbara, and the Faulding Hotel, one of the only remaining SROs in Santa Barbara. It has eighty-one units offering permanent supportive housing and is centrally located downtown. A notorious pot smoker, Ed is unable to abide by the Faulding's no smoking rule and eventually leaves and goes back to a combination of unstable locations, most of which are far from downtown, so he walks, bikes, or takes public transportation back and forth. It is riding his bike that eventually proves fatal, when a driver hits him head-on and he dies instantly. His obituary in 2016 describes him as "homeless rights advocate, street person," and his death as a "random, freak accident," but if you ask anyone on the streets during this time, it is anything but random. In fact, the death toll between 2014 and 2017 among homeless people in Santa Barbara is over 160, with the leading causes ranging from addiction to blunt-force trauma (*Santa Barbara Independent,* November 22, 2017; March 16, 2019).

Learning something from these tragedies is difficult. Ed never thought of himself as someone predisposed to give lessons in anything, except perhaps Irish folk music, and even then, he was always willing to hear someone else's opinion. Watching the trajectory of his life unfold shows how his quality of life—particularly without legitimate prospects for work, apartment living, or even sobriety—is central to his against-all-odds survival. In a music class with a talented local musician, Ed values himself as a member of the group, he cleans up, he pays attention, and he is grateful to share the class with everyone. His teacher also shows him how to be less aggressive, using a metaphor of swords, which resonates with Ed, a long-time knife wielder. "You don't have to give your swords (your defenses) up completely," she tells him, "you don't have to drop them, just put them down." This comes as a revelation to Ed, who has had to defend himself against several violent, random attacks over the years. Taking guitar class helps Ed manage his aggression and his personal appearance. To me, this seems priceless.

But offering classes does not help Ed with employment. In fact, he never holds a job in the time I know him, not even shadow work. He survives on a small monthly SSDI check and has a representative payee who disburses the money to him.[4] I never understood the extent of Ed's disability until we went to an ATM machine in Montecito during one of my return trips to Santa Barbara. As we approached the bank, Ed handed me his card and said, "Can you do it for me? I can't enter the numbers, Michele, I don't know what to pick," and I don't really understand what he means at first so I say, "You do this all the time, right?" and he answers, "No, the card is new. I usually get a check because I never know how to work these machines." Ed gives me his pin number and I take out $160 of his money, hand it to him with his receipt, and say, "You don't do this with other people, right?" "I haven't survived this long out here by being stuck on stupid," he replies, and I feel good for being worthy of his trust. Maybe classes won't help Ed manage his money and maybe the milk truck isn't the best place for a person to live. All of these are the fragile trappings of his home, his stability, his masculinity, and his fierce independence, but they are threatened every day by law enforcement, business owners, and even his friends on the street. Chipping away at these resources makes Ed unstable.

About eight years before he dies, I return to Santa Barbara and talk with Ed about the dangers of street living. I pick him up near the Bird Refuge and we go for a long car ride through Montecito, a wealthy estate community in the hills adjacent to Santa Barbara. He no longer takes classes or showers, so I keep my windows rolled down. Ed tells me about his long-standing relationship with another street person, whom I will call "Red," even though this is not what everyone else calls him. Red is bipolar and suffers from several injuries he sustained in the Vietnam War. When he is in depressive mode, Red becomes erratic and aggressive. He was in the Safe Parking Program, designed to offer safe parking in church and non-profit lots throughout the city, for people living in their vehicles. I ran this program from 2004-2005, and every month or so, Red would come into my office, sweating and red-faced, ready to tell me his troubles at the top of his lungs. He barely waited for me to say anything before losing his temper completely, yelling at me, and running off. Although Red is friends with Ed, Red also beats him up from time to time, and he does it from behind or with his face covered, so Ed never sees him. Once it was so bad that Ed had to have his eye stitched back into its socket.

Ed doesn't have proof that Red is his attacker. "I know it's him, though," he tells me. "I saw the color of his hair and I know the way he smells, what he wears, it couldn't be anyone else." Ed explains the beatings as a result of Red's dislike for him. "Why does he hate me so much?" he asks me, and I tell him that from my perspective, "he doesn't hate you. I think you are one of his only true friends. But sooner or later, he will go off. Sooner or later, he will find a reason to attack you. It's not because of you, but he won't ever stop." My rudimentary explanation of Red makes sense to Ed, and for a moment he feels better. "Wow, Michele, I never had anyone explain it to me like that," he says. "I just thought he hated my guts." "I don't think he does," I tell him, "but I also don't think you can be friends with him without becoming a target for him sooner or later." Because Ed lives on the street, he is easy to find, and Red always looks for him. "I don't think I can do that (avoid Red)," he says. "I don't know what to do, though, because I think one day he will kill me," he confides. But Red never has his chance. When Ed loses the trappings of home, the milk truck, the classes, even the community he was used to, it is only a matter of time before he succumbs, like Moms and Ricky and so many others before him. Of course, there is a mix of mental illness, addiction, violence, incarceration, but these are par for the jungle's course.

Put Up a Parking Lot

In contrast to the 1980s jungle, when homeless people felt entitled to protest in the city's most prominent public spaces, jungle protest today is muted or nonexistent. People living in today's jungles are typically hiding and not calling attention to themselves through protest. They are already resisting by opting out of emergency shelters, if they are even available, or by creating other makeshift sleeping areas, or by merely surviving, making friends, and hiding from authorities. Only those who are marginally more self-sufficient, who are living in vehicles and RVs, are able to make some headway in contesting sleeping and camping citations, but even their victories are measured. Once they lose legal advocacy, the city steps up its enforcement, many people lose their homes, and they slip closer and closer toward the magnetic pull of the jungle.

When I arrive the meeting is just starting. There are about twenty or thirty people gathered in a small corner of a large public parking lot downtown; many are sitting in lawn chairs, some are standing, and there are two tables behind which the hosts stand, ready to begin. The hosts are two well-dressed, obviously housed women, one of whom is a city councilor (Cathy) and the other a longtime advocate for the homeless (Deborah). The audience is made up of people living in their vehicles, most of which are standard-sized RVs; advocates include members of the Committee for Social Justice; a reporter from the *Santa Barbara News Press*; and me. The purpose of the meeting is to warn people living in their RVs of impending regulation and offer assistance on how to avoid it. The meeting begins with a laundry list of complaints from business owners about RVers, the first of which is their location, size, and visibility. In a surprising complaint coming from a homeless advocate, Deborah claims that RVs park in front of downtown businesses and block storefronts from view for tourists. As if this is not egregious enough, she asks RVers to empathize with the discomfort they cause wealthy homeowners. "Imagine walking out of your multimillion-dollar home and seeing that." From her point of view, the mere visibility of homeless people in paradise causes such offense that it seems only natural that everyone can empathize, even homeless people themselves. The bewildered and frustrated faces of RVers in the audience show just how little Deborah's complaint resonates with them.

Most people at the meeting simply roll their eyes as this line of thought continues and RVers are associated not just with visual blight but with excrement and waste. "One woman was dumping every week at the Bird Refuge," Deborah complains, and Cathy too says she has heard of people in RVs leaving urine or excrement in bottles or bags on people's front lawns. To remedy this situation, they remind RVers that there is a local dumping station where they can dump their tanks for free, which everyone in attendance already knows. They also offer some guidelines for RVers, a kind of behavior lesson for the stigmatized: "if you see another RV, don't park on that street, two or more is excessive." Imagine the same advice being given to wealthy businessmen: "Please cluster in small groups to avoid making people uncomfortable, as your conspicuous wealth is offensive." To avoid regulation, RVs need to stay away from each other and remain highly mobile— "Police want you to move around"—and they outline what the seventy-two-hour parking rule means and how long seventy-two hours is in days. There is also a ban on RV parking between 3:00 a.m. and 6:00 a.m., and a daily two-hour parking limit, but these restrictions are not mentioned. In this case, mobility is rewarded and enforced through the threat of ticketing, but putting down roots becomes more and more difficult, as even sleeping through the night is off limits.

To underscore how serious police are about towing vehicles in violation of this limit, Deborah and Cathy tell the group about "a Hispanic family with three or four kids and the dad was just getting back to work after a broken back—mom was out as a maid working—their vehicle was towed because of unanswered tickets." Rather than questioning a policy that evicts an intact working family struggling with medical issues, this serves as a warning that no matter who you are or what you are going through, as long as you live in an RV, you are fair game for targeting and removal. Of course, here the issue is not merely one citation but multiple, unanswered citations, which are easy to get for someone in daily violation of local parking restrictions, whatever the reason. Cathy adds that if people don't know if they have outstanding tickets, they can go to the police station to check. Needless to say, asking homeless people to remain in constant motion in vehicles that are costly to move and maintain and to check in regularly with the police to be sure they are still ticket-free is not feasible.

The only solution that Cathy offers is for everyone living in RVs to register for the Safe Parking Program, which is full to capacity, with forty people on the waiting list. In her view: "This gives you a status, it lets the city know you are legal and want to stay." Although signing up for the program is not officially tied to any moratorium on ticketing, and arguing for one never makes it to the list of things to do, she suggests that the police "may choose to exempt vehicles on the list or in the program." I look around at the people listening to her, wondering if they feel belittled by the etiquette lesson followed by the lack of any viable solution except applying for a parking program that has no vacancies and might not offer protection even if it did. I also wonder why Cathy, a city councilor, does not offer to approach the police and ask them to work with RVers to offer an official endorsement of the program and a moratorium on ticketing. Why not work with her fellow councilors to increase the number of parking lots to make it proportionate with the population? Perhaps Cathy does not offer these solutions because her intention is to inform rather than entertain a change in policy or approach. And perhaps she, like homeless people who work with city councilors, is seen as someone homeless people relate to, or relate to more than other local politicians. In any case, her best advice is to stay contrite, move often, and stay out of sight.

A man in the audience, sharing my indignation, stands up and asks, "Does city council know how much money they are kicking to the curb? There are nice RVs that want to park here," referring to tourist vehicles. His argument doesn't resonate with Deborah or Cathy at all, in part because there is no shortage of tourist dollars in Santa Barbara and also because excluding tourist RVs is not the intention. "Our best advice is to sign up for the Safe Parking Program," Cathy reiterates. This pisses him off even more, and he asks the question many of us have been wondering: "Why do we as human beings have to live in a fucking program?" No one has an answer, but many people nod their heads in agreement. Deborah and

Cathy tell him to calm down, but this just adds fuel to his fire. "This meeting ain't gonna solve anything," he shouts, pointing at his friends in the audience, "*She's* gonna get a ticket—*he's* gonna get a ticket. We are the last fucking Indians in the fucking reservations. You DO NOT speak for us!!!" Apparently, this man has appeared at city council meetings before, sharing similar views, and has a ten-year restraining order against him. Although he can no longer share his views publicly in certain venues, speaking his truth calms him down. "I got my voice out," he says, motioning to the listening crowd, "these are my brothers and my sisters, and I will defend them to the fucking death."

The attack he is defending RVers from is a new ordinance by the city that bans vehicles longer than twenty-five feet, higher or wider than eighty-two feet, and apparently very few are smaller than this. Vehicles are either too tall or too wide, so now even constant mobility won't save people from losing their homes. There is some leeway in the application of this ordinance. As Cathy indicates, delivery trucks are exempt and "if you have a handicapped placard, you will be given some leeway," which is, in fact a federal provision.[5] Cathy goes on to suggest that people attend and speak at the upcoming city council meeting devoted to reviewing the ban, but not just anyone—someone who represents RVers well, a good one. To illustrate, she points to a man in the audience, a well-dressed, contrite, white male RVer, "someone like yourself," she says, "not a drug addict, does not dump, tries not to bother residents." The man shakes his head, as if he is at least flattered that she thinks he is not a drug addict.

Her suggestion makes explicit the good-bad distinction as a moral evaluation in which "good ones" can speak and be listened to only marginally more than "bad ones," in part because they adhere to spatial and behavioral norms. These norms brand RVers and homeless people in general as a blight to society. Regardless of the risks people pose to themselves and each other by living in RVs or on the streets, housed society sees visibly poor people as a nuisance and a threat because they interfere with tourism, wealth, and, as Deborah points out, the pleasure of a million-dollar ocean view. Paradise itself feels tainted by their presence, and maybe even by its own production of an underclass it cannot, does not, want to rehabilitate. Instead, the cycles of addiction and incarceration, trauma and abuse keep this underclass in place, filling the prisons and employing hundreds of service workers, police and corrections officers, and health care employees. RVers are only marginally safer than people living in the jungle. They have a slightly better chance if they comply with behavioral norms, are contrite, apologetic, able to move constantly, and willing to submit to a program. Then they might get lucky, but with a price this high and no guarantee, many wonder why they should have to submit.

The irony of this conversation is that the people in the audience see themselves as "good ones" and cannot understand why police are targeting them and forcing them to remain in constant motion or lose their homes entirely. Ready to voice this concern, a woman who has been quietly listening the entire time stands up and shouts, "This is emergency housing in a brutal housing market, don't you get it?" Another man, sitting next to me, quietly tells the assembly, "There has to be a solution beyond banning people's houses." But the only solution the speakers offer, in addition to the above, is to have another meeting. "I can get this parking lot blocked off again," Cathy proudly announces. "Can we have a safe lot to park in, though?" comes another shout from the audience. A woman named Magda is sitting next to me and she is clearly upset by the whole discussion. She whispers under her breath, "What are we supposed to do?" and then in a slightly louder voice, she asks the group, "Would they rather everyone go to shelter and have to pick themselves back up again?" She feels the jungle calling.

Homes on Wheels

Of course, there are the more articulate, together, "normal" people living in their vehicles who are part of the movement to gain increased rights and privileges. They are the good ones, the professional ones, the ones who can get things done. Some of them are the same people who were living in the jungle in the 1980s, including Nancy and Bob. Bob's protest activity has receded, but Nancy remains a fixture in the local advocacy arena and is frequently called on to represent the interests of various groups of homeless people, most of whom do not know she is doing so. Her work is voluntary, and she also holds two part-time jobs to support herself, her family, and maintenance on the vehicles she owns with Bob. They have grown further and further away from the jungle and even the community around Casa Esperanza, where they rarely visit. Lyn is Nancy's close friend, who also lives in her RV in the immediate shelter neighborhood. When they work together, Lyn accompanies Nancy to public meetings, but Nancy is clearly the leader. Lyn has also lived in the Santa Barbara area off and on since the 1980s and has raised several children with various husbands with whom she shares custody.

In April 2002, Nancy and Lyn form a group called Homes on Wheels (HOW) and submit an application to become a nonprofit 501(c)(3) organization. Besides Lyn and Nancy, there are four other people listed as directors of the organization. Two of them are local people living in their RVs, one is the current mayor of the City of Santa Barbara, and I am the fourth. They also rely on the Committee for Social Justice for assistance with the application. The goals of the group are to provide assistance to people living in vehicles, to promote greater awareness of homelessness within the larger community, and to develop and operate an RV park. Their first step is to secure office space in the basement of the Lobero Theater, the building that also houses the Committee for Social Justice. They also receive two small grants from the McCune Foundation and the Fund for Santa Barbara and hold regular office hours to begin the work.

Bob visits the office regularly, bringing friends with him and annoying other people who work in the building. Because the HOW office is in the basement, close to the back entrance, when small groups of haggard-looking men cluster there to smoke cigarettes and hang out, it is only a matter of time before HOW loses the space. In addition, their initial interest in an RV park becomes a larger conversation with the city, directed to study and explore the problem. Without the resources to provide organized, ongoing assistance to RVers, HOW's remaining goal of raising awareness and developing a greater understanding of homelessness becomes its main focus. In a moment of insight that highlights the longer view of homelessness in Santa Barbara, HOW chooses to commemorate Lillian Child's protection of the men of the jungle. To do this, HOW purchases a plaque that is installed on a utility building in the Santa Barbara Zoo, thanking Lillian Child for "giving shelter and respect to homeless men." It is posted on the same building that was constructed for the men of the old jungle as a recreation room, bathroom, and laundry.

This memorialization underscores the importance of place and the meaning of the jungle in this community, as well as its changing role over time. The plaque represents an early acceptance of homelessness and poverty that has largely faded from view, aside from the money donated by advocates. But today, advocates stay safely in their mansions, writing checks and occasionally attending meetings, but not visiting, interacting, or lending their property. Even the events held by HOW are full of "good ones," most of whom are not living in the jungle today. A sense of historical preservation is what saves the jungle from obscurity, as the zoo does not otherwise preserve or commemorate its humble beginnings. Instead, HOW gives permanence to a city space that has always been thought of as belonging to homeless people and a sense of importance and entitlement that business owners, police, and city officials cannot take away. People experiencing homelessness still cluster along the same boulevards and only the faces and places have changed, and even then, not so much. But shacks are almost unheard of, except for the occasional ramshackle one on the beach, and the proper place for homeless people is the shelter, jail, or prison.

In contrast with the men of the jungle, Nancy has lived in a camper for many years. She has the protection of multiple vehicles, including a small truck with a sturdy cage on the back that houses her dogs, huge beasts that are part wolf, part dog, always bucking against their confinement. With more than twenty years of experience, Nancy understands how social protest works; she interacts regularly with housed citizens and is a fixture in advocacy circles. This allows her the credibility to get things done on behalf of homeless people, and it stands in marked contrast to the kinds of resistance found in the jungle. Ricky always talked about deeding his property to Edwin, but he never took a first step to make it happen. He was also driven by the immediate concern of protecting Edwin and not the larger goals of social awareness and community recognition. Nancy, with the support of Lyn and HOW, achieves what Ricky could not, establishing a permanent public record of the jungle tied to the place of its origin and a degree of acceptance that the building signifies. But she does so with a sustained measure of stability that most of today's jungle residents do not enjoy.

A Long Way to Normal

The nature of advocacy relationships between supporters, benefactors, business owners, politicians, and people living in the jungle is far removed from what it was in earlier years. People in the jungle do not interact with normals, aside from service and shelter. Nancy is one of the few people who is used to and comfortable with mixed contacts; in fact, they go a long way toward helping her feel normal. And for the normal, she is delightful though befuddled, sometimes sharing eloquent insights and sometimes making less sense. Her participation on the Coalition board, unlike Moms's mostly silent presence, is always eventful. She is not asked her opinion as much as Moms is, in part because she doesn't hesitate to give it. Yet sometimes, in what she says and how she says it, you can tell she is from a different world: she will begin a long story when the meeting is almost over, making business owners roll their eyes, or she will opine when she has not been asked and is kindly redirected. Still, Nancy's relative stability in comparison to others, her longevity in the homeless community, and her ability to sustain mixed contacts all make her the default spokesperson for homeless people.

Most advocates today who have been in Santa Barbara since the 1980s no longer visit homeless places regularly, and none of them frequent the jungle. They visit the shelter on dedication days, for grand openings, and for meetings, but not to have conversations, meals, or interactions. They descend for a moment, like the man in the Fleetwood, to see how the other half lives. Then they retreat to safety and comfort and feel good that they are giving a version of it to "those people," even if they don't use that wording. To illustrate this, on a typical day in the shelter, I had been in the field for months and knew that photographers would be coming to take photos for the upcoming gala to raise money for the second phase of our expansion project. I was standing with Elf and Russell when a young woman approached and asked Elf if he wanted to be photographed. She didn't ask me or Russell—I think we looked too clean. Elf, on the other hand, had visible dirt marks on both of his cheeks. Bad ones make great poster children. They did not pay him for his time but photographed him, told him how to stand and whether he should smile, which of course was a no.

As a member of the Coalition Board, I was invited to its fundraising gala and told that I could bring a guest. I brought Louie, my street dad and longtime informant (Wakin 2014). I knew this was a bold move, and when Louie asked me, "Is there an open bar?" I worried I had made an error in judgment. Protest Bob was there when we arrived, standing on the sidewalk in front of the building, burning incense and wearing a sandwich board that read: "People should not be placed in shelters." This was all to the embarrassment of the Coalition chairperson, who, when she saw him, exclaimed, "Bob, you *promised*!" I walked in slightly behind Louie and saw the photo of Elf mounted on poster board and hanging to one side of the podium, with dirt still on his cheeks. We were being served cassoulet because it was something the attendees would consider rustic and people were arriving and filing in to be seated. A white-haired man sat next to Louie and introduced himself. Louie responded politely, and I thought, *Oh God, I hope he can handle this.* The man turned to Louie and asked, "If there is any bread, can you pass it over," and then, to explain, he said, "I can't see at all, you know, I'm legally blind." The night was saved!

We talked about politics, shelter over street living, and the current state of things in Santa Barbara, and everyone was at ease. I doubt this would have happened without this organic version of a blind experiment. It showed me firsthand how strong bias and prejudice are, how unconsciously, despite whatever else we believe or think we believe, most of us act on what we see and the immediate impression it conjures. In today's world, especially in the United States, there's room for little else. This knee-jerk reaction closes many doors and is part and parcel of how homeless people experience mixed contacts. This interactional stigmatization affects their sense of self and quality of life and is a barrier to reintegration. Intentional or not, figuring out how to create and normalize mixed contacts is an important part of making homeless people feel as if they matter and are part of a community beyond their own. RVers achieve this sense of status only marginally more than people living in the jungle and only because of their greater resources and how these affect their sense of self and ability to engage in social protest.

6

Paradise Revisited

In the first chapter of this book, I describe the experiential categories used to understand life in the jungle and show how access to mainstream housing and employment gradually becomes out of reach for people on the lower end of the wealth and income spectrum. Using firsthand accounts written by and recorded with people living in the jungle, along with extensive research on policies designed to shelter and serve homeless people, I offer a sustained profile of a jungle community in Santa Barbara, California. I trace the evolution of the space and meaning of the jungle for people who live there and for the local community. Because there is such heavy focus on categories of experience, perhaps the portrayal suffers from a lack of precision over the definition of the jungle or demands a more comprehensive nationwide profile of encampments and jungle settings. Although I address the latter concern, at this point I hope it is clear that the jungle is undefined on purpose. Binaries and definitions haven't gotten us very far to begin with.

The jungle is the name everyone uses for the little camps they live in around the waterfront and along creeks and railroad tracks, as they have always done, since the original jungle on the Child Estate. The word *jungle* is also used to refer to camps in Ventura, Santa Cruz, and Sonoma Counties, and throughout the Pacific Northwest. Beyond this, the jungle is used as a metaphor to understand how people are drawn into, or further into, a web of illness, addiction, and disease, coupled with criminalization, shelterization and other structural components of a system created for a group seen as fundamentally different, wholly apart. The jungle is what threatens to consume, either by chewing one up in the machinery of capitalism, or by the organic threats of sickness and the elements that eventually close in on people living outdoors. Calling it a vortex, as I do several times throughout this book, is a way of describing the funnel we have created in a society that makes it increasingly difficult to reintegrate and ever easier to get caught in the spinning, falling maelstrom.

Sociologists make sense of homelessness by splitting it into individual and structural causes. We either blame society or the individual or, more often than not, a combination of the two. Splitting causes is a way of placing blame, and it is usually done by those with the power to say who is at fault and what should be done about it. Overlooking the interactional dimension of homelessness is a grave mistake because it denies our similarity and reinforces difference. My work here emphasizes interaction because it views the experience of homelessness as paramount, over moral judgment or placing blame, or even determining causes or identity characteristics. Yes, people experiencing homelessness have faced individual and structural challenges that cause them to lose their homes. But once they are homeless, the death by a thousand paper cuts that makes up most mixed contacts deals ongoing blows to their self-esteem, which eventually brings trouble. Understanding how this happens and what it feels like is part of the explanation for why people choose the jungle over other alternatives and why it remains a marginal zone.

My work also examines how homeless people survive and make it out of the jungle. In earlier years, the jungle community permits the Bookman's survival and allows the prestige of a jungle mayor. By the 1980s, jungle leaders focus on social change as well as mere survival, and they develop a protest-based collectivity focusing on grassroots action. In the millennial jungle, the relationships between Moms and Russell, Ricky and Edwin, and Cuba and Martin show a degree of caring and community they carve out for themselves that is surprising and uplifting, amid a dearth of alternatives. It is the search for a version of domestic life, for comfort and protection from crime and hate, that is a reason people live in the jungle and preserve relationships and build community there.

Returning to Santa Barbara, I examine how Hopper becomes a case manager, how Nancy organizes to commemorate the jungle, how Crazy Ed responds to classes, and all these stories give hope to the idea that change is possible. Even the fleeting transformations that take place through offering access to mainstream routines, short of mainstream spaces, are substantial. Together they demonstrate the resilience of the human spirit and the importance of basic comforts and routines in making stigmatized people feel normal. These are the jungle's constant positive and enduring features, carved out using strategies that seem counterintuitive to shelter and service policies.

Getting lost in deciding who deserves help seems the inevitable trap of a service industry mired in organizational and funding challenges, particularly regarding the unsheltered, for whom the best argument for housing them is that it's cheaper than other forms of public support (Culhane, Park, and Metraux 2011). Focusing on judgments of moral worth inherent in the binaries good-bad and deserving-undeserving underscores the overall idea, prevalent within our society and the homeless service industry, that poor people are poor because they are deficient. We don't interrogate the unequal conditions of education, employment, training, housing, or health care that continue to polarize society and perpetuate inequality. We convince ourselves that we have privilege because we've earned it, we're worth it, and homeless people are not.

Jungle Spaces, Jungle Cycles

Examining the jungle over time shows the key role that spatial control plays for members of society with nowhere else to go. The jungle in the 1940s and 1950s offers protection and community in an era when skid row undergoes redevelopment, labor camps close, and poverty and transience are no longer the nation's main focus. The men living there during this time build a relatively orderly community and are left alone until the land is sold and developed. They are in control of their days and routines, for the most part, and can more easily access mainstream employment. People understand the men as either drunken outcasts or as productive members of society, once removed. Either way, they have the use of Child's land and her protection. As a result, the Bookman and Mayor Anderson both live there as long as they can, until they recover from or succumb to illness.

In the 1980s, the jungle is on public land, more fragmented and impermanent, and is loosely associated with pockets of homeless people clustering on lower State Street, the Fig Tree, City Hall, and sometimes the Salvation Army or Rescue Mission. Without anywhere else to go, homeless people in public spaces in Santa Barbara and nationwide in this era become synonymous with social disorder, chaos, and threat, inspiring a host of punitive measures designed to minimize or eradicate their presence. Arguing for the right to shelter or to sleep outside without citation, homeless people work with advocates during this decade to win important concessions, including the right to vote. Shelter is the one spatial provision that advocates and homeless people agree on, and it becomes synonymous with homelessness itself.

In California, National Guard armories are opened as emergency shelters in 1987, and, at least in Santa Barbara, they are staffed with people currently living on the streets. For Ricky and Edwin, this leads to the feeling of incorporation, participation, and agency, and the satisfaction of giving back to their community. Although this is an important first step, shelters still do not offer autonomy or freedom, and community leadership does not always mean good decisions or safe spaces, a steady paycheck, or a transition to being housed. In addition, the armories are only open in cold weather, so for the rest of the year, the jungle is full. During the 1980s, SROs close, addiction and incarceration skyrocket, and homeless people are trapped and punished in a cycle that worsens over time.

Starting in the year 2000, Santa Barbara develops a plan to provide for homeless people and simultaneously clean them out of the State Street area and have a reason to regulate them in other parts of the city. Mirroring the armory in many respects, the city's first emergency shelter is a warehouse in the industrial area without heat, bathrooms, a kitchen, or a roof. Even when construction is complete, it is only open for part of the year, and no other local emergency shelter offers more than episodic stays. So people split their time between shelters and streets or, if they are lucky enough, they purchase vehicles with their SSI or SSDI checks, which keeps them only marginally safer. Drugs are everywhere at this point, without a medical detox facility, and there is a liquor store selling cheap beer on the corner where the shelter is located and another one along the border of the jungle. Opportunities to leave town for employment are virtually nonexistent, except for day laborers, and those jobs come with accompanying risks. And settling in town is also difficult, as rental prices make the market prohibitive for anyone making minimum wage or on SSI or SSDI. In the new millennium, there is nowhere for most people to go to sleep undisturbed for any length of time for the majority of the year. When shelters close, homeless people spend their days going around and around the same circles, usually making things worse instead of better.

I use the idea of a nexus between time, space, and mobility to talk about the changes in how people living in the jungle experience it. As a private and then a public space, the jungle eventually prohibits permanent structures or accumulation, beyond what people can carry on their backs or in shopping carts or bicycle tow-behinds. This means that someone like the Bookman would have no choice but to submit to shelter or succumb to the elements. He would have no barrier from law enforcement or poor health. He would not plan for the future, he would survive in the present, ducking and covering to the best of his ability, as Cuba and Martin do later on. This creates a feeling of being trapped in a fishbowl, the distorted faces of normals on the outside, and one's own waste and that of others on the inside. The only mobility is cyclical. It does not lead to a feeling of agency, the literal or figurative sense of going somewhere. It magnifies frustration as it requires physical stamina, current bus schedules, a way to keep track of time, and these factors make keeping simple appointments far more difficult. Eventually, people give up.

Over time, society's response to homeless people has changed from regulating the unchecked movement of hoboes, their jungles, and skid row areas to encouraging mobility in cities struggling to provide for their homeless populations. The idea of homeless people as a flawed and lawless breed apart, not welcome to settle, has only widened since theories of disaffiliation first suggested their voicelessness relative to agencies designed to serve them and to organizations in general. Opportunities for reintegration gradually become out of reach, and homeless people are nickel-and-dimed for the assistance they do receive, as if their very comfort is something undeserved. Of course, this takes a toll on identity, as the mere concept of home implies a certain balance between control over space, time, mobility, and insulation from negative looks and interactions, which reinforce stigma. Jungles are an attempt to build the temporal and spatial control that homes provide and that shelters take away, but they don't typically lead to greater social mobility, or even to protest and resistance.

Binaries and Reintegration

Over time, certain groups of homeless people are considered worth saving, as if some people are okay and some don't belong and should be shut out or crushed. Young men in the early 1900s are seen as an important part of the team, like families fleeing the Dust Bowl in the 1930s, women and children in the 1980s, and veterans today. All of these groups receive a larger share of government resources and are targeted for better, more innovative programs. This is an effective strategy for reintegrating people considered unable to help themselves, "just like us," or who directly serve us. But focusing on specific groups is often fleeting and does not take into account the rest of the homeless population. So even if ending veteran homelessness is successful, and everyone hopes it will be, what about ending child homelessness, or focusing on people with disabilities and addictions, and many other categories, not to mention the always incoming tides of new and diverse homeless groups?

Trying to help one group over others reproduces the binary thinking that says some homeless people are good and some are bad, some are worth saving and some are not. Or, it is simply a way of managing an overwhelming issue. Either way, we still have not moved beyond binary thinking in our policies to serve homeless people. In fact, they are typically seen as so bad, so damaged and despondent, that even simple choice seems beyond them, and most of us, except those with the insight of Sam Tsemberis, founder of the Housing First initiative, don't even ask them what they want. Focusing on one group over another silences some homeless voices and labels some lives as unimportant, and then distributes resources accordingly: some get housing, some get prison, some get death. This strategy devalues a large part of the population it attempts to serve, and it couldn't misunderstand the experience further.

Reintegration is simply a folding back into the rhythms and routines of normal life, whence most homeless people came in the first place and to which many will return. In the 1930s, the first time in the twentieth century that homelessness and poverty reached epic proportions and the first time families were so frequently afflicted, the goal was to return people to settled, community life. Of course, who they were figured prominently in the host community's willingness to accept them. Many families moved west, settled down, and blended in. Young men were also overrepresented in a group of men traveling in search of employment. As a result, both the country and the youth themselves panicked over the idea that perhaps they would not ever reach the goals of domestic prosperity. Post–World War II policies ensured a future, at least for America's white soldiers, who settled in suburbia and began to build their fortunes, leaving the inner city a darker, more impoverished core.

The 1950s renewed hope for domestic ideals and prosperity, however rigid and confining. The jungle's few remaining "oldsters" could simply move on in search of employment or cluster in the remaining skid row areas not yet redeveloped. Those with employment pensions or Social Security income could move into town. Retired jungle mayor Edward Anderson does just that and keeps up a lively social commentary in the local paper and participates in the affairs of the city, leaving behind several scrapbooks with the Santa Barbara Historical Society that show that he thought of himself as someone with something to contribute. The return letters in his scrapbook, as well as his correspondences about the utility building for the men of the jungle, show that he is taken seriously and listened to by the larger community, even its most prominent citizens.

By the 1980s, only certain people are seen as worthy contributors and they are typically not the people living in the jungle, at least not in the long term. Yet the homeless community is able to martial the support of advocates and the momentum of the national spotlight focusing on homelessness to make substantial gains, including the right to vote. This is monumental, and this win, along with the provision of National Guard armories, buoys up protest among homeless people as something that will get them somewhere. But where to go after that is anyone's guess. Jungle leaders like James can climb telephone poles and protest at City Hall or get married in the jungle, but they don't translate well with housed people. They don't go to meetings, and when they do, they are drunk and end up either crying or giggling. The first time I witnessed this was at a screening of the film *First, Last, and Deposit*, released in 2000, in which the title refers to housing rental requirements. James sat on the stage, barely able to focus, reaffirming everyone's fear and loathing of him and of street people in general. If this is his one shot at getting his point across, it doesn't go well, and by 2006, he collapses and dies on the ground in Hopper's arms, outside the bathrooms at Pershing Park.

Nancy and Bob, also leaders in the 1980s, manage to sustain several vehicles throughout their relationship and support their biological daughter and a son of Nancy's from a previous marriage. At one point they even purchase a small house to live in, which they give to their daughter, but it doesn't last long, as it was never legally owned. Nancy works in the neighboring city of Montecito and has a paper route she has maintained for years. She enjoys being part of advocacy circles, and Santa Barbara embraces her, in part, as the new mayor in charge of articulating the needs and wants of homeless people. She is conversant with authorities and has just enough funk to give her street cred. People feel as if they are talking to a homeless person when they talk to her, or at least someone close to it. Bob is another story. As Santa Barbara mayor Marty Blum put it, "He can behave when he has to," but Bob is distrustful of authorities and although he is smart and wickedly funny, he does not translate well in most mixed-contact situations. Although Bob spent some time in the jungle in the 1980s, neither he nor Nancy have lived there in years.

The good-bad split that becomes ever wider in the 1980s is tied to resources and space and also social policy, as those who are bad are out of opportunities. There is no rationalizing the effects of trauma, addiction, mental illness, and disability as reasons for jungle living. In the face of staggering need and violent social protest, the service industry acts in emergency mode, getting lost in the weeds, and the government offers no solution for the majority of people experiencing homelessness, except that maybe sleeping on grates is enough. A war on drugs is declared, which ravages people already enmeshed in addiction, as well as those involved in its shadow economy. So some of the people on the street wind up in prison and the rest are pushed into shelters or shuttle back and forth between jail and the streets until they crack under pressure.

One way to see the good-bad split in action in the 2000s is through interaction. When Moms attends meetings of the Santa Barbara Homeless Coalition, she doesn't participate in the same way that everyone else does. She is not used to this kind of meeting. She makes strange noises. She speaks too slowly or too quickly or not at the right time. She offers non sequiturs and is then embarrassed when no one responds. Everyone tries to be nice to her, but they don't always understand or have time for her comments, so she is often politely ignored or shuffled along to get back to business. Nancy is received in a marginally better way, although most of her suggestions, too, are ignored and pushed aside, as Hopper's are to the present day. But this is only interactionally. Policies complement the stereotypes as they are increasingly split between good ones and bad ones, and the latter are not part of the team, even more so than in previous decades.

People living in today's jungle use the shelters when they must, along with several meal programs, hospitals, and the county clinic. Section 8 housing has a three-year waiting list, and the rolls are intermittently closed because of too many applicants and too few units. Forms of assistance people pursue include SSI, SSDI, and workers' compensation. Sometimes people challenge the citations they receive, mostly for sleeping and camping offenses. They interact with law enforcement frequently, sometimes daily, and spend time in jail or prison. Beyond this, they do not interact with housed citizens in any other capacity, and increasingly, they stop trying and everyday survival eclipses all else. A few are able to leave the jungle and purchase RVs to live in, but that lifestyle comes with its own risks and the expense of ongoing maintenance, typically afforded through SSI or SSDI payments. The jungle takes its toll on all who live there, and only the strong survive, like James and Crazy Ed. And they have some amazing adventures, but they never leave, and both of them die tragically.

Irony and Identity

The irony of a homeless identity is evidenced by the fact that many, if not most people experiencing homelessness have also experienced house or apartment living. Although going back and forth between the two may not be unusual, the judgment and stigma that accompany being homeless are often striking, leading many people to question the authenticity of social ties among the normal. Irony, as a signifier, states the opposite of what is intended and can be used humorously or tragically. Homeless people, as social signifiers, are considered offensive, dangerous, and diseased. Yet at the heart of it, even when the system rejects them, most strive to protect one another as best they can, to eat and sleep, bathe and dress. This is not to sanctify the truly gruesome details of lives lived on the street—the filth, disease, violence, and addiction—but it is striking that signs of suffering among homeless people inspire punishment and correction instead of safety and comfort.

People who are housed should understand the need for basic comforts and the struggle to keep up with the Joneses, get a house with curb appeal, drive a newer car, take the right vacations, post it all on Facebook. If you are homeless, you see the sham in this, you criticize the smooth veneer, the sneer lurking behind the image. There is no pretending when you're homeless, because everyone sees the condition you're in and presumes a lot about who you are. This is so much the case that homeless people have been compared to celebrities because of the public stir they cause. Being homeless in public is heavily stigmatized, and everything—from your personal appearance to what you carry with you, to your behavior—is suspect. People don't want your autograph. They can't help but see the state that you're in, and reactions vary from kindness and handouts to fear, hate, and citations for an array of "nuisance crimes" targeted to remove you from public places, even if you're not doing anything. If you are not already nervous or depressed, and you don't already have addiction issues, now might be the time you start.

And once you are living in the jungle and you develop or worsen the maladies that go along with long-term street living, exiting the jungle becomes increasingly difficult. The cyclical survival routine of meal-shelter-jungle-jail-repeat becomes a downward spiral, and most people are eventually pulled down completely and wind up dead or in prison. Your quality of life is not a feature of most programs designed to serve you, nor is asking you your preferences or treating you like a person. Any comfort or self-esteem you have resides in the company you keep, in looking out for people where you can, resisting authority, and generally trying to get by—sometimes on faith. For many people living in the jungle, it involves being kind to others the world has forgotten, the ones with broken teeth, drug habits, those who talk to themselves, and generally smell, look, and act the part. No one criticizes your appearance in the jungle.

The reality of jungle living might be ugly for the people who do it, but it's better than pretending or dressing it up to be something it's not. It's better than buying into the logic of a society that would throw you away, when you know you have such promise. People on the street accept each other or are at least loosely bound together because they share the knowledge of society's other side, its double, cutting edge. They know that there are reasons for homelessness that go far beyond the failings of individual people, and that they are still seen as dirt until they do question their own worth, and then it's only a matter of time. The rigors and danger of the jungle mean that nothing is surprising and nothing lasts, except, perhaps, the persistence of such a marginalized and resilient community in the middle of paradise.

Understanding jungle living as a rational response to poverty that implicates others as well as the self is part of its irony. A common starting point for people in the jungle involves critiquing normals and normal society, resisting shelters and police, and sharing the experience of stigma in general, but moving from survival-based to resistance strategies usually takes help. That involves facing the society that you have shunned and that has shunned you, and then searching for your place. When you achieve this and reenter society, and there are notable examples of people who have, you feel like an even better, more enlightened person than you otherwise would have been. But fitting back into society is a complex negotiation, as it always involves mixed contacts, the juxtaposition of stigmatized and normal. It is always uncomfortable, and it takes a heavier toll on people who are already voiceless, powerless, and traumatized. If they are not that way when they enter the jungle, living within it underscores marginality through punishment and regulation, making the pain of mixed contacts that much more difficult to face. Yet learning to manage mixed contacts is essential for resistance and reintegration.

Identity and Survival

Identity work is used to describe a set of strategies homeless people use to make themselves feel better, safer, and more in control or to convince others that they are more than what they appear to be. The strategy employs identity as a personal and social concept, what one thinks of oneself and the image the world reflects (Snow and Anderson 1993). These exist simultaneously but often, for the stigmatized, in marked contrast. A homeless person, degraded in society, may be hurt by this treatment, knowing his or her own personal experiences, accomplishments, and sense of self-worth. This does not mean that all people experiencing homelessness think of themselves as worthy, only that they strive to be seen in this way. Talmadge Wright (1997) elaborates on the concept of identity work by including place-making strategies. This is an important addition, as it recognizes the multiple ways homeless people work to salvage the idea that they are worth something.

Most of the evidence in identity work focuses on identity talk, the verbal avowal of personal identity. This usually occurs during mixed contacts, as homeless people are striving to prove to normals that they are, or were, just like us. But is anyone really convinced? When Ricky talks about his past adventures or Brett tells me he has a BA degree, even if these things are true, they hardly matter for men living in the jungle, one on his way back to prison and the other heading toward death. This is not to minimize the survival strategies that homeless people use to manage an unmanageable, stigmatized life but rather to say that these are not enough. Merely valorizing them keeps homeless people in their place, where they can develop ways of feeling better personally while they stay locked in a cycle of poverty that keeps them on the social margins. Examining mixed contacts shows how interactions between homeless people and nonhomeless people (shelter staff, business owners, homeless advocates, and others) keep those living in the jungle at a distance.

Punishing and correcting, common in the shelters, jails, prisons, and institutions in which homeless people spend much of their time, does not nurture strategies that salvage the self in the same way that safe spaces, community integration strategies, and education and training opportunities do. And it isn't their purpose to begin with. Instead of fostering these resources, housed normals reflect moral indignation about the appearance and behavior of homeless people, which translates into policies and programs with the same ideology. It is as if we don't understand how they, the tainted and stigmatized, could possibly behave as they do, and if we could only show them the way through punishment and correction, they would reform and be just like us. Despite this moral judgment, research shows that many of the same things common in people experiencing homelessness—for example, addiction, depression, stress, and poverty—are also prevalent in general society, sometimes in epidemic proportions.

In this sense, perhaps the overlap between the Occupy Wall Street movement and homelessness in general can help us understand where this moral indignation comes from. In the context of the Occupy movement, homeless people are initially shut out of even the 99 percent. Perhaps this is because OWS campers see themselves as entitled to public space and because they have the resources to sustain social-movement activities and their consequences, including arrest. Invested in their own form of identity work, which rationalizes privilege as something deserved, OWS campers were initially reluctant to work with homeless people. Yet integrating homeless people into social-movement activities is one example of developing similar feelings of entitlement in them, leading to a sense of self-worth and willingness to participate in group activities, even to pursue housing. The effectiveness of reintegration strategies like these are echoed through the classes offered by The People's Institute. These classes focus on quality of life over employment and housing, none of which are realistic goals that can be accomplished in an eight-week session for people who are developmentally and physically disabled, or who have never worked. Perhaps they are merely an important first step.

Understanding what sets the stage for resistance, for a fundamental questioning of society on the grounds that homelessness and inequality are unacceptable and that something beyond personal failure is to blame, is a complicated task. In a discussion of the political possibilities that can be seen as alternatives to the alienation of modern consciousness, sociologists suggest sympathy with "the urge to be liberated from the structures of exploitation and misery . . . it comes out of the protest against the increasing domination of wide areas of life by the technological and bureaucratic institutions" (Berger, Berger, and Kellner 1973, 234). The urge to be liberated from corporate domination today is evidenced by OWS, as it was by the IWW in the early 1900s. People experiencing homelessness are dominated by the institutions and structures that, though designed to serve them, rarely involve equal participation. Without a voice to question or protest conditions, people living in the jungle in the early 2000s simply rail self-destructively against the machine. Action is prevented by the absence of a political movement or the resources or wherewithal to engage in long-term protest, planning, and advocacy. In addition, the almost complete lack of services to manage addiction and mental illness, or offer year-round shelter or permanent housing, are also significant barriers to resistance.

Surviving within the criminal justice and homeless service systems typically means the erosion of community among homeless people, whose voices and opinions do not inform policy and whose possessions and companions are frequently lost or compromised in the struggle. Fitting in means submitting, and the days of the Santa Barbara Homeless Coalition and protesting on the steps of City Hall with vocal advocates, national support, and media attention are long gone. So too is the protection of private property. Today's advocates support shelters, legal advocacy, and small loans. But they do not visit the jungle, and anyone lucky enough to own private property in paradise does not jeopardize it by allowing a critical mass of homeless campers.

Resistance to anything is immediate and reactionary. It does not involve strategic planning or community organizing, except for those with comparatively greater resources. The jungle is a place to hide out; it isn't a place for notebooks and pamphlets, despite the fact that many people living in the jungle, including Ricky, Russell, and Martin, are avid readers. The jungle is a place to run from authority and society, not embrace it—just use it as you need to and leave the rest alone. This is truer than ever in today's jungle. Prez Ed summarizes the lack of community organizing by saying that "today, it's just all individualized. Everyone wants their own piece of the pie." In the 2000s, Prez Ed is tired, addicted, and suffering from tuberculosis. After Ricky leaves, he drifts further and further into the jungle, without a companion to protect him, even a fragile one. Everyone else, besides Hopper, is dead or in prison or their days are numbered.

Just Like Us

When people experiencing homelessness are listened to, valued, given a safe space, a job, a role within a community, things begin to change and lives are transformed. Why is listening to and working with people experiencing homelessness so difficult? Why is it not the cornerstone of the entire service and shelter industry? Why are public spaces, at the very least, not seen as zones of inclusion that permit a momentary shedding of one's stigma and a chance to interact with diverse people under a canopy of civility, however limited (Anderson 2011)? Why are these things reserved, primarily, for those with greater resources? And how can we stop policies from reflecting these interests so that having shelter is mainly about safety and comfort over moral judgment and punishment?

In the early 1900s and again in the 1980s, street living and camping in jungles signaled a systemic crisis. The first period associated with itinerant labor, and the second with a failed welfare and safety net. "Encampments" are becoming a crisis again, both nationwide and along the Pacific Coast, where they proliferate. But Santa Barbara is not a global city. It is a sleepy, Spanish Colonial–looking one, where the average rent is inaccessible and only the "newlywed or nearly dead" can afford to settle. The fact that the vast majority of the homeless population lives there unsheltered, that until the early 2000s there was no emergency shelter, that groups of homeless people sleep nightly in public parks, on beaches, and in jungles makes it a familiar and well-worn crisis. But, in Santa Barbara and elsewhere, it is one that we sustain and deepen through various forms of regulation, which push homeless people to the brink and keep them there.

Creating and maintaining a group of people living in camps that surround cities, who are depressed and addicted, sick and tired, and with nothing to lose, isn't good for anyone. It makes people feel unsafe and on edge. No one wants to feel this way. Arguing for the rights of people experiencing homelessness is not an argument for legal street sleeping or permissiveness regarding behavior that is threatening. It is to say that the laws of civility apply to all. Think of urban sociologist Jane Jacobs's eyes on the street, those who are watching and being watched (Jacobs 1961). To change the way homeless people feel about themselves, we have to create environments that offer control over space, a place to feel comfort, to be alone and backstage, and to create low-barrier opportunities to develop social ties and practice handling mixed contacts. The effects on identity can be transformative. Imagine if homeless people had control over their time and routines, a chance to be inside when they want to, as opposed to obeying staff mandates, and above all, if they had the feeling of mobility, agency, of going somewhere, being master of their own fate, something that may be harder to achieve than mere comfort. Would this lead to reintegration? Is that even what we as a society want? When faced with the gritty reality of homelessness, many of us normals shut down, believe the stereotypes, stop listening. And if we don't engage, why would they, particularly when control over the immediate is all they have.

Many people would be out of work if the prison industrial complex shut down, particularly in California, which the US Department of Labor, Bureau of Statistics ranks second only to Texas in terms of the number of corrections officers and jailers. Hollywood would have less to go on to depict a future like the one portrayed in the film *The Hunger Games* (2012). But this is about more than mere portrayals. Focusing on the lived reality of jungle living, even within this book's limitations, is a way of highlighting the words and opinions of the Bookman, Mayor Anderson, James and Hopper, Nancy and Bob, Ricky and Edwin, Moms and Russell, Cuba and Martin, and Crazy Ed. They show how living in the jungle makes sense to them, given their personal histories with addiction, trauma, abuse, and incarceration, and how they can possibly carve a way out.

Who are the people of the jungle? They are good and bad, they are victims and perpetrators, they are characters and introverts, generous and stingy, friendly and hostile, beautiful and disgusting, smart and not so smart. The point is not to emphasize their racism, violence, and addiction as winning out over their kindness, generosity, and pain, or vice versa, or to decide which parts of the individual or the system are to blame or worth saving. It is to omit moral judgments and arguments in favor of equal access to basic human comforts, even for the bad ones. It is asking people what they want, even when it seems they might not be coherent enough to know, and then developing services and housing around this. It is about keeping everyone safe and forsaking sympathy and pity for the common ground of experience, as a basic starting point. How, in the face of any of the things that homeless people in this book face, would *you* feel? How would *you* behave? Despite the seemingly pervasive categories and binaries people experiencing homelessness are divided into—female/male, deserving/undeserving, sheltered/unsheltered, chronic/nonchronic—it is the intangible sense of belonging, inclusion, and safety that we're all looking for and that defines our sense of home.

Experiencing Marginal: Fieldwork in the Jungle

Doing fieldwork in a place so far from my East Coast home in Boston and working with such a marginalized group of people made me, too, feel marginal. The things I saw and experienced were so dark, so disturbing, so traumatic and unfair, that I can only write about them now, years later, when I can better place them within the context of my life and research, when they no longer threaten to take them over. Experiencing, even vicariously, how homeless people feel when their homes are taken away, when they are beaten and jailed, when they experience trauma and rejection, even when they present themselves for shelter, meals, or services, is almost too heartbreaking to take in all at once. Because homelessness is so visceral, so emotional, the experience of it seems more illustrative than theories or statistics. Of course, in most of this book, I attempt to blend emotional and experiential insights with sociological description and analysis, but here in this appendix, I can explain in more detail what being in the field *felt* like and how, through conducting fieldwork, I too experienced a sense of withdrawal from the mainstream.

Visiting the jungle was a world away from shelters and vehicles, city parks and beaches. It was both public and private, usually a few minutes' walk to the nearest street. People lived in twos, fours, and small groups, many of which endured for months or years. But this work does not present a comprehensive inventory of jungle spaces. I never slept in the jungle and usually had no one protecting me and no cell phone with me when I went there, except for my first visit to Ricky's camp. Although I was safe with Ricky, when I visited Russell's camp, I knew I had gone too far. The thought of it still gives me chills. There was no way I could do a more comprehensive ethnographic study of the jungle without spending more time there, sleeping there, and eventually getting hurt. In this appendix I can begin to explain, without excusing it, why this is the case and in doing so provide insights into the boundaries I established and maintained in the field, how people tried to cross them, and what I did about it.

Other researchers are willing to brave New York City subway tunnels (Toth 1993) or get punched in the face to understand the role of the boxing gym in the lives of black men in inner city Chicago (Waquant 2004). Still others have elements of safety and privilege infused in their work through having famous fathers (Goffman 2014) or research buddies who accompany them in the field (Snow and Anderson 1993; Wasserman and Claire 2010). I too had white, scholarly privilege, but no one famous, no buddy-collaborator, no consistent mentors. Along with my whiteness, being a woman infused every aspect of my work in the field. It is my own "master status" that defines my role in the world, how others act toward me and how I in turn react.

It was clear early on that unwanted attention from all men, housed and unhoused, was a constant and daily feature of this work. Unlike the smooth onetime brush-offs that allow other researchers to gain respect (Dordick 1997), I worked for it every single day, often in misguided ways and with failed attempts. I remember meeting with Mitchell Duneier in the early stages of my research on vehicle living, published as *Otherwise Homeless* (2014), and he suggested that I give up my apartment and buy an RV to live in so that I could experience this form of homelessness firsthand. Without the funding to pursue this, a contingency he hadn't considered, I couldn't manage it, but it was also physical danger that made me think twice. Even when they are living in vehicles, even when they are over sixty-five and missing teeth, women are harassed on a daily basis. Can you imagine the toll this takes on a woman's self-esteem and ability to cope with everyday life? Research shows that the physical reactions alone that women have when they become homeless are formative in shaping their experience. As Julia Wardhaugh (1999) shows, when homeless women lack "access to that second skin, the home, the homeless body becomes the first and often only line of defense against a dangerous world" (1999, 102).

In this context, it is not surprising that shelters are populated by more women than men. Women are not safe on the streets. And the jungle is still its own special breed of lawlessness. One in five housed women will be raped at some point in her lifetime, and the rates of physical and sexual violence among homeless women are far higher (Goodman et al. 2006). The result of constant victimization means high degrees of substance abuse, depression, mental illness, stress, and trauma. Interactionally, this often comes across as highly volatile, defensive, and aggressive behavior, particularly toward other women, who are seen as competition.

To illustrate this latter point and further explore my relationships with women in the field, one of my main informants, A—— was dating Donny, whom I describe in the section below called Love Letters from Jail. She and I had been hanging out for about four months in the shelter neighborhood. She introduced me to many of the people living in vehicles and jungles, whom I eventually interviewed, and she often accompanied me throughout the day, all day, while I pursued various leads. Because she is a native Spanish speaker, originally from Mexico, I also hired her to translate several interviews related to this work. Donny and I are both white and relatively close in age. Although Donny always flirted with me, he gave me a wide berth, and he enjoyed my questions. He had been dating A—— for a few weeks, although she was pregnant at the time and another man was the father. When they started dating, it was clear that A—— felt lucky to be with Donny, as if every other woman must want her man.

One day when I was eating lunch at the shelter, A—— and Donny walked in to get in line, and she made a big show of stopping him right across from me to hold and kiss him and then looked at me to see my reaction. I was uncomfortable but just waved at them and continued eating, yet this and other signs told me that A—— viewed me as a threat. A few days later, she arrived wearing a ring with a small, curved blade attached and asked me, "Michele, you want to box?" I said no, and she accepted it, but being ready to box or get boxed was a constant feature of life in the jungle, even if you're just visiting, even if you're friends. The violence that characterizes life on the street also characterizes interpersonal relations therein. This is not to say that every relationship is violent, but violence is par for the course and something I had to navigate with all men and all women with whom I came into contact.

Slapped and Schooled

I had several "Aha!" moments during my fieldwork. The most poignant one was when I realized that fieldwork was affecting me, changing my reactions to people, making me defensive and aggressive. Although I can honestly say that I've been sexually harassed in every job I've ever held, in most cases, I said nothing, did nothing. I got out of the situation as well as I could and then moved on. But after several months of fieldwork, I started to toughen up, to react defensively, to stop taking it. I remember meeting with a faculty adviser during this time and showing him a set of field notes from an incident in which I talked tough when approached by someone in the field, an event I describe below. My adviser obviously thought I was losing my grip. But the incident and my reaction stuck with me as a central part of what it is to be a woman in the jungle: if you don't have someone with you, protecting you or threatening to, sooner or later you will be victimized. So you need people to know that someone has your back. It also helps to have people sense that despite your small stature, you might be a little "off the rails," so being aggressive, even overly aggressive, sometimes works well.

As a graduate student in California, going out to dinner and to dance with friends was a welcome distraction from ongoing fieldwork, at least in the beginning. On one such night, I was waiting in line when a club-owner friend came up behind me and slapped my backside in greeting, an indignity I have endured since the days of Jordache jeans. But in this case, my reaction was immediate, unforgiving, and violent. Without a moment's hesitation and without knowing who did it, I turned around and slapped him in the face. The force of my hit matched his, and we were both speechless, not knowing how to react to the encounter we were now having. This was one of the first times I realized how much the jungle was affecting me. The entire time I was conducting fieldwork, my physical being and safety were always an issue, always at risk, always something to guard against attack. When you have to do this 24/7, it's hard to switch off.

During my time on the street, I learned that I had better be on the defensive, through my actions or my words or by having someone protecting me. But I was lucky. I always had a car or bicycle I could use to escape to my comfortable apartment or anywhere else I chose to go. I had freedom and mobility and the legitimacy of being someone from the outside world, a researcher, definitely a more risky mark than a homeless woman. Of course, I wasn't completely safe. My car was keyed, my CDs stolen, my apartment broken into. I was catcalled daily, grabbed on several occasions, pawed at, and offered drugs and sexual favors often. I was threatened physically by several women and several men, yelled at incessantly by several others, some of whom suffered from extreme mental illness and did it all day long. I was exposed to more filth, disease, and despair than I can relate, even in several books.

In the face of all this, sustained fieldwork was only possible because of the people who did protect me. They were often the same people who grabbed or harassed me or stole from me, but the good usually outweighed the bad. Developing an understanding with several key informants was the most rewarding part of this work. It taught me that people living on the street want what everyone wants: some comfort, food, a place to be alone and still safe, to have one's things, people who care, and to provide these things for others. There are very few people experiencing homelessness, whatever the cause or condition, past or present, who don't want these things. Focusing on commonalities over binaries can bring us as a society into a better understanding of one another, of reciprocal action, of human emotion, of home as something everyone is striving for. Trying to figure out who deserves it and who doesn't is like asking which birds should fly. Think of the little gray sparrow: "Either you can or you can't."

After several weeks of fieldwork, I was more comfortable in the shelter environment. The after-meal silences were soothing, and I learned to observe in the quiet moments when nothing seemed to be going on and I was invited to do things in conspiratorial whispers. It was on one of these days that a new, overly talkative man named Larry showed up bragging about the dusty rocks he had collected and continuing to make comments about how one rock was particularly "naked and sexy," looking at me lustily from the chair next to mine every time he said it. I listened for a while and found him annoying but not threatening. I got up to get some coffee and bread from the lunch leftovers. Russell, Donny, and Louie were all close by, so I left my bag and DAT recorder sitting on the chair next to Larry, and although I glanced back at it, I knew they were safe. Larry knew I was recording, as was evident from the remarks he made while I was gone, but I didn't hear that until later.

When I came back to sit down, Larry decided to "school me" on how to protect myself in the shelter setting, something I thought I had accomplished pretty well by then. He started off with, "What is your name, hon?" and then using it: "Michele, can I give you a bit of advice?" after which he told me to carry my things with me at all times. I told him that I had an eye on my things, but he kept persisting "No, no—no, you didn't—you had your back turned to us," to which I responded with a threat, telling him: "If you did take it, there are about three huge guys who'd" beat you down. So he backed off, wanting me to know he had no plans to take it: "I'm not saying me or anything." But, distancing himself from other homeless people who are not to be trusted, he continued, "I'm just giving you a word of advice," to which I responded, "No, I'm just giving *you* advice. I'm not as unprotected as I look." Being on the street was definitely affecting me.

My reaction to getting schooled by Larry is, perhaps overly aggressive, but being on the streets all day, annoyed and hungry and surrounded by misery makes it easier to "pop off" and do things you might regret. Things I often overlook in everyday life, like slapping or schooling, became harder to ignore, and I began to wonder why I should have to. Shutting Larry up felt good. But when I played back the tape from that day, I heard the conversation Larry had with his friend in my absence. He said, "I would never steal from another person," noting "she probably figured that out," but he still wanted to offer me some advice, still wanted to school me. And I realized that when you have to be on the defensive to survive, your sense of others and your relationship to them is shaped by immediate necessities over anything else. Because Larry was suggesting my vulnerability, I needed to put him down; to school *him* in what kind of a victim I would be, in case he thought I was easy prey.

If I could go back to that moment with Larry, I would have used it to talk to him about safety, to initiate a conversation about his trajectory with women or why he was so flirtatious. I would let him school me about life on the street. But the immediate need to protect myself, whether misplaced in that moment or not, overshadowed the overarching goals of fieldwork. I was beginning to understand this knee-jerk aspect of "the life." When all else fails, and usually if you're living on the street, it has, you focus on your physical self and safety above all else. But I was not used to reacting to people on this kind of visceral level; it was frightening and thrilling.

Although I felt badly about overreacting with Larry, if I had to go back to that moment with the club owner, I would slap him again. Managing sexual harassment and advances from all sides of the fence was one of the most difficult aspects of this work. The men in the shelter blew kisses at me constantly, calling me *güera* (white girl), "cookie," and many other things both complimentary and insulting, and asking if they could follow me home. Those in the homeless service industry asked me on dates or made passes at me, always mistaking me for an "intern" or "secretary." All of these advances and put-downs were more difficult to ignore than just schooling. In many cases, I pretended not to hear or understand the overt flirtation and innuendo directed toward me. Someone who needs to be schooled might not understand it anyway. But which is more offensive: the homeless men who hit on me or the lawyers and activists who thought they were somehow entitled to me? At least the former treated me well, like someone special, someone they still couldn't quite believe would spend time with them, someone they should defend and protect. The latter treated me like a subordinate, even when we held the same degree or when I outranked them, as if I owed them something, as if they were getting away with something, or hoped to, by spending time with me.

I understood later on that offering advice and protection are part of what some men on the street see as their role and that overt flirtation is a predictable aspect of the life. I gradually learned to manage attention and aggression in a more nuanced way, using gender as a window instead of a barrier; allowing shelter staff, clients, local politicians, homeless activists, and people on the street to instruct me on what they thought were appropriate ways of managing homelessness, and in many cases, inviting them to do so. I let people believe what they wanted to, in some cases, about my research. When police assumed, for example, that I was riding along with them because I wanted to become a police officer or because I agreed with their point of view, I was slow to reveal the truth. I let them, for the most part, feel like they were schooling me. It was a better way to draw out their expertise, motives, and opinions without imposing my own, although I did this too with people I was closer to, whom I grew to trust.

Knowing that gender is a status I cannot escape, making the best of it in the field means viewing it as both a barrier and a window. It is a barrier because it inhibits the people, places, and situations in which I can safely conduct research. Because of this, I never slept in the jungle. There were literally no women who did who were not prostitutes or girlfriends and/or the victims of physical and sexual violence. Violence against women is par for the jungle's course, and several women were raped or beaten there during the time of this research. As its name conjures, the jungle is a place beyond rules, structure, or order. It is tangled with addiction, mental illness, and the night and the train that threaten to close in. My gender was a window into what other women experience in jungle settings, how they are viewed and treated by their male counterparts, and how they manage relationships.

Love Letters from Jail

Donny is twenty-seven when I meet him, with a lengthy criminal record for burglary offenses. He had recently absconded from parole, meaning that now he is rarely in one place for long. I spend a lot of time with Donny, as he is forthcoming about his life, about jail and parole, and because we get along well. Because A—— is his girlfriend for most of this time, we all hang out together. I drive back and forth from the shelter to the travel trailer they are sleeping in and to visit various vehicles, jungles, and makeshift sleeping sites. On one of these rides, I must have left some movie rentals on the seat of my car. After returning from a short visit to the East Coast for the holidays, I stop in at the video store and find out that several movies have been charged to my account. They are movies such as *Hell Raiser* and *Bride of Chucky*, which my rental history confirms are not my cup of tea. I point that out to the clerk, but it is my East Coast plane ticket that proves these were not films I had rented—I wasn't there at that time. It had to be Donny.

I don't say anything to him until about a week later. I had arrived at the shelter and was at the front desk, just checking in and saying hello when Donny walked up. I leaned in close to him, making eye contact, and said, "Seen any good *movies* lately?" I felt him squirm and watched his face flush, and then I walked away before he could say anything. I didn't have to pay for the movies and was not angry, but I wanted him to know that I knew what he did. I wanted him to consider it a warning.

Donny was eventually rearrested on a parole violation and charged with giving a false name, absconding, and possession. His immediate removal from the street is traumatic for A——, who is six months pregnant. Although the baby is not Donny's, his support of A—— and his interest in her during this time are important for her self-esteem. She and I become closer in his absence, but her own criminal history and outstanding warrants make visiting him impossible. By contrast, my record is clean, so I visit Donny and put $10 on his books, and from March to May we send letters back and forth, from Wasco State Prison to my university address. I didn't realize what an impact this would have on Donny. In his first letter, he explains, "There isn't anything I wouldn't do for you now. I don't care what the problem is, even if you're right or wrong, I'll be there for you rain or shine, day or night." In his second letter, he tells me that he got a five-month sentence and will be out before his birthday. He also asks me to spend his first free night with him, an invitation I am not prepared for.

His invitation compromises my friendship with A——, as I don't want to hurt her by telling her about it. So, I stop writing to him. He continues to send me short letters and clippings from the newspaper that he thinks I might be interested in and a graffiti pencil drawing of my name, which he spent hours on. Eventually, he is transferred from jail to prison to serve the remainder of his term. His first letter from Wasco simply asks, "Are you mad at me?" because I did not visit him before his transfer. He also sends requests from friends on the inside, to contact their loved ones. I respond to his letter and his invitation to ask questions about prison. He tells me that he is "celled up" with someone of his race, as is common in prison. "High profile convicts are sent to the hole (administrative segregation)!" he explains. Donny is not high profile and describes the routines of prison life: "We get a chance to shower at least once every three days. We get a hot breakfast and dinner daily and we get a snack at lunch. We get to go to the yard twice a week and we get dayroom when they feel like giving it to us. But most of all, we stay in our cells." In all the time I had known him, Donny never stayed put.

In this letter, he also confesses that he has feelings for me. He writes, "You see I fell in love with you the very first time I saw you and I mean that. You see it's not just jail or prison talk. I really do mean it when I say I love you and I really do love you as a friend," and he asks again for pictures, which I never send. I receive two additional letters from Donny before his release, asking me to be there for him at the bus station, where A—— plans to be. I never tell her about his confessions, and he and I never talk about them face to face. For a few weeks after he gets out of prison, he talks about inheriting his grandmother's house and inviting A—— and me to live there rent free, a story that eventually dries up. After A—— has her baby, Donny is no longer interested in her. They split up and life goes on until Donny is locked up again.

I also receive letters from Russell and Brett, while they are in jail. Brett's is sad. He reaches out because I am one of the few people he knows who might write back. "My family gave up on me a long time ago," he tells me, "and I'm learning to deal with that." Brett scares me, and I don't write back to him. When I don't respond, he becomes violent and sends a letter telling me that he thinks I'm a bitch. Russell, Donny, and Brett all take my research interests personally and respond to them personally, which is hard to manage. Like Brett, Russell confesses, "It's been a long time since I've had anyone in my corner with any bit of sincere concern. I was touched and moved more than you even know." Later in the same letter, he confides, "From the moment I first met you, I held you in reverence." Then, he writes, in uncomfortable detail, that he is physically attracted to me too but that he doesn't want to lose my "friendship, loyalty, or solidarity." Again, this is awkward for me, as I've become closer to Judy in his absence, and I don't know what to tell her. I say nothing about Russell's confession, but the first time I see him after his release, I don't know what to do. He and Judy are standing outside of the shelter, waiting in line for beds when I walk up, and I immediately start talking with Judy, not sure what to say to Russell.

He stares at me, knowing what he wrote and enjoying my discomfort, and he leans over and taps me on the shoulder, wanting to play, and says, "You're not even going to say anything to me?" He is trying to be jovial, but I'm hating this moment, and I say, "I said hi, didn't I?" And he says, "Not really, huh? huh?" jumping around and looking like he wants to spar with me, to play-fight, but I'm not interested. Then he approaches me and I turn away, but he grabs me in a bear hug and lifts me off my feet. I hate this completely and I feel powerless. He eventually puts me down, but it's never the same again. Making sense of these advances, beyond the fact that they are physically intimidating, shows that men in the jungle have difficulty managing mixed contacts with women, and relationships in general. They have roles to play and allies on the street, but friends are often few and far between, and family ties vary from person to person. These letters emphasize how important personal connections become, in the absence of all else, and the changing, uneasy nature of relationships in the jungle.

Relating to Normal

In the 1991 film *The Fisher King*, Jeff Bridges plays radio DJ Jack Lucas, whose off-the-cuff remark on the air leads to a shooting. The victim is the wife of a professor at Hunter College. The professor is brilliantly played by Robin Williams, who becomes homeless and experiences mental illness as a result of witnessing her death. The two men meet and form an unlikely friendship, getting to know each other's friends and spending increasing amounts of time together. In a moment of comic relief, after a particularly dirty-looking homeless man greets him by name, Lucas says, "I can't believe I'm on a first-name basis with these people." I know the feeling. When you hang around with visibly homeless people, you can feel the stir they cause by the way you are also treated.

Police officers will stop you randomly, even when you aren't doing anything, and then ask, "Where do you live?" as if that alone is enough to stop you. They will yell at you on the street for things like jaywalking or riding a bicycle on the sidewalk. People in town will yell hostile things at you out of car windows, like "Get a job," or "You'll never afford it," if you stop to look at something expensive. This kind of treatment extends to friends and colleagues as well. When Moms took me out to lunch to thank me for helping her get a motel room in Oxnard, a school friend of mine walked past as we were eating. "I never thought you would do that," she told me later, looking at me with a mix of disgust and admiration. Still in graduate school during the early stages of this work, I withdrew from classes. The immediate life-and-death concerns of people on the street began to replace the world of normalcy I was used to, and I began to understand and resent its double-sidedness.

Feeling a sense of withdrawal from the mainstream is not only personal but social. It is the same sense of judgment homeless people face in the eyes of friends, family, and housed normals. You withdraw, and people, in turn, withdraw from you, and the effects are cumulative. Even in a one-week homeless simulation called "tent city" on a college campus, a student shared his paranoia about his appearance, wondering, "Are people staring at me?" and by the end of the week feeling the need to hide. If this is the effect of a mere simulation, what about the lived experience? At the end of this work, I have come to think it is the commonality of lived experience through which we can understand our similarity to people living in the jungle, and we can use this concept as a starting point to develop strategies for reintegration.

Notes

Chapter 1

1. I use various terms to refer to people experiencing homelessness. Using "homeless people" over "people experiencing homelessness" seems, in some cases, like too much of a compromise, as if this research reaffirms the idea that homelessness is an identity characteristic rather than the lack of a controlled, protected space. But the use of "homeless people" is merely simpler in text, particularly as some version of this phrase is used multiple times throughout this book, and other terminology is too wordy to repeat without taking away from the book's overall meaning.

In the same sense that my use of terminology varies with respect to "homeless," "homeless people," and "people experiencing homelessness," I also discuss the deserving/undeserving split in two ways. Traditionally, it refers to people seen as worthy or unworthy of assistance. The present usage also refers to people seen as deserving/undeserving of poverty itself. This varying usage is made clear through its interpretation in the text.

2. Research on Santa Barbara's Day Labor Line was funded by grants from The Fund for Santa Barbara in 2002, and the Institute for Labor and Employment in 2003. Both awards included stipends for participant experts from Santa Barbara's Day Labor Line to assist in translation and data collection for a longitudinal study of a small set of workers, including extended interviews with six workers. A portion of this data is examined in Wakin (2008). This is an important aspect of this work, as approximately 45 percent of Santa Barbara's population is Hispanic/Latino (www.census.gov) and is overrepresented in the unsheltered homeless population since 2015, the first year these demographics were reported in the annual point-in-time count.

3. James Eads How, known as the "millionaire hobo," organizes the International Brotherhood Welfare Association (IBWA) along principles similar to those of the Industrial Workers of the World, in that both organizations

view hoboes as having the potential to liberate society from the bonds of capitalism (DePastino 2003). They diverge because of their differing means of achieving these goals, as IBWA uses education and respite as the cornerstones of its philosophy. Hobo Colleges offer meeting places for men to cluster in the winter months and classes on topics of interest or that would instruct or train hoboes for gainful employment. Aside from federal funding for K–12 students through McKinney-Vento, there are very few efforts to use education as a tool for transformation, particularly for unsheltered homeless adults. This is despite the overwhelming evidence that training and education offer pathways not only to employment but to self-respect and reintegration into group life and community settings.

4. Female hoboes hold a special place in the literature on hoboing, as they are fewer in number and are understood in the context of both mainstream hobo culture and mainstream culture in general, both of which view women's independence, employment, and sexuality as dangerous and threatening (Manne 2018). Women are read through a binary lens that sees them either as housewives offering handouts or prostitutes offering sexual favors (Hall 2010) or as people from whom these things can be taken. Traveling women are typically placed in one of these two categories. Although the reality of poor women who travel is far more complex and varied, stereotypical images popularized in literature (Reitman 2002) and film (for example, Scorsese's *Boxcar Bertha* from 1972) suggest a more limited, sensationalized view of the reasons for and conditions of life on the road.

Other accounts (Starke 1931; Uys 1999) are less lurid, offering more detail on survival and employment for female hoboes, showing that women on the road traveled together or in disguise to avoid unwanted attention, that they were protected and provided for, and that they had good, wholesome adventures on the road, in addition to the more popular horror stories. The strategies that homeless women develop to stay safe and gain needed resources are the subject of several accounts summarized in Hall (2010). Wardhaugh's (1999) ethnographic study of homeless women also eloquently describes the dual notion of home as respite and home as prison, an irony reflected in the experiences of young women on the road, and a primary reason for homelessness then and now.

5. In *The Hobo: The Sociology of the Homeless Man* (1923, 89), Anderson describes five types of homeless men: seasonal workers, occasional workers or hoboes, the tramp who "dreams and wanders" and works only when it is convenient, the bum who seldom wanders or works, and the home guard, who lives in hobohemia year round. This is a more complex version of the original and often-cited quote by Ben Reitman, who wrote "the hobo works and wanders, the tramp dreams and wanders and the bum drinks and wanders" (Anderson 1923). In reality, many hoboes worked, dreamed, drank, and wandered. Perhaps these categories are tied to determining whether or not hoboes should be seen as productive or nonproductive, deserving or undeserving, good or bad. Or perhaps they show the penchant for order and categorization that characterizes the work of the early Chicago School with which both Reitman and Anderson were affiliated (Geis 2008). Although these categories order hoboes into groups based on

behavior and mobility, they don't capture the experience of life in the jungle as much as Anderson's later work does.

In a book referred to as a handbook for hoboes (1930), Anderson, writing as hobo Dean Stiff, describes the rules and etiquette of the jungle over the main stem as its primary, distinguishing features. This is an important distinction, as there is very little written on life in the jungle itself. He writes: "This is the law of the jungle. On the main stem the hobo is an individualist and a law unto himself, but in the jungle he must be a social animal" (Anderson 1930, 21). It is the rules of the jungle and how they are enacted in practice, among one's fellows, that captures jungle life and distinguishes it from the hustle and bustle of the main stem. For this reason, categories of experience over identity better capture jungle living, relationships among the men, and how they develop and sustain their makeshift lifestyle.

6. The experience of black hoboes is given far less attention than white and immigrant hoboes in the early 1900s because of the everyday, taken-for-granted nature of racial discrimination. Particularly in the South, the threat of violence prevents black hoboes from traveling freely, a privilege other hoboes enjoy with abandon. When they do find work, it is often in the most menial, dangerous conditions and for the lowest pay. Black hoboing overlaps with the Great Migration, in which 6 million African Americans moved from the rural South to northern cities and to western states, including California (Wilkerson 2011). With racial violence and discrimination as "push" factors, black hoboes had to be particularly careful on the road, which they used as a place of last resort. Their experiences of threat, want, and fear, along with the search for employment, the conditions of employment, and life in the jungles and on the road, gave rise to poetry and music, particularly the blues tradition. Garon and Tomko (2006) provide an important exploration of the development of blues music as directly informed by these aspects of hobo life for black men in the early 1900s.

7. The sense of fear and threat that men feel in this era is embodied in film noir, a genre known for its portrayal of a male protagonist at risk. Shot in dark, threatening urban environments, often in black and white even though color was available, films in this era depict men feeling adrift in corporate America, not knowing whom to trust (Copjec 1993) and fearing both internal and external threat. They also show the drudgery of marriage and wage labor as something men do but which makes them miserable. Women in film noir are an overly stylized combination of desire and danger—black widows who lure their victims or drab and boring housewives and mothers. We see this wartime image of insecurity and instability replaced with the embrace of suburban ideals both on television and in film in the 1950s (Haskell 1973). Wives and mothers become a bit less drab, a bit happier to be housewives, with a multitude of appliances and kitchen gadgetry to distract them, and men become responsible workers, heads of the household who sacrifice for the good of the team and are revered for it.

8. Comparing census data from the general population with the Annual Homeless Assessment Report (AHAR) for 2009–2010 shows that African Americans are overrepresented in the homeless population. The AHAR, unfortunately, does not provide a demographic breakdown of the unsheltered

homeless population in 2010 because of the difficulty of collecting this information on the single night of the count and because of a lack of resources to support this effort. Instead, numbers of sheltered homeless people and demographics are recorded through the Homeless Management Information System (HMIS), a feature of most shelter intake. The 2010 AHAR reports a 2.8 percent increase in unsheltered homelessness from 2009 to 2010 and estimates that 40 percent of individual homeless people are unsheltered.

AHAR Table 1 2009–2010 Annual Homeless Assessment Report to Congress

2009–2010 Estimates	Percentage of Sheltered Population	Percentage of Total US Population
White	41.60	64.90
Black/African American	37.00	22.00

The most recent AHAR, from 2017, shows that although white people (47 percent) are slightly more prevalent than African American people (41 percent), Latinos (22 percent), or people identifying as multiracial (7 percent), when compared with the general population, white people are underrepresented and black/African American people are overrepresented.

AHAR Table 2 2017 Annual Homeless Assessment Report to Congress

2017 AHAR Census Estimates	Percentage of People in Unsheltered Locations	Percentage of All Homeless People	Percentage of Total US Population
White	55	47	76.6
Black/African American	30	41	13.4

9. Detailed descriptions of hobohemia can be found in the Bughouse Square Series by Charles H. Kerr Publishers and in Beck (1956). *Bughouse* is a slang term for a mental institution, and Bughouse Square is the popular name for Chicago's Washington Square Park, where soapbox orators came to argue and uphold the ideals of free expression throughout the 1920s and 1930s, when it was at its most popular point. Although not all

of skid row was quite so inviting to outsiders, the Bughouse Square area was one of the few places where people of different social classes used to meet and share ideas, if not openly at least on a more level playing field. Detailed in academic and popular literature, a well-worn gimmick of the time was for a man to head to the soapbox and shout, "I've been robbed!" and once he drew a crowd, he would add, "I've been robbed by the capitalist system" (DePastino 2003). Leftist politics, revolutionary leanings, and the Industrial Workers of the World all found a safe haven in Bughouse Square, and because of its proximity to the rest of the city, bohemian normals could visit for adventure.

10. For a summary of narrative films on homelessness from 1980 to 2002 and a comprehensive list of publications on homelessness, scholarly and otherwise, see Levinson (2004).

11. Produced by Indecline Films, four *Bumfights* videos were released from 2002 to 2004, until felony and misdemeanor charges were filed against the filmmakers in the state of California. In the videos, filmmakers pay homeless men to beat each other or harm themselves while drunk, even supplying the alcohol. Protests against the dehumanizing, degrading aspects of these films led to their banning in several countries, and the National Coalition for the Homeless criticized them for fostering hate against homeless people.

12. Musician Tom Waits appears in the film *The Fisher King* (1991) as a disabled homeless person asking for change inside one of the entrances to New York City's Grand Central Station. In one scene, he is in his wheelchair panhandling during rush hour, and a man in the passing crowd tosses a quarter at him without looking and it lands on the floor. He strains to get it and when one of his friends criticizes the man for throwing the coin at him, Waits says, "It's okay. He's paying so he don't have to look." Then Waits describes a worker he calls Bob, who has a boss who demands his subservience. In the voice of Bob, he imagines what it would be like to assault his boss, "to see the look on his face when I jam this pair of scissors into his arm." But Bob thinks twice, puts the scissors down, and says, "Wait a minute. I got both my arms, both my legs, at least I'm not beggin' for a living." And then Bob does exactly what his boss wants. Explaining this in the context of himself, Waits says, "I'm what you call a moral traffic light, really. It's like I'm saying, '*Red*—go no further,'" suggesting that the fear of becoming homeless keeps the rest of us in line, kowtowing to bosses, fitting into traditional domestic and social routines, suppressing our true feelings and selves in favor of adhering to societal conventions and their incipient rewards.

13. In the state of California in 2017, 65 percent of the overall homeless population was unsheltered. Eighty-two percent of people in homeless families were sheltered, but 78 percent of homeless individuals remained unsheltered and the vast majority were men. Although there has been some attempt to separate homeless people by the subpopulations that HUD has identified (chronically homeless, severely mentally ill, chronic substance abusers, persons with HIV/AIDS, victims of domestic violence, unaccompanied youth [under eighteen]), disorganized, underfunded, and inconsistent count methodology means that the numbers are often inaccurate.

Figure A.1 HUD Count Selected California Homeless Population Change, 2005–2017

As the point-in-time (PIT) counts from Santa Barbara show, drastic fluctuations in count methodology make it look as if the number of unsheltered homeless people drops by about 2,000 from 2010 to 2011. Similarly, when looking at fluctuations in the number of unsheltered homeless people in six comparison counties across the state, there are similar dramatic changes. San Luis Obispo, for example, saw an increase of about 3,000 people from 2008 to 2009, and Sonoma saw a similar increase from 2008 to 2011. These changes are reflective of a shifting count methodology rather than programmatic or policy changes or actual changes in population.

Chapter 2

1. From the mid-1800s to the late 1970s, the East Beach area was known for a diversity of uses, with about 15 percent of the land sitting vacant. The remaining land was used for commercial and industrial purposes and as public recreation land (Kahn 1982, 98–99) with very little residential property. The East Beach neighborhood is divided into three distinct neighborhoods: the fishermen's neighborhood, the estate area, and the inland East Beach/lower east side area. The jungle is in the center of the waterfront's most opulent and coveted land in the estate neighborhood, making its existence that much more controversial (Kahn 1982). This is the part of the same area that will earn the nickname the Golden Triangle in the 2000s.

2. Between 1920 and 1930, $2,301,000 was spent on projects and properties designed to preserve the natural beauty of the Santa Barbara Waterfront. A tragic earthquake in 1925 offered an opportunity to rebuild Santa Barbara in a romantic, Spanish Colonial style supported by some of its main proponents. Wealthy citizens, including business owners Max Fleischmann, Thomas Storke, noted conservationist Pearl Chase, Andrée Clark, Lillian

Child, and Dwight Murphy, were largely responsible for the combination of natural beauty and peaceful luxury still maintained in Santa Barbara's waterfront today (Bookspan 1982; Hartfield 2007).

3. The rules that Child imposed have several versions. The one cited in this text is from the Bookman's diary. The reference to "negroes" in this version does not appear in any of the official publications, which cite the rules as: "1) No intoxicating liquor to be consumed on the premises; 2) No loud noise or rough stuff at any time, day or night; and 3) The area must be kept neat and sanitary at all times" (Tomkins, *West Santa Barbara News Press,* March 21, 1971). Other accounts suggest that Child wanted the residents limited to men over thirty-five.

4. Child's generosity was well known, perhaps too well known. One report describes a Christmas when more than 100 men showed up in hopes of receiving a fifty-cent piece. Child showed up in the jungle, saw the crowd of men, and went back to her mansion. When the men had dispersed, she returned to pass out the money to the men she already knew.

5. The jungle is listed as one of several locations of interest in a tourist pamphlet from 1953, announcing that "Childs City," along with the wharf, breakwater, courthouse, botanical gardens, El Paseo, El Presidio, and the Old Mission, would be visited, followed by a picnic at Oak Park. It was also written about in the *Los Angeles Times*, local newspapers (the *Santa Barbara Independent* and *Santa Barbara News Press*), and *Stars and Stripes* as an odd but quaint tourist attraction.

6. It is worth noting that from many of the balconies of the Mar Monte, the jungle was only visible using binoculars or "field glasses" and that it was the sight of the men engaged in domestic chores that proved most objectionable.

7. Before her death in 1951, Lillian Child deeded the land to the Santa Barbara Foundation, with the stipulation that she be allowed to retain lifetime residence on the property and that after her death it be developed into a city park. Although her desire to protect the men and insure their lifetime residence on the property was well documented during her lifetime, it was never included in her will, making the jungle's future uncertain.

8. The Bookman's notes include brief definitions of terms common in the jungle and forty-nine names that the men in the jungle are known by. The nicknames include:

Whiskers, Handsome Harry, Cockney Al, Highclimber, Wino Art, The Astrologer, Chicken Henry, The Mayor, Crippled Joe, Pancho Villa, The Poet, Galloping Swede, Deafy, Oklahoma Scissorbill, Soldier Shorty, The Cowboy, Leo the Guzzler, Dirty-Shirt Al, The Vulture, Hoosegow Paddy, Squinty, Thunder-Mug Jimmie, Shoemaker Scotty, Long and Short Brown, The Dutchman, Pop, The Weasel, The Frenchman, The Cricket, Gabby Louie, Tam-o-shanter, Old Toothless, Indian Joe, Slue-Foot Louie, Open Roof Andy, One-Eyed Chappie, The Midget, Barber Jim, The Bookman, Marble George, Lompoc Eddie, The Midget, Barber Ed, One-eyed Frank, Baldy, Scotty the Bum, Top of the Morning Pat, Fish Face Fred, The New York Junker.

Part of what characterizes the culture of the jungle is that men take on new, anonymous selves in which given names are less important than observable characteristics, habits, national origins, or other details that men use to rename one another. This underscores the different and marginal nature of the community in the jungle.

9. All of the quotes in this chapter that are attributed to the Bookman and Edward Anderson are directly excerpted from the series of notes and letters that are included in the archives of the Santa Barbara Historical Museum, Gledhill Library (Folder 4, "Child Estate"). Any errors in grammar are left entirely as written, to preserve their unique voices as writers and the colloquialisms of the time period in which they were writing.

10. In 1956, police officer Noah E. (Stormy) Cloud was chosen as Young Man of the Year by Santa Barbara's 20–30 Club for his work organizing the Cavaliers to assist in constructing the utility building for the men of the jungle (*Santa Barbara News Press,* January 17, 1956). His willingness to take on this project and defend the men of the jungle lent an air of legitimacy to an otherwise controversial project. Nevertheless, the majority of the donations that came in were left anonymous.

11. Buildings from the hobo jungle are reported to have existed, vacant and decomposing on unused land, until the mid-1970s. The original utility building constructed in the 1950s remains on zoo property with a plaque dedicating it to the memory of Lillian Child.

Chapter 3

1. Women, and particularly women with children, are seen as victims of homelessness, an "undeserving" segment of the population, who face more danger if left on the street. Services and shelters are therefore more readily available to women and families. It is also common for women to be offered protection and shelter by men they are romantically involved with, despite the fact that these relationships are often exploitative and abusive (http://vawnet.org/material/no-safe-place-sexual-assault-lives-homeless-women). As Underwood starkly notes, "all women on the street live under the dark shadow of physical abuse, assault, and rape" (1993, 207).

In Santa Barbara, at the same time that the Homeless People's Alliance (HPA) formed, so did the Single Parent Alliance (SPA), composed primarily of women and children living in vehicles, doubled up, and in other makeshift housing. The SPA, with its more sober and articulate membership than the HPA, and its greater sympathy for women and children overall, inspired the city's first shelter for homeless families, Transition House, which opened in 1984 and remains open today in 2020. It evolved from a rotating set of church basements and public buildings to several emergency and transitional housing locations to a licensed child-care facility, opened in 2012. Of course, along with a better space, the rules and requirements are also greater, as is the surveillance of families. The result is the loss of parental authority that comes with answering to staff over parents in family shelters (Crowley 2003).

2. There is one tragic case of a child dying in the shelter in the 1980s. Nicknamed "the littlest hobo," infant Joshua Flowers was camping in front of City Hall with his parents and living in a combination of makeshift loca-

tions including the jungle, until he died of sudden infant death syndrome at four months old. Prior to his death, the child protective services agency was called twice, and although he was determined to be healthy, he was taken away from his parents. Only when they agreed to move into a religious-run family shelter, the early version of Transition House, were they reunited, before tragedy struck. In a newspaper report, the couple says they wish they had not moved around so much and endured such instability.

3. A video of James's marriage is available online, along with commentary on homelessness in Santa Barbara in the 1980s (https://www.youtube.com/watch?v=whx6cNLEx-Q; https://www.youtube.com/watch?v=mXpPKEdwd0o).

4. When I conduct an extended interview with Edwin, he describes being attacked by two young men while sleeping at the Fig Tree. He was severely beaten during the attack and although he managed to stumble onto State Street, he had trouble convincing a local merchant to call the hospital. When he arrived there, he realized that both of his arms had been broken.

5. The West Beach Merchant's Association attempted to make life more difficult for homeless people by urging the city to pass ordinances criminalizing dumpster diving and regulating food programs like the one led by Westmont College (*Santa Barbara News Press*, August 14, 1988). They also fenced in the area around the Fig Tree, hoping that this would deter homeless people from spending time there.

6. See http://www.nationalhomeless.org/projects/vote/court.html for an overview of legal decisions on voting rights.

7. See Irvine (2016) on the importance of dogs in homeless people's lives.

Chapter 4

1. By 2002, the shelter expanded to include a thirty-bed transitional shelter, open from April 1 to November 30. The emergency shelter is open during the interim, meaning that people who do not fit into the transitional program sleep outside or for ten nights per month at the Rescue Mission. All participants in the transitional program must receive income from employment or federal forms of assistance and must pay a portion of this amount to remain.

2. Despite the fact that this is a hidden population, there is definitely something larger than life about the trials of homeless people in Santa Barbara. Perhaps being so close to Hollywood, to the opulence of Montecito, home of Oprah, and to the impossible dreams brought to life on the South Coast makes everything a little larger than life. One evening, James and Hopper decide to light a fire on the beach and barbecue a tri-tip cut of beef. Hopper leaves to buy beer and when he returns, a helicopter follows him all the way back, with a spotlight trained on him the whole way. The incident made the local newspaper and James and Hopper bragged about it for weeks.

3. The artworks made by homeless people in The People's Institute were made into a calendar with captions highlighting the haunting nature of the photographs, drawings, and paintings, taken while paradise is sleeping, capturing its lonelier, moodier side. This is in contrast with the palm trees and blazing sun in tourist calendars.

4. One day, Ricky and Edwin show me a collection of sleeping and camping tickets that Edwin jokingly tells me they are saving to make wallpaper. Most of the tickets are for having an open container, and several are for sleeping and camping violations. Both men have between five and seven tickets, issued during a ten-day window, meaning significant legal complications and outstanding warrants for nonpayment. Repeat ticketing is par for the course for chronically homeless people living in the jungle. In testimony to this, the local paper estimates that James Magruder, longtime homeless "street person," was arrested 848 times since 1982, mostly for public intoxication (*Santa Barbara Independent*, February 2, 2006).

5. There are three insights to be gained from the 1926 novel *You Can't Win* by "burglar and hobo" Jack Black that are relevant to the story of Russell: (1) Time in prison, particularly hard time, can leave inmates more hostile and more damaged than when they entered; (2) if you go around asking questions, you often get misinformation; and (3) adhering to the code of the underworld makes it that much more difficult to reintegrate. To illustrate the last point, Black says, "The more strictly a criminal adheres to the underworld code, the greater will be his handicap if, and when, he decides to mend his ways" (1926, 310). This shows how the skills one learns to survive on the streets or in prison affect one's ability to handle mixed contacts.

6. The types of work men are hired for includes moving, cleaning, gardening, construction, painting, and digging. It is physically grueling work, and those who are small in stature, older, sick, or injured, or otherwise not in tiptop shape often lose out (Wakin 2008, 430). Without access to benefits or health insurance of any kind, physical strength remains a key feature of surviving life in the jungle for men at the labor line.

7. I was invited to the police station several times to discuss how the police might address the concerns of business owners in the shelter neighborhood. I was a member of the police review board for several months of this work and also made several presentations on the recently developed program to provide safe parking for people living in their vehicles. During one of our meetings at the police station, I watched as an officer returned from issuing citations at the labor line. "I got five more," he triumphantly told his sergeant, giving him a raucous high five, without any discussion of the circumstances of the citations.

Chapter 5

1. My brief literary reference in the title of this section—"Paradise Revisited"—offers a useful metaphor for understanding how we treat homeless people in US society. In the epic poem *Paradise Lost,* Milton (1968) describes paradise as the Garden of Eden, and it is lost when Eve is tempted by Satan into eating an apple that would give her the one thing she does not have: knowledge. Although it is Eve's original sin that is to blame in this narrative, Adam also succumbs, tastes the fruit, and is subject to

God's punishment, which is destruction. Because they do not stay in their place, behave in allowable ways, accept limits and constraints in childlike dependence, Adam and Eve are punished with death, and God repents having made them (p. 107). This is similar to the way homeless people are treated in their own paradise, as if their very poverty is a scourge on humanity, and ridding the world of them, particularly the commercial world that makes us feel untouchable, and even omnipotent, is the overall goal. Those who will not humble themselves and who cannot be wiped out entirely shall be confined to a hell of our making and shall remain trapped in its confinement, going around and around, until eventually they go down.

2. For a glimpse at Hopper's "crew," see: https://www.youtube.com/watch?v=mXpPKEdwd0o.

3. When I return to Sonoma County in 2008, their veteran's outreach program has really taken off. I attend a meeting in a local park and see about twenty men clustering around a barbecue pit, talking and laughing as if it is a family party. When I ask the person in charge of street outreach to veterans, "How did you get such a good turnout?" he responds, "One of the things I found is not to push anybody to talk about anything when you first meet 'em . . . it's all by word of mouth, having other vets say you're an okay person. You have to just be patient, keep going to the drop-in sites—the shelters—and it gets around by word of mouth." There is also preference, as veterans are prioritized for both available and designated beds. Of course, by 2010, ending veteran homelessness had become an explicit goal of the Obama administration. Although not fully achieved, the influx of HUD-VASH vouchers offers a partnership between HUD and the VA that offers both housing and supportive services to the tune of 90,000 vouchers and $635 million expended (Associated Press, January 5, 2017).

4. A representative payee is someone designated by a beneficiary of Social Security and appointed by the Social Security Administration. People who need representative payees are those deemed incapable of managing their money because of prior felony convictions, mental illness, or other stipulations. When a beneficiary receives supplemental security income, the payee sets up a custodial account and receives and disburses the funds and assists the beneficiary in managing the money.

5. In 2018, the Committee for Social Justice filed a lawsuit on behalf of several RV plaintiffs, claiming that the City of Santa Barbara was in violation of the Americans with Disabilities Act in its pursuit of RVs and disregard for the rights that DMV disability placards afford.

References

Amster, R. 2008. *Lost in Space: The Criminalization, Globalization, and Urban Ecology of Homelessness.* New York: LFB Scholarly Publishing.

Anderson, E. 1999. *Code of the Street: Decency, Violence, and the Moral Life of the Inner City.* New York: W. W. Norton.

———. 2011. *The Cosmopolitan Canopy: Race and Civility in Everyday Life.* New York: W. W. Norton.

———. 2012. "Toward Knowing the Iconic Ghetto." In *The Ghetto: Contemporary Global Issues and Controversies,* ed. R. Hutchison and B. Haynes, pp. 67–82. Boulder: Westview Press.

Anderson, N. 1923. *The Hobo: The Sociology of the Homeless Man.* Chicago: University of Chicago Press.

——— (as Dean Stiff). 1930. *The Milk and Honey Route: A Handbook for Hobos.* New York: Vanguard Press.

Anderson, N. 1940. *Men on the Move.* Chicago: University of Chicago Press.

Arnold, K. 2004. *Homelessness, Citizenship, and Identity: The Uncanniness of Late Modernity.* Albany: State University of New York Press.

Bahr, H. 1973. *Skid Row: An Introduction to Disaffiliation.* New York: Oxford University Press.

Bahr, H., and T. Caplow. 1973. *Old Men Drunk and Sober.* New York: New York University Press.

Baumohl, J. 1996. *Homelessness in America.* Phoenix, AZ: Oryx Press.

Baxter, E., and K. Hopper. 1981. *Private Lives/Public Spaces: Homeless Adults on the Streets of New York City.* New York: Community Service Society.

Beck, F. O. 1956. *Hobohemia.* New Hampshire: Richard R. Smith Publisher, Inc.

Berger, P., B. Berger, and H. Kellner. 1973. *The Homeless Mind: Modernization and Consciousness.* New York: Vintage Books.

205

Black, J. 1926. *You Can't Win.* New York: Macmillan.
Blakely, E. J., and M. G. Snyder. 1997. *Fortress America: Gated Communities in the United States.* Washington, DC: Brookings Institution Press.
Blumer, H. 1969. *Symbolic Interactionism: Perspective and Method.* Englewood Cliffs, NJ: Prentice-Hall.
Bogue, D. J. 1963. *Skid Row in American Cities.* Chicago: Community and Family Study Center, University of Chicago.
Bookspan, Rochelle, ed. 1982. *Santa Barbara by the Sea.* Santa Barbara, CA: McNally and Loftin, West.
Boothe, D. 2007. *Why Are So Many Black Men in Prison? A Comprehensive Account of How and Why the Prison Industry Has Become a Predatory Entity in the Lives of African-American Men.* Memphis, TN: Full Surface Publishing.
Borchard, K. 2005. *The Word on the Street: Homeless Men in Las Vegas.* Reno: University of Nevada Press.
———. 2010. "Between Poverty and a Lifestyle: The Leisure Activities of Homeless People in Las Vegas." *Journal of Contemporary Ethnography* 39 (4): 441–466.
Brundage, S. 1997. *From Bughouse Square to the Beat Generation.* Chicago: Charles H. Kerr Publishing.
Bruns, R. A. 1980. *Knights of the Road: A Hobo History.* New York: Methuen.
Burgess, E. 1925. "The Growth of the City: An Introduction to a Research Project." In *Urban Ecology* 18, ed. J. M. Marzluff et al., pp. 85–97. Publication of the American Sociological Society.
Burgess, E., and D. Bogue. 1964. "Research in Urban Society: A Long View." In *Contributions to Urban Sociology,* ed. E. Burgess and D. Bogue, pp. 1–14. Chicago: University of Chicago Press.
Burt, M. 1991. "Causes of the Growth of Homelessness in the 1980s." *Housing Policy Debate* 2 (3): 901–936.
———. 1992. *Over the Edge: The Growth of Homelessness in the 1980s.* New York: Russell Sage Foundation.
———. 2016. "Three Decades of Homelessness." In *Ending Homelessness: Why We Haven't, How We Can,* ed. D. Burnes and D. DiLeo, pp. 47–66. Boulder: Lynne Rienner Publishers.
Caplow, T. 1940. "Transiency as a Cultural Pattern." *American Sociological Review* 5 (5): 731–739.
Carr, L. 1994. "The Can't Move–Must Move Contradiction: A Case Study of Displacement of the Poor and Social Stress." *Journal of Social Distress and the Homeless* 3 (2): 185–201.
Chambliss, W. 1964. "A Sociological Analysis of the Law of Vagrancy." *Social Problems* 12 (1): 67–77.
Conard, R. 1982. "From Private Philanthropy to Public Resort: Waterfront Tourism and Recreation, 1920s to the Present." In *Santa Barbara by the Sea,* ed. R. Bookspan, pp. 185–213. Santa Barbara, CA: McNally and Loftin, West.
Conrad , J. 1899. *Heart of Darkness.* New York: Global Classics.
Copjec, J. 1993. *Shades of Noir.* New York: Verso.

Cress, D. M., and D. A. Snow. 1996. "Mobilization at the Margins: Resources, Benefactors, and the Viability of Homeless Social Movement Organizations." *American Sociological Review* 61: 1089–1109.

Cresswell, T. 2001. *The Tramp in America.* London: Reaktion Books.

———. 2006. *On the Move: Mobility in the Modern Western World.* New York: Routledge.

Crowley, S. 2003. "The Affordable Housing Crisis: Residential Mobility of Poor Families and School Mobility of Poor Children." *Journal of Negro Education* 72 (1): 22–38.

Culhane, D., J. M. Park, and S. Metraux. 2011. "The Patterns and Costs of Services Use Among Homeless Families." *Journal of Community Psychology* 39 (7): 815–825.

Danielson, C., and J. A. Klerman. 2008. "Did Welfare Reform Cause the Caseload Decline?" *Social Service Review* 82 (4): 703–730.

Davenport, C. 1915. *The Feebly Inhibited: Nomadism, or the Wandering Impulse, with Special Reference to Heredity.* Washington, DC: Carnegie Institution of Washington.

Davis, M. 1990. *City of Quartz: Excavating the Future in Los Angeles.* London: Verso.

Dear, M., and J. Wolch. 1987. *Landscapes of Despair.* Princeton, NJ: Princeton University Press.

Dehavenon, A. L., ed. 1996. *There's No Place Like Home: Anthropological Perspectives on Housing and Homelessness in the United States.* Westport, CT: Bergin and Garvey.

DePastino, T. 2003. *Citizen Hobo: How a Century of Homelessness Shaped America.* Chicago: University of Chicago Press.

DeVerteuil, G. 2003. "Homeless Mobility, Institutional Settings, and the New Poverty Management." *Environment and Planning* 35: 361–379.

DiFazio, W. 2006. *Ordinary Poverty: A Little Food and Cold Storage.* Philadelphia: Temple University Press.

Donley, A., and J. Wright. 2012. "Safer Outside: A Qualitative Exploration of Homeless People's Resistance to Homeless Shelters." *Journal of Forensic Psychology Practice* 12: 288–306.

Dordick, G. 1997. *Something Left to Lose: Personal Relations and Survival Among New York's Homeless.* Philadelphia: Temple University Press.

Duneier, M. 2000. *Sidewalk.* New York: Farrar, Straus and Giroux.

Ehrenreich, B. 2001. *Nickel and Dimed: On Not Getting By in America.* New York: Henry Holt.

Ellickson, R. 2001. "Controlling Chronic Misconduct in City Spaces: Of Panhandlers, Skid Rows, and Public-Space Zoning." In *The Legal Geographies Reader,* ed. N. Blomley, D. Delaney, and R. T. Ford, pp. 19–30. Oxford: Blackwell.

Feldman, L. 2004. *Citizens Without Shelter.* Ithaca: Cornell University Press.

Fisk, D. M. 2003. "American Labor in the Twentieth Century." Washington, DC: Bureau of Labor Statistics.

Flynt, J. 1972 [1899]. *Tramping with Tramps: Studies and Sketches of Vagabond Life.* Patterson, NJ: Smith Publishing.

Foote Whyte, W., D. Greenwood, and P. Lazes. 1991. "Participatory Action Research." In *Participatory Action Research,* ed. W. Foote Whyte, pp. 19–55. London: Sage Publications.

Gabbard, W., C. Snyder, M. Lin, J. Chadha, J. D. May, and J. Jaggers. 2007. "Methodological Issues in Enumerating Homeless Individuals." *Journal of Social Distress and the Homeless* 16 (2): 90–103.

Garon, P., and G. Tomko. 2006. *What's the Use of Walking if There's a Freight Train Going Your Way? Black Hoboes and Their Songs.* Chicago: Charles H. Kerr Publishing.

Geis, G. 2008. "Ben L. Reitman, MD: Colorful Critical Criminologist." *Contemporary Justice Review* 11 (3): 271–285.

Goffman, A. 2014. *On the Run: Fugitive Life in an American City.* New York: Picador.

Goffman, E. 1959. *The Presentation of Self in Everyday Life.* New York: Doubleday.

———. 1963. *Stigma: Notes on the Management of a Spoiled Identity.* New York: Simon and Schuster.

Gomez, R., and T. Ryan. 2016. "Speaking Out: Youth Led Research as a Methodology Used with Homeless Youth." *Child Adolescent Social Work Journal* 33: 185–193.

Goodman, L. A., K. Fels, C. Glenn, and J. Benitez. 2006. "No Safe Place: Sexual Assault in the Lives of Homeless Women." *VAWnet: The National Online Resource Center on Violence Against Women.* https://vawnet .org/material/no-safe-place-sexual-assault-lives-homeless-women.

Gould-Wartofsky, M. A. 2015. *The Occupiers: The Making of the 99 Percent Movement.* Oxford: Oxford University Press.

Gowan, T. 2010. *Hobos, Hustlers, and Backsliders: Homeless in San Francisco.* Minneapolis: University of Minnesota Press.

Gravelle, R. 2015. *Hooverville and the Unemployed: Seattle During the Great Depression.* Self-published.

Gregory, C. 1974. *Women in Defense Work During World War II: An Analysis of the Labor Problem and Women's Rights.* New York: Exposition Press.

Gregory, J. N. 1989. *American Exodus: The Dust Bowl Migration and Okie Culture in California.* New York: Oxford University Press.

Grigsby, C., D. Baumann, S. E. Gregorich, and C. Roberts-Gray. 1990. "Disaffiliation to Entrenchment: A Model for Understanding Homelessness." *Journal of Social Issues* 46 (4): 141–156.

Haggstrom, J. 1994. "The Santa Barbara Sleeping Law Controversy: A Study of the Empowerment of the Homeless." PhD diss., University of California, Santa Barbara.

Hall, J. 2010. "Sisters of the Road?: The Construction of Female Hobo Identity in the Autobiographies of Ethel Lynn, Barbara Starke, and 'Box-Car' Bertha Thompson." *Women's Studies* 39: 215-237.

Hartfield, E. A. 2007. *California's Knight on a Golden Horse: Dwight Murphy, Santa Barbara's Renaissance Man.* Santa Barbara, CA: Studio E. Books.

Harvey, D. 1989. *The Urban Experience.* Baltimore: Johns Hopkins University Press.

Haskell, M. 1973. *From Reverence to Rape: The Treatment of Women in the Movies.* Chicago: University of Chicago Press.

Heben, A. 2014. *Tent City Urbanism: From Self-Organized Camps to Tiny House Villages.* Eugene, OR: The Village Collaborative.

Herring, C. 2014. "The New Logics of Homeless Seclusion: Homeless Encampments in America's West Coast Cities." *City and Community* 13 (4): 285–309.

Herring, C., and M. Lutz. 2015. "The Roots and Implications of the United States' Homeless Tent Cities." *City: Analysis of Urban Trends, Culture, Theory, Policy, Action* 19 (5): 689–701.

Higbie, F. T. 2003. *Indispensable Outcasts: Hobo Workers and Community in the American Midwest, 1880–1930.* Chicago: University of Illinois Press.

Hoch, C., and R. Slayton. 1989. *New Homelessness and Old.* Philadelphia: Temple University Press.

Hopper, K., E. Susser, and S. Conover. 1985. "Economies of Makeshift: Deindustrialization and Homelessness in New York City." *Urban Anthropology* 14 (1–3): 183–236.

Hudson, C. G. 2015. "Churning in the Human Services: Nefarious Practice or Policy of 'Creative Destruction'?" *New England Journal of Public Policy* 27 (1): 1–11.

Humphries, B., D. M. Mertens, and C. Truman. 2000. "Arguments for an Emancipatory Research Paradigm." In *Research and Inequality,* ed. C. Truman, D. M. Mertens, and B. Humphries, pp. 3–23. Abingdon, UK: Routledge.

Industrial Workers of the World. 1905. Preamble to the 1905 Constitution. http://xroads.virginia.edu/~MA05/cline/preamble.htm.

Irvine, L. 2016. *My Dog Always Eats First: Homeless People and Their Animals.* Boulder: Lynne Rienner Publishers.

Jacobs, J. 1961. *The Death and Life of Great American Cities.* New York: Vintage Books.

Jones, N., and C. Jackson. 2012. "You Just Don't Go Down There: Learning to Avoid the Ghetto in San Francisco." In *The Ghetto: Contemporary Global Issues and Controversies,* ed. R. Hutchison and B. Haynes, pp. 83–110. Boulder: Westview Press.

Kahn, A. 1982. "Santa Barbara Harbor and Waterfront Residents." In *Santa Barbara by the Sea,* ed. R. Bookspan, pp. 91-115. Santa Barbara: McNally and Loftin, West.

Kelling, G. L., and C. M. Coles. 1996. *Fixing Broken Windows.* New York: Martin Kessler Books.

Kerr, D. 2016. "Almost Like I Am in Jail: Homelessness and the Sense of Immobility in Cleveland, Ohio." *Cultural Studies* 30 (3): 401–420.

Kim, M. M., J. D. Ford, D. L. Howard, and D. W. Bradford. 2010. "Assessing Trauma, Substance Abuse, and Mental Health in a Sample of Homeless Men. *Health and Social Work* 35 (1): 39–48.

Kimmel, M. 2012. *Manhood in America: A Cultural History.* New York: Oxford University Press.

Kipling, R. 1984. *The Jungle Book.* New York: Macmillan.

Krakauer, J. 1996. *Into the Wild.* New York: Anchor Books.

Kusmer, K. L. 2002. *Down and Out, On the Road.* New York: Oxford University Press.

Levinson, D. 2004. *Encyclopedia of Homelessness.* Thousand Oaks, CA: Sage Publications.

Liebow, E. 1993. *Tell Them Who I Am: The Lives of Homeless Women.* New York: Penguin Books.

Lippert, A., and B. Lee. 2015. "Stress, Coping, and Mental Health Differences Among Homeless People." *Sociological Inquiry* 85 (3): 343–374.

Lyon-Callo, V. 2008. *Inequality, Poverty, and Neoliberal Governance: Activist Ethnography in the Homeless Sheltering Industry.* Toronto: University of Toronto Press.

Maher, N. 2008. *Nature's New Deal.* New York: Oxford University Press.

Manne, K. 2018. *Down Girl: The Logic of Mysogyny.* New York: Oxford University Press.

Marin, P. 1988. Unpublished manuscript on the Santa Barbara jungle.

Marr, M. 2012. "Pathways Out of Homelessness in Los Angeles and Tokyo: Multilevel Contexts of Limited Mobility Amid Advanced Urban Marginality." *International Journal of Urban and Regional Research* 36 (5): 980–1006.

Mattice, W. A. 1941. "The Weather of 1941 in the United States." *Monthly Weather Review.*

Milton, J. 1968. *Paradise Lost.* ed. Alistair Fowler. New York: Longman.

Mitchell, D. 2001. The Annihilation of Space by Law: The Roots and Implications of Anti-Homeless Laws in the United States." In *The Legal Geographies Reader,* ed. N. Blomley, D. Delaney, and R. T. Ford, pp. 6–18. Oxford: Blackwell.

———. 2003. *The Right to the City.* New York: Guilford Press.

Monkkonen, E. 1984. *Walking to Work: Tramps in America, 1790–1935.* Lincoln: University of Nebraska Press.

Morris, L. 1994. *Dangerous Class: The Underclass and Social Citizenship.* London: Routledge.

Murphy, J., and K. Tobin. 2011. *Homelessness Comes to School.* Thousand Oaks, CA: Corwin Press.

National Alliance to End Homelessness. 2018. "Addressing Chronic Homelessness: What the Research Tells Us." Guest post by Jill Kadduri. Washington, DC: National Alliance to End Homelessness.

National Coalition for the Homeless. 2004. *Illegal to Be Homeless: The Criminalization of Homelessness in the United States.* Washington, DC: National Coalition for the Homeless.

———. 2010. *Tent Cities in America: A Pacific Coast Report.* Washington, DC: National Coalition for the Homeless.

National Law Center on Homelessness and Poverty. 2013. *Cruel, Inhuman, and Degrading: Homelessness in the United States Under the International Covenant on Civil and Political Rights.* Washington, DC: National Law Center on Homelessness and Poverty.

———. 2017. *Tent City USA: The Growth of America's Homeless Encampments and How Communities Are Responding.* Washington, DC: National Law Center on Homelessness and Poverty.

National Law Center on Homelessness and Poverty and the National Coalition for the Homeless. 2009. *Homes, Not Handcuffs: The Criminalization of Homelessness in US Cities.* Washington, DC: National Law Center on Homelessness and Poverty and the National Coalition for the Homeless.

National Low Income Housing Coalition. 2019. *Out of Reach.* Washington, DC: National Low Income Housing Coalition.

O'Connell, J. J. (MD), S. C. Oppenheimer (ScM), C. M. Judge (MS), R. L. Taube (PhD, MPH), B. B. Blanchfield (CPA, ScD), S. E. Swain (MDiv, MPH), and H. K. Koh (MD, MPH). 2010. "The Boston Health Care for the Homeless Program: A Public Health Framework." *American Journal of Public Health* 100 (8): 1400–1408.

Onkst, D. 1998. "First a Negro . . . Incidentally a Veteran: Black World War II Veterans and the G.I. Bill of Rights in the Deep South, 1944–1948." *Journal of Social History* 31 (3): 517–543.

Oyserman, D., and J. K. Swim. 2001. "Stigma: An Insider's View." *Journal of Social Issues* 57 (1): 1–13.

Ozawa, M. N., and H. S. Yoon. 2005. "'Leavers' from TANF and AFDC: How Do They Fare Economically?" *Social Work* 50 (3): 239–249.

Pacific Rural Press, vol. 20, no. 9, August 28, 1880. "New York Anti-Tramp Law," p. 29.

Padgett, D. K., B. F. Henwood, and S. J. Tsemberis. 2016. *Housing First: Ending Homelessness, Transforming Systems, and Changing Lives.* New York: Oxford University Press.

Park, R. E. 1925. "The Mind of the Hobo: Reflections upon the Relation Between Mentality and Locomotion." In *The City,* ed. R. E. Park and E. W. Burgess, pp. 156–160. Chicago: University of Chicago Press.

Passaro, J. 1996. *The Unequal Homeless: Men on the Streets, Women in Their Place.* New York: Routledge.

Piven, F., and R. Cloward. 1979. *Poor People's Movements: Why They Succeed, How They Fail.* New York: Vintage Books.

———. 1993. *Regulating the Poor: The Functions of Public Welfare.* New York: Vintage Books.

Purser, G. L., O. P. Mowbray, and J. O'Shields. 2017. "The Relationship Between Length and Number of Homeless Episodes and Engagement in Survival Sex." *Journal of Social Service Research* 43 (2): 262–269.

Reed, E., and E. Potter. 1934. *Federal Transient Program: An Evaluative Survey, May to July, 1934.* New York: The Committee on Care of Transient and Homeless.

Reitman, B. 2002 [1937]. *Sister of The Road: The Autobiography of Boxcar Bertha.* Oakland, CA: AK Press/NABAT.

Reitzes, D., T. Crimmins, J. Yarbrough, and J. Parker. 2015. "Home or Office: The Homeless and Atlanta's Downtown Park." *Sociological Focus* 48: 28–48.

Roberts, J. J. 2004. *How to Increase Homelessness.* Loyalpublishing.com.

Rosenthal. R. 1994. *Homeless in Paradise: A Map of the Terrain.* Philadelphia: Temple University Press.

Rossi, P. H. 1989. *Down and Out in America: The Origins of Homelessness.* Chicago: University of Chicago Press.

Sakai, J. 2014. *Settlers: The Mythology of the White Proletariat from Mayflower to Modern.* Dexter, MI: Thomson-Shore.

Schein, R. 2012. "Whose Occupation? Homelessness and the Politics of Park Encampments." *Social Movement Studies.* 11 (3–4): 335–341.

Shaw, C. 1930. *The Jack-Roller: A Delinquent Boy's Own Story.* Chicago: University of Chicago Press.

Sinclair, U. 1906. *The Jungle.* New York: Doubleday, Page.

Smith, C., E. Castañeda, and J. Heyman. 2012. "The Homeless and Occupy El Paso: Creating Community Among the 99 Percent." *Social Movement Studies* 11 (3–4): 356–366.

Snow, D., and L. Anderson. 1993. *Down on Their Luck: A Study of Homeless Street People.* Berkeley: University of California Press.

Solenberger, A. W. 1911. *One Thousand Homeless Men: A Study of Original Records (1911).* New York: Russell Sage Foundation.

Spradley, J. 1970. *You Owe Yourself a Drunk: An Ethnography of Urban Nomads.* Boston: Little Brown.

Starke, B. 1931. *Touch and Go.* London: Jonathan Cape Ltd.

Stone, C., D. Trisi, A. Sherman, and R. Taylor. 2018. *A Guide to Statistics on Historical Trends in Income Inequality.* Center on Budget and Policy Priorities. Washington, DC.

Suzik, J. 1999. "Building Better Men: The CCC Boy and the Changing Social Ideal of Manliness." *Men and Masculinities* 2 (2): 152–179.

Tate, M. 2015. "Comfortable While Homeless: Resistance to the 'Annihilation of Space by Law.'" Paper presented at the Annual Meeting of the American Sociological Association, Chicago, IL, August 2015.

Thernstrom, S. 1964. *Poverty and Progress: Social Mobility in a Nineteenth Century City.* Cambridge, MA: Harvard University Press.

Toth, J. 1993. *The Mole People.* Chicago: Chicago Review Press.

Tsemberis, S., L. Gulcur, and M. Nakae. 2004. "Housing First, Consumer Choice, and Harm Reduction for Homeless Individuals with a Dual Diagnosis." *American Journal of Public Health* 94 (4): 651–656.

Udelsman, A. 2011. "Surviving the Forest: Ethnography of New Haven's Tent City." *Yale Journal of Sociology* 8: 153–180.

Underwood, J. 1993. *The Bridge People: Daily Life in a Camp of the Homeless.* Lanham, MD: University Press of America.

United States Congress. 1944. Servicemen's Readjustment Act of 1944. Public law 346, chap. 268, S.1767.

United States Department of Housing and Urban Development. 2004. *A Guide to Counting Unsheltered Homeless People.* Washington, DC: Office of Community Planning and Development.

———. 2007. *Defining Chronic Homelessness: A Technical Guide for HUD Programs.* Washington, DC: Office of Community Planning and Development.

———. 2008. *A Guide to Counting Unsheltered Homeless People.* Washington, DC: Office of Community Planning and Development.

———. 2009. *Annual Homeless Assessment Report (AHAR) to Congress.* Washington, DC: Office of Community Planning and Development.

————. 2010. *Annual Homeless Assessment Report (AHAR) to Congress.* Washington, DC: Office of Community Planning and Development.

————. 2017. *Annual Homeless Assessment Report (AHAR) to Congress.* Washington, DC: Office of Community Planning and Development

United States Interagency Council on Homelessness. 2015. *Ending Homelessness for People Living in Encampments: Advancing the Dialogue.* Washington, DC: US Interagency Council on Homelessness.

Urry, J. 2007. *Mobilities.* Cambridge, UK: Polity Press.

Uys, E. L. 1999. *Riding the Rails: Teenagers on the Move During the Great Depression.* New York: TV Books.

Valenzuela, A. 1999. *Day Laborers in Southern California: Preliminary Findings from the Day Labor Survey.* Los Angeles: Center for the Study of Urban Poverty, University of California at Los Angeles.

Valenzuela, A., N. Theodore, E. Meléndez, and A. L. Gonzalez. 2006. *On the Corner: Day Labor in the United States.* http://www.uic.edu/cuppa/uicued/Publications/RECENT/onthecorner.pdf, August 2006.

Van Maanen, John. 1991. "Playing Back the Tape: Early Days in the Field." In *Experiencing Fieldwork: An Inside View of Qualitative Research,* ed. William B. Shaffir and Robert A. Stebbins, pp. 31–42. Newbury Park, CA: Sage Publications.

Vitale, A. E. 2005. "Innovation and Institutionalization: Factors in the Development of 'Quality of Life' Policing in New York." *Policing and Society* 15 (2): 99–124.

Von Mahs, J. 2013. *Down and Out in Los Angeles and Berlin: The Sociospatial Exclusion of Homeless People.* Philadelphia: Temple University Press.

Wagner, D. 1993. *Checkerboard Square: Culture and Resistance in a Homeless Community.* Boulder: Westview Press.

————. 2005. *The Poorhouse: America's Forgotten Institution.* New York: Rowman and Littlefield.

Walker, I. 1985. "A History of Homelessness in Santa Barbara: How a Spirited Group of Homeless People Took On City Hall." Unpublished manuscript. Santa Barbara, CA.

Wakin, M. 2008. "La Barda: Documenting Conditions and Exploring Change at Santa Barbara's Labor Line." *Journal of Workplace Rights* 13 (4): 421–448.

————. 2014. *Otherwise Homeless: Vehicle Living and the Culture of Homelessness.* Boulder: FirstForum Press.

Waquant, L. 2004. *Body and Soul: Notebooks of an Apprentice Boxer.* Oxford: Oxford University Press.

————. 2012. "A Janus-Faced Institution of Ethnoracial Closure: A Sociological Specification of the Ghetto." In *The Ghetto: Contemporary Global Issues and Controversies,* ed. R. Hutchison and B. Haynes, pp. 1–32. Boulder: Westview Press.

Wardhaugh, J. 1999. "The Unaccommodated Woman: Home, Homelessness and Identity." *Sociological Review* 47 (1): 91–110.

Wasserman, J. A., and J. M. Clair. 2010. *At Home on the Street: People, Poverty and a Hidden Culture of Homelessness.* Boulder: Lynne Rienner Publishers.

Western, B. 2001. "Incarceration, Unemployment, and Inequality." *Focus* 21: 32–36.

Wilkerson, I. 2011. *The Warmth of Other Suns: The Epic Story of America's Great Migration.* New York: Vintage.

Willse, C. 2015. *The Value of Homelessness: Managing Surplus Life in the United States.* Minneapolis: University of Minnesota Press.

Wolch, J. 1995. "Inside/Outside: The Dialectics of Homelessness." In *Populations at Risk in America,* ed. G. J. Demko and M. C. Jackson, pp. 77–90. Boulder: Westview Press.

Wolch, J., and M. Dear. 1993. *Malign Neglect.* San Francisco: Jossey-Bass.

Wright, T. 1997. *Out of Place: Homeless Mobilizations, Subcities, and Contested Landscapes.* Albany: State University of New York Press.

Wyatt, I. D., and D. E. Hecker. 2006. "Occupational Changes During the Twentieth Century." *Monthly Labor Review/U.S. Department of Labor, Bureau of Labor Statistics* 129 (3) (March): 35–57.

Wyman, M. 2010. *Hoboes, Bindlestiffs, Fruit Tramps, and the Harvesting of the West.* New York: Hill and Wang.

Index

About the Book

For many decades and for many reasons, people who are homeless have chosen to live in camps or other makeshift settings, even when shelters are available. Is this an act of resistance? Of self-preservation? Or are they simply too addicted, too mentally ill, or too criminal to adapt to the rules and regulations of shelter life?

To address these questions, Michele Wakin explores the evolution of unsheltered homelessness through an evocative portrait of a jungle encampment that has endured since the Great Depression in one of the most opulent cities on California's south coast.

Michele Wakin is professor of sociology at Bridgewater State University. She is the author of *Otherwise Homeless: Vehicle Living and the Culture of Homelessness*.